AFRICAN AMERICAN SATIRE

AFRICAN AMERICAN SATIRE

The
Sacredly Profane
Novel

DARRYL DICKSON-CARR

University of Missouri Press

Columbia and London

i 082621325)

Copyright © 2001 by
The Curators of the University of Missouri
University of Missouri Press, Columbia, Missouri 65201
Printed and bound in the United States of America
All rights reserved
5 4 3 2 1   05 04 03 02 01

Library of Congress Cataloging-in-Publication Data

Dickson-Carr, Darryl, 1968–
African American satire : the sacredly profane novel / Darryl Dickson-Carr.
p.   cm.
Includes bibliographical references and index.
ISBN 0-8262-1325-1 (alk. paper)
1. American fiction—Afro-American authors—History and criticism.
2. Politics and literature—United States—History—20th century.
3. American fiction—20th century—History and criticism.   4. Political
fiction, American—History and criticism.   5. Political satire,
American—History and criticism.   6. Satire, American—History
and criticism.   7. Afro-Americans in literature.   I. Title.

PS374.N4 D53   2001
813'.509896073—dc21
00-066598

∞™ This paper meets the requirements of the
American National Standard for Permanence of Paper
for Printed Library Materials, Z39.48, 1984.

Jacket Designer: Susan Ferber
Typesetter: BOOKCOMP, Inc.
Printer and binder: The Maple-Vail Book Manufacturing Group
Typeface: Palatino

Quotations from *Jazz* by Toni Morrison reprinted by permission of International
Creative Management, Inc., copyright © 1992, Toni Morrison. Quotations
from *Invisible Man* by Ralph Ellison, copyright © 1947, 1948, 1952 by
Ralph Ellison. Reprinted by permission of Random House, Inc.

For

MAYA

YVONNE

CONTENTS

ACKNOWLEDGMENTS

When I started the research for this book, I found myself faced with a daunting task. A study of African American satirical novels is not easy; the topic has received little critical attention. Yet drawing on the collective knowledge, skill, and resourcefulness of a great many individuals and institutions, I was able to surmount the obstacles that came with the project. I owe the greatest debt of gratitude to the countless people who offered continuous encouragement as I negotiated the project's more difficult passages. What follows is but a partial list of the individuals and institutions who have aided me in this endeavor.

First, I would like to thank Drs. Elliott Butler-Evans, Robert Erickson, Giles Gunn, Carl Gutiérrez-Jones, Everett Zimmerman, Travis Dixon, Karen Chow, Parker Douglas, Tiffany Ana López, and Wei Ming Dariotis, all of whom offered their most candid and thoughtful advice as I developed the bases for this project many years ago as a graduate student at the University of California, Santa Barbara. Dr. Butler-Evans, in particular, acted as a caring, yet challenging and provocative, mentor and advisor.

At Florida State University, several of my colleagues in the department of English questioned me about a number of theoretical and philosophical problems within the manuscript. First and foremost, I owe heartfelt thanks to Dr. Jerrilyn McGregory for reading the entire manuscript and for offering her extremely thorough and insightful advice and criticism. She helped me to clarify my theoretical bases, pointed out grammatical and stylistic errors, and suggested many helpful resources that shifted the direction of crucial sections of the manuscript for the better. It was surely an enormous undertaking, one that has had an incalculable effect upon this book's direction. Carol Batker, Barry Faulk, Chanta Haywood, and Maxine Montgomery read and critiqued drafts of selected chapters and other documents. In addition, Marcy North, David F. Johnson, Laura Rosenthal, Helen Burke, James O'Rourke, W. T. Lhamon, and Dennis Moore maintained serious interest in my project and helped strengthen it through their support and advice. At the Florida State University Black Studies Program, William R. Jones, Monifa A. Love, and the late Ed Love provided necessary guidance and constructive criticism.

Dr. Dolan Hubbard of Morgan State University critiqued the original book proposal and consequently helped me to clarify the project's direction. It was he who suggested I send the manuscript to the University of Missouri Press, advice I have never regretted following. Drs. Richard C. De Prospo and Jacqueline Jones of Washington College suggested a number of helpful texts and resources. I am also indebted to Dr. Winston Napier of Clark University (Massachusetts) for suggesting several key primary and secondary resources. Mr. Michael D. Hill offered additional constructive feedback on the project as a whole and gave continuous support. All of my colleagues' analyses of logical, formal, and philosophical problems, suggestions of primary and secondary texts, and delightfully new ideas and approaches helped solve a number of problems I had not initially recognized. In sum, then, they helped turn a once daunting project into one that was considerably more focused and therefore closer to my original vision and intent. Again, to all of those named here and many others, I express my deepest gratitude.

I wish I could name all of the students, graduate and undergraduate, who shrewdly challenged my original thoughts on this topic in various classes over the last few years at Florida State University. Let it suffice to say that all of their contributions have been invaluable. I am particularly grateful to a select few students who worked closely with me on several different projects that helped shape sections of the book: Dr. Stephanie D. Powell, Dr. Christopher Okonkwo, William A. Hobbs III, Robin A. Nixon, Dr. Charles D. Martin, Rachel Davis, Dr. M. Genevieve West, and Paul M. Reifenheiser.

As with any long-term project, financial support was crucial to making this book possible. For that reason, I am grateful for grants from the Florida State University Council on Faculty Research Support, the Council on Research Support for Black Faculty, and the English Department Research and Creative Activity Committee for summer support, the purchase of a laptop computer for archival research, and travel monies, respectively. Special gratitude must go to the office of the Dean in the Florida State University College of Arts and Science, which provided summer support and release from teaching duties at crucial junctures.

This book clearly would not exist if it were not for the vast archival and other library resources available. The staff at Strozier Library at Florida State University patiently assisted me in finding and using the library's rich resources. Certain stages of this project required extensive use of primary source materials in the United States' best university archives. I am therefore grateful to the staff at Yale University's Beinecke Library, who retrieved endless volumes of material from the James Weldon Johnson Collection with the utmost courtesy and professionalism. During my visit to John Hay Library at Brown University, the staff went out of their way to find rare, but essential, information about Rudolph Fisher. Finally, the professionalism of the staffs at the Schomburg Center for Research in Black Culture and Howard University's Moorland-Spingarn Research Center is matched only by their collections' riches.

Beverly Jarrett and the staff at the University of Missouri Press have been ever gracious, expeditious, and thorough at all stages of the editing process. They have made the production process smooth and pleasant.

Portions of *African American Satire* were adapted from previously published essays. The discussion of Wallace Thurman in chapter 2 appeared in *Studies in Contemporary Satire;* chapter 5 combines essays published in *The Critical Response to Ishmael Reed,* edited by Bruce Dick, and *Canadian Review of American Studies.* I wish to thank the editors of each publishing venue for permission to use these materials here.

Most important, I would like to thank my wife, Carol Dickson-Carr, who tirelessly read and corrected portions of the manuscript through the intelligent scrutiny of a layperson's lens, and never flagged in her enthusiastic support of a lengthy project. Members of the Carr, Dickson, and Barnett families listened to my concerns, urged me forward, gave their emotional support, and offered important feedback. I am also grateful for the active encouragement and support Dr. Mary Cardenas of Harvey Mudd College offered at all stages of the book's development.

Finally, this book might not have been possible without the inspiration my daughter, Maya Yvonne Carr, provided. She was born as this project was entering its later stages, and her very presence challenged me to work with greater fervor and enthusiasm. For that reason, I have dedicated this book to her.

ABBREVIATIONS

The following abbreviations are used in common citations throughout the book:

BNM	*Black No More: Being an Account of the Strange and Wonderful Workings of Science in the Land of the Free, A.D. 1933–1940,* by George S. Schuyler
B&W	*The Harlem Renaissance in Black and White,* by George Hutchinson
CLC	*Contemporary Literary Criticism: Excerpts from Criticism of the Works of Today's Novelists, Poets, Playwrights, Short Story Writers and Other Creative Writers,* ed. Roger Matuz, et al.
Cotillion	*The Cotillion, or One Good Bull Is Half the Herd,* by John Oliver Killens
DLB	*Dictionary of Literary Biography,* ed. Trudier Harris and Thadious Davis
Fables	*Fables of Subversion: Satire and the American Novel, 1930–1980,* by Steven Weisenburger
Faces	*Faces at the Bottom of the Well: The Permanence of Racism,* by Derrick Bell
GSS	*George S. Schuyler,* by Michael W. Peplow
Infants	*Infants of the Spring,* by Wallace Thurman
IM	*Invisible Man,* by Ralph Ellison
JBS	*Japanese by Spring,* by Ishmael Reed
LDP	*Lord of Dark Places,* by Hal Bennett
LLH	*Life of Langston Hughes* (vols. 1 and 2), by Arnold Rampersad

Lonely	*Lonely Crusade*, by Chester Himes
MJ	*Mumbo Jumbo*, by Ishmael Reed
Moses	*Moses, Man of the Mountain*, by Zora Neale Hurston
Negrophobia	*Negrophobia: An Urban Parable*, by Darius James
NSS	*Not So Simple: The "Simple" Stories by Langston Hughes*, by Donna Akiba Sullivan Harper
Reckless	*Reckless Eyeballing*, by Ishmael Reed
RGD	*Race, Gender, and Desire: Narrative Strategies in the Fiction of Toni Cade Bambara, Toni Morrison, and Alice Walker*, by Elliott Butler-Evans
Twos	*The Terrible Twos*, by Ishmael Reed
Ways	*The Ways of White Folks*, by Langston Hughes
WBS	*The White Boy Shuffle*, by Paul Beatty
WOJ	*The Walls of Jericho*, by Rudolph Fisher
ZNH	*Zora Neale Hurston: A Literary Biography*, by Robert E. Hemenway

A NOTE ON USAGE

In *African American Satire* I move interchangeably between the terms "African American" and "black." The reader should not construe such a move as ideological confusion on my part. "African American" is, of course, the term that many native-born people of African descent have chosen as the one that most accurately describes both their heritage and identity. I agree with the logic behind this term and therefore use it frequently here. At the same time, however, I am equally comfortable with the term "black" when used as a synonym for African American, since it is still used and accepted widely by and about African Americans. The acceptance of both terms has depended largely upon substantial shifts in African American cultural politics, some of which I discuss in subsequent chapters. Except when it is used as part of a proper name or title, though, I do not capitalize "black," again in keeping with current usage. I do not use such decidedly outmoded terms as "Negro" or "colored" unless, again, I am quoting these terms as part of a name, title, or literary passage. On occasion I use the term "people of color" as a general descriptor of the major ethnic minority groups in the United States of America, including African Americans, Asian-Americans, and Hispanics/Latinos or Chicanos, among others.

I use all of these terms fully conscious of the fact that their acceptability and accuracy depend largely upon the reader's own political orientation and sensibilities. I hope the reader will note that I have neither the desire nor the intent to offend via my use of this terminology.

AFRICAN AMERICAN SATIRE

INTRODUCTION

Satire manages to fascinate, infuriate, and delight us to the extent that it transgresses boundaries of taste, propriety, decorum, and the current ideological status quo. As the literary genre whose primary purpose is to criticize through humor, irony, caricature, and parody, satire is nothing if it does not aggressively defy the status quo. For this reason, African American novelist, essayist, and satirist Ishmael Reed has repeatedly bristled whenever he has sensed anyone trespassing upon his satirical premises. In an interview with Reginald Martin, Reed alleges that "there was a nonaggression pact signed between the traditional liberal critics and the black aesthetic critics" that prevented the latter from engaging in intellectually honest critiques of African American authors—especially Reed—and limited the exposure of work by some exceptional authors.[1] In effect, Reed accuses Black Nationalist critics of doing precisely what is made unthinkable for the satirist in African American culture by virtue of his or her ethics, conscience, and the literary occupation itself. It is therefore appropriate that Reed would find the alleged collusion of Black Nationalism with American liberalism to be a deal with the devil that threatens the position of voices that go beyond that pact.

In that spirit, the present study foregrounds those authors and works that have used satire to scrutinize different political positions in African American communities. Many of the texts under exploration here have either suffered from varying degrees of obscurity or have been analyzed in ways that minimize the important role satire plays within their pages. To examine the way satire operates in the context of African American literature and culture, I plan to provide a running critique of dominant political and social ideologies at all points within African American history. Although the focus is on texts written in the twentieth century, I also will be referencing nineteenth- and eighteenth-century satirical texts, African and

1. Reginald Martin, "An Interview with Ishmael Reed," 177.

1

African American folklore, and other works that have influenced or contributed to African American satire.

I therefore privilege earlier scholarship on satire as well as on African American literature, calling for the advancement in our understanding and study of both. Numerous scholars of African American literature have researched and discussed the traditional literature as an outgrowth of different literary genres and styles in America—when it was not establishing those genres or styles itself—or of various ideologies historically informed by the extreme socioeconomic circumstances that African Americans have frequently endured. This study does not necessarily seek to negate any of this remarkable scholarship. Mel Watkins's virtually exhaustive history of African American humor, *On the Real Side,* adds greatly to our knowledge and understanding of how humor, irony, and satire have informed and enriched African American culture. No one, however, has concentrated solely on the many satirists in African American literature. This oversight is especially puzzling given the extensive work produced on satire from other cultures. Studies concentrating on Restoration and eighteenth-century English satires alone provide a wealth of insight into what it means to write satire, to be satiric, and to surmise satire's social or political purposes. Most theorists of satire, however, have not focused their attentions on African American literature, which is clearly a fertile area for literary discussions. We must ask why this is so, even as we wonder why scholars of African American literature have underutilized these larger theories of satire.

The answer to our first query lies among the same reasons that African American literature in general has but recently come close to receiving the serious scholarly attention it deserves. That is, the Western literary canon tends to deem African and African American literature and culture as primarily social protest literature, a restrictive designation not normally given to traditional, European literatures and cultures. Judged by the standards established by Western scholars, they have been declared patently inferior, decried as hopelessly derivative, deracinated from their cultural contexts, or unduly romanticized. Each of these treatments is effectively as dangerous as openly declaring the traditions inferior; if they cannot be seriously examined to the same degree as their European contemporaries, this is a *de facto* denial of their worth on their own terms. In short, black traditions have frequently been throttled by critics far too eager to either curse or bless the traditions and, by extension, the *people* from which they sprang, in the absence of fair, contextualized standards.

Ironically, in the last thirty years or so in which African American scholars have finally been taken seriously as authorities on their own cultural and literary traditions, we have seen black critics dole out some of the same fallacious critical treatments described above toward African American literature: viewing it either through the limited lens of Western cultures or ascribing narrow, romantic qualities to it. To the extent that personal or political ideologies are almost certain to influence a reading, this is certainly inevitable. Moreover, given the fact that African American literature and literary criticism have enjoyed acceptance beyond the strict boundaries previously set around them, we should expect oversights from a relatively new field of serious inquiry. Nonetheless, it is still curious that satire within African American literature has not received more extensive inquiry.

It is inarguable that humor infused with slapstick, double entendre, and a healthy dose of irony has played a central role in African American culture. The ontological condition of most African Americans during the era of chattel slavery alone normally precluded the free and direct expression of the black individual's ideas. Enslaved Africans and their descendants, their lives circumscribed by racist economic systems that reduced them to property, peons, and exploitable subjects, but rarely found the opportunity to confront either the whites who controlled this system or their agents, white and black. African Americans were forced to create various complex coded languages and expressions that allowed for the indirect expression of their frustration. Bitingly satiric humor was as much a part of these codes as any other rhetorical element, written into a language of indirection that often satisfied those who held power even as it stymied them. I explore some examples of this coded discourse in the first chapter, but suffice it to say for now that it became part of African American culture, including its literature, from the outset.

African American satire's earliest purpose in both oral and written form was to lampoon the (il)logic of chattel slavery and racism itself. Every individual or institution that kept human beings in bondage on the North American continent, ranging from the United States government, to the state house, to the individual slaveholder or anyone else who somehow aided in slavery's continued existence, was suspect. The satirist's goal was to expose the sheer absurdity of slavery itself, and in meeting this goal he gave American literature some of its finest satire, whether it be in the form of caustic passages within slave narratives or antislavery pamphlets. Even after the abolition of chattel slavery in 1865, true, unmitigated freedom and equality still evaded African Americans in a culture and government that were not originally designed to include them. Since that time, African Americans have continuously struggled to achieve the ideals promised within the Declaration of Independence and the Constitution, arguably the United States' most hallowed foundational documents. This struggle has been both a rich fount and frequently the primary focus of the satirical works I study here.

Yet the sort of overt and covert satire to be found at many points in African American literature's history remains tangential in most critical discussions. One reason for this relative silence is connected to Steven Weisenburger's assertion that "[o]ne of the remaining, unchallenged shibboleths of formalist criticism is that the satirist cannot 'speak for the twentieth century' because satire itself has allegedly 'gone stale and mouldy.' "[2] This assertion, which opens a critique of Northrop Frye's reading of satire, has arisen at least partially out of a lingering, outdated belief that satire must necessarily call for conformity to a normative morality, that it is restrictive and narrow, and therefore cannot address the problems of Western societies that have embraced liberal humanism. To put it bluntly, satire can seem rather old-fashioned and conservative. Many satires seem either to want a prelapsarian world in which humans behaved rationally and society was balanced and just or to believe that in the absence of utopia, humanity is disgusting and unworthy.

Translated into the terms of African American critical discourse, Frye's belief materializes as a curious disdain of selected satire and satirists as either too restrictive and conservative or as conforming to cultural definitions and stereotypes stemming from American racism. This last is frequently based upon two fallacies: conflation of different types of humor with satire or confusion of the representation of an offensive stereotype with advocacy of that stereotype. The first fallacy, of course, is the result of an assumption that "satire" and "humor" are completely synonymous terms and is less common. Satire's purpose

2. *Fables*, 1.

frequently extends beyond that of mere entertainment; its primary purpose is to act as an invaluable mode of social and political critique. Yet some critics may deem this same mode a threat when the "wrong" parties are satirized, which happens fairly often. Without a doubt, satire tends to be "politically incorrect," to use a rather trite term loosely. It is iconoclastic and frequently offensive on personal and political levels. It can be simultaneously too pointed and too diffuse in its targeting of cultural icons, popular ideologies and ideologues, political movements and parties, or other widely accepted ideas. What is worse is that satire has tended to be associated most closely with male writers and is therefore dominated by men. Perhaps inevitably, then, certain types of sexism have dogged satirists and besmirched their reputations almost as frequently as their general iconoclasm. At select points, this study will reveal and discuss the ways in which women have often been dismissed as sexual objects, decried as ide-ological *femmes fatales*, and assigned a hefty part of the blame for the demise of civilized discourse in at least a few African American satires. The result has been controversy and condemnation—both deserved and undeserved—at best, and critical rejection or individual authors' virtual erasure from the literary world at worst.

Given the generally offensive nature of satire and the irritating frequency of glib sexism found within it, the reader might ask why I would bother with works that assault my own personal beliefs, as some certainly do. The reader may notice, in addition, that an over-whelming majority of the authors studied are male, and at least one of them, Ishmael Reed, has been strongly criticized since at least the 1970s but particularly in the 1980s for allegedly being an antifeminist. The easy conclusion to be drawn from these two facts would be that I am either an apologist for male chauvinism or that my own selection of authors has been sexist. I vigorously contend that neither is true. When I began this project years ago, I performed a wide search for satire by and about African Americans. I was especially interested in the satirical *novel* because of my long-standing personal preference for the novel as a genre. In conducting this research, I had no trouble finding novel-length satires by African American men, but I uncovered little work by women. This is not to say that black women have not contributed heavily to African American *humor* and satire in general: as examples, there are the brilliant comedic routines of Jackie "Moms" Mabley and her innumerable descendants, including

Whoopi Goldberg. In fact, Goldberg herself recently published an autobiography, *Book,* that is as scathingly satirical as any novel studied in this volume. The same must be said of selected poems of Gwendolyn Brooks, Nikki Giovanni, Carolyn Rodgers, Sonia Sanchez; the drama of Ntozake Shange, and arguably parts of the later novels of Terry McMillan, especially *Waiting to Exhale* (1992). Of equal significance is Daryl Cumber Dance's *Honey, Hush!: An Anthology of African American Women's Humor* (1998), the first collection of its kind and one rife with satirical commentary. With such a wealth of women's humor at hand, then, why is this study restricted almost exclusively to the novel? Why not include drama, poetry, autobiographies, comedy routines, and television shows, thereby opening up greater opportunities for women to have a voice as they always have in African American literature and culture?

The first reason, as I explained above, is that I privilege the satirical *novel* because of my personal enjoyment of it. M. M. Bakhtin's basic definition of novelistic style applies not only to what the novel is but also to why I focus upon it. Bakhtin argues that the novel's "compositional-stylistic unities" break down into the following types:

(1) direct authorial literary-artistic narration (in all its diverse variants);

(2) stylization of the various forms of oral everyday discourse;

(3) stylization of the various forms of semiliterary (written) everyday narration (the letter, the diary, etc.);

(4) various forms of literary but extra-artistic authorial speech (moral, philosophical, or scientific statements, oratory, ethnographic descriptions, memoranda, and so forth);

(5) the stylistically individualized speech of characters.

Bakhtin goes on to say that the novel's tendency to incorporate these forms of discourse opens up a space for heteroglossia—diverse voices—to enter the novel.[3] The novel thus allows through these voices opportunities for sustained investigations and/or critiques of a wide range of subjects and permits an author to develop her or his plot, characters, and potential messages or arguments—thoroughly and in a unified manner. Obviously, the essay, short story or novella, long

3. Mikhail Mikhailovitch Bakhtin, "Discourse in the Novel," in *The Dialogic Imagination: Four Essays,* ed. Michael Holquist; trans. Caryl Emerson and Michael Holquist, 262, 263.

poem, and play also possess some of these qualities and therefore some of the same potential. The novel's greater length, however, extends the process that facilitates development of ideas, characters, and discourses, whether simple or intricate, over hundreds of pages. In this process, the complex and bewildering system of characters and their discourse enter the scene, all making mad stabs at approximating a particular representation of the real. The novel's attempt "to portray all the varieties of human experience, and not merely those suited to one particular literary perspective" defines it as arguably the most fecund genre.[4] The *satirical* novel, then, poses an extra opportunity for fascination precisely because it frequently develops material that is arguably even more difficult to sustain: the ironic joke. George Schuyler's *Black No More,* for example, takes an outrageous idea long discussed in African American intellectual discourse—racial amalgamation—and creates a fantasy in which virtually every African American is turned white, thereby upsetting the entire American social order. The results are sometimes uneven, but the process is endlessly fascinating and therefore allows endless possibilities for study.

The second reason is more practical than personal. This study focuses upon a mere selection of twentieth-century satirical novels. As I developed this project, it became clear that to include and study every form in which satire appears would, on the one hand, be tantamount to reinventing the wheel. Mel Watkins's aforementioned *On the Real Side* (1994) already covers the breadth of African American humor in one excellent volume. Only one chapter of Watkins's book, however, is devoted to the African American novel. On the other hand, my research led me to conclude that despite Watkins's impressive circumspection, one chapter was not enough to give the satirical novel in general and individual novels in particular the attention they deserved. More disturbing was the disappearance of some impressive novels mentioned in *On the Real Side* or Bernard W. Bell's *The Afro-American Novel and Its Tradition* (1987) from publishers' catalogs and/or critics' eyes. As of this writing, John Oliver Killens's *The Cotillion, or One Good Bull Is Half the Herd* (1971) is out of print and has but rarely been mentioned, much less studied closely, in twenty years. With the sole exception of

---

4. Ian Watt, *The Rise of the Novel,* 11.

Lord of Dark Places (1970), which came back into print in 1997 after a twenty-five–year absence, Hal Bennett's impressive novels from the 1960s and 1970s are all out of print. As with Killens, virtually no one has written about Bennett in decades; the last critical article on his work was published in 1974. On the other hand, Rudolph Fisher's *The Walls of Jericho*, Zora Neale Hurston's *Moses, Man of the Mountain*, William Melvin Kelley's *dem*, Trey Ellis's *Platitudes*, and Darius James's *Negrophobia* are mostly still in print. None of these, however, have been studied with any appreciable frequency, and only half are studied *as satires.*

Despite these basic reasons for restricting this study to the satirical novel, I am fully aware of the influences of other genres upon this form. If the etymology of "satire" begins with the Latin *satura*—a mix—then the satirical novel sits atop the generic mountain, mixing everything below it. The aforementioned *Black No More*, for example, owes its successes and shortcomings as much to George Schuyler's skills as a freelance journalist and essayist as it does to the novel form; Hurston developed *Moses, Man of the Mountain* from her 1934 short story "The Fire and the Cloud," itself a revision of an African American version of the biblical Mosaic myth; Ralph Ellison credited an earlier version of his short story "Flying Home" as the inspiration for *Invisible Man*; Ishmael Reed's 1993 novel *Japanese by Spring* sometimes reads as an extension of his columns and essays, mixing in mythology, folklore, film conventions, and historiography; Darius James's *Negrophobia* is a novel written in the form of a screenplay; and so on. In short, virtually all of the novels studied here owe their existence to or incorporate other genres. In fact, so far as my interest in Langston Hughes's Jesse B. Semple stories is concerned, I am not, in the strictest sense, dealing with a novel at all. These stories began as one feature of a column, "Here to Yonder," Hughes wrote for the *Chicago Defender* for well over twenty years. Hughes, however, slowly developed the Semple stories into an identifiable cycle, one coherent enough to make it eligible for this study.

This book, then, returns African American satirical novels to the centers of our conceptions of black literature and culture. Along the way, I examine the numerous influences and antecedents of the satirical novel. I begin by examining how African American satirists have used their rhetorical skills to negotiate the political and social terrain at crucial points throughout black history. Beginning with African

folktales and their cousins developed by enslaved Africans, this negotiation has been part of an ongoing process to prescribe possible
solutions to the so-called "race question," or America's continuing
reluctance to extend full equality and justice to African Americans.
Although I mark African American satire's origins within the traditions of African American folktales and folk culture, I do not argue that
African American folklife always has a direct influence on authorial
style or content. In fact, several works studied here question the very
existence of African American folk culture and/or the way certain
authors have occasionally privileged folklife in their works as a purer
form of black life.

I chose the twentieth century as the focus of this project for two
major reasons. First, with the exception of folklore, the eighteenth
and nineteenth centuries yielded a rather limited number of texts
by African Americans that could legitimately be called satirical. As I
mention above, abolitionist texts and slave narratives certainly owe a
great deal of their rhetorical efficacy to careful uses of irony and invective. Yet blatant satire is relatively rare and hardly ubiquitous enough
within individual texts to allow me to consider them satires *per se*.
Certainly, selected parts of Frederick Douglass's written and spoken
oeuvre would qualify, as would passages of William Wells Brown's
Clotel (1853), the first African American novel, selected poems by Frances E. W. Harper, or David Walker's *Appeal* (1829), which parodies the
format and content of the U.S. Constitution. These selections, however,
do not make up a satirical tradition for the reasons stated above. The
short stories of Charles W. Chesnutt, written as they were in the local
color tradition and possessing subtle satirical messages, constitute
perhaps the sole consistent body of ironic and often satiric literature by
an African American in the nineteenth century. Second, the twentieth
century, by contrast, was the first period in which a number of African
American authors went beyond irony in order to craft works that were
clearly satiric in intent and by design. It was also the century in which
the novel came into its own in the African American literary tradition
as select publishing houses either aggressively pursued black authors
or slowly opened their doors to them. This last development coincided
with America's movement into modernity, a movement that carried
African American culture with it. As the generation that had direct
experience with slavery passed away, younger generations hungry for
freedom in the American context reinterpreted the struggle against

oppression in new terms that depended less upon the spectre of chattel slavery and more upon recognizing the desperately slow but real progress African Americans were achieving in the social and political realms on their own terms. These developments combined with the century's most extraordinary historical events to give rise to a new, polyglot facet of African American letters that diversified the literature, priming the literary scene for satire.

Within the twentieth century itself, I have chosen to focus upon specific periods and movements rather than span the era's breadth. So far as I have been able to determine, flowerings of black satire have coincided with flowerings of African American fiction in general or, in the case of Langston Hughes's Jesse B. Semple cycle and Ralph Ellison's *Invisible Man* (1952), growing political activism. The first chapter reviews the theoretical implications driving my study of these texts. In the second chapter, I offer a short history of the "New Negro" or Harlem Renaissance (ca. 1919–1940), then proceed to place the satirical novelists of the period, including Rudolph Fisher, Zora Neale Hurston, Wallace Thurman, Langston Hughes, and George Schuyler, in this context.

In the third chapter, I continue to the period from the middle of World War II through the publication of Ralph Ellison's classic *Invisible Man* (1943–1952). Besides Ellison's landmark work, I also draw upon Donna A. S. Harper's work to historicize Langston Hughes's remarkable Jesse B. Semple stories, one of the few non-novelistic bodies of work studied. In the fourth chapter, I shift from the milieu of the 1950s to that of the mid-1960s and early 1970s, with its resurgence in black literature and arts, which included the rise of a new crop of black satirists. Foremost among those were Ishmael Reed, John Oliver Killens, Hal Bennett, Charles S. Wright, Douglas Turner Ward, Cecil Brown, and William Melvin Kelley. Finally, I turn to the 1980s and 1990s, when Ishmael Reed established himself as one of the preeminent black satirists—and lightning rods of controversy—alongside such authors as Toni Morrison, Derrick Bell, and, most recently, Darius James, Trey Ellis, and Paul Beatty.

I should stress again that the authors and works studied here make up a sort of honor roll of African American literary satire. I have purposely avoided works that, while containing satirical or humorous *passages,* do not qualify as satires *in toto.* Even if, for example, works like Chester Himes's early novels *If He Hollers Let Him Go* (1945) and

Lonely Crusade (1947) contain figures who are clearly made to look ridiculous in the context of the novel or evince a rather sharp, sardonic tone at many points, their primary mode is not satire. The critique that satire offers is present, but a consistent acerbic humor is missing. For this reason and others, I have consciously excluded texts that a reader might find satirical only at remote points (had I not, an overwhelming number of African American literary works might have swelled this project beyond any viable bounds). Finally, I should note that even at the moment that *African American Satire* is published, it is highly possible that other satirical novels will appear or be reprinted and therefore cannot be studied here. It is my fervent wish, then, that this book be seen as a foundation upon which other scholars interested in African American satire may build. I would hope, for example, that a study of satire in other forms of African American literature outside of the novel will soon follow, or that close analyses of newer works or older works brought back into print will soon emerge.

On the other hand, I have included a select number of works that are not normally considered satires, such as Hurston's *Moses, Man of the Mountain* and Toni Morrison's *Jazz,* and argued that they can and should be read as complex allegories that frequently rely upon heavily ironic voices and satirical rhetoric. While not *satires,* they are *satirical* and force us to reconsider our definitions of satire itself. Not coincidentally, these texts were also written by women authors, only one of whom—Hurston—has consistently been noted and praised for her biting humor and sharp critique of purported fallacies within the African American body politic. As I analyze selected works, I will address the question that continues to loom over the African American satirical novel: Why aren't more satirical novels written by African American women?

One possible answer to this question is linked inexorably to the project's focal points. Traditionally, satire has tended to point its barbs at a very selective array of targets, with cultural, social, and political corruption squarely within its sights. *African American Satire* reveals that African American satirists consistently focus upon the first two types of corruption as the bane of black survival in the land Claude McKay called a "cultured hell" in his poem "America."[5] Consequently,

5. Claude McKay, *Selected Poems,* 59.

my primary goal in *African American Satire* is to draw the links within this pattern of works written by African American authors whose primary foci are issues affecting African Americans or dealing with their experiences. This is not to say that no individual examples of satire by African Americans exist that do *not* focus on black cultural and political issues; however, such works are outnumbered by texts focusing on black issues. These texts also use rhetorical strategies common in satire while occasionally privileging African American folklore, folk culture, and black vernacular discourse. This last qualification is especially important, for not only does it distinguish black satire from its extracultural counterparts, but it also reveals the degree to which I find folklore central to the creation of African American culture and literature. Ralph Ellison's dictum on this point is especially instructive:

> [Folklore] offers the first drawings of any group's character. . . . It describes those rites, manners, customs, and so forth, which insure the good life, or destroy it; and it describes those boundaries of feeling, thought and action which that particular group has found to be the limitation of the human condition. It projects this wisdom in symbols which express the group's will to survive; it embodies those values by which the group lives and dies. These drawings may be crude but they are nonetheless profound in that they represent the group's attempt to humanize the world.[6]

While folklore and folk culture are clearly not the only formative agents in African American culture and thought, they influence a crucial part of the written literature, especially the portion of that literature that simultaneously uses the rhetoric of satire to create its critique and, as Ellison avers, to "humanize the world."

I also recognize, however, that while folklore yields rich understandings of what constitutes folk thought, we cannot read folk thought as a reductive synecdoche for all African American experiences. Nonetheless, black folk thought and culture are inextricably linked to the bases of African American literature and especially African American satire. Folk and vernacular forms, as products of African folk culture and the oppressive state of slavery, display subtle and overt cynicism, sarcasm, and irony toward both natural

---

6. Ralph Ellison, *Shadow and Act*, 172.

and man-made adversity, particularly slavery and other forms of racism. Folklore was instrumental in easing the psychological and social tensions these conditions engendered while critiquing the fact that such adversities existed at all. A substantial portion of black satire pursues these same purposes, among others. But why is satire specifically well suited to these purposes? What *is* satire, and why is it so important for fulfilling many of the goals of African American literature? Let us first attempt to understand satire in general, and then we shall see how it is relevant to African American literature.

CHAPTER 1

✦

Sacredly Profane

Toward a Theory of African
American Literary Satire

You want to know where black humor came from? It started
on the slave ships. Cat was rowing and dude says, "What you
laughin' about?"
[The first cat replied,] "Yesterday, I was a king."

—Richard Pryor, *Pryor Convictions, and Other Life Sentences*

Whenever a literary critic embarks upon a project seeking to understand satire or specific satirical texts, he or she is inevitably faced
with choosing from among definitions that build upon the concepts of
satire developed in antiquity. This would not be problematic if each of
these definitions helped focus and narrow our conception of satire. All
too frequently, though, elaborations on the core classical conception of
satire have produced endless controversies about what satire is, what
it does or *should* do, who creates it and why, and how it works on
rhetorical and political levels. It is all one can do as a critic to decide
which definitions and conceptions should be excluded, to say nothing
of actually picking one definition. This is perhaps appropriate since
nearly all elements of satire, ranging from the satirist to the plot and the
characters within, reflect degrees of ambivalence toward the objects
satirized. In that light, each time we define satire, we must look to our
backs and sides, wishing to incorporate the other definitions into our
own. In discussing African American satire, this effort may be more
difficult given the cultural factors that we need to take into account. In
this chapter, I would like to outline basic definitions of satire itself then

14

proceed with definitions and discussion of *African American* satire in particular.

I should state outright that I do not argue that satire by African Americans is inherently different from all other forms of satire or that it shares no characteristics with other forms. To make such an argument would be disingenuous and counterintuitive at the very least since African American culture and literature are themselves products of continuous links and struggles among African, European-American, and Native American traditions. Moreover, a few of the authors studied in *African American Satire,* especially George Schuyler, Wallace Thurman, and Ralph Ellison, vocally denounced the idea of African American literature and culture being so discrete as to merit no comparison. While I do not take these authors at face value—indeed, Schuyler's unremitting iconoclasm precludes taking him at his word—they raise challenging, if controversial, questions about the ways we define African American identity and culture. These same challenges and controversies, however, also provide the impetus for the authors' satirical enterprises.

Since defining satire can be a challenging and frequently confusing endeavor, I would like to begin with a fairly lucid definition that is both close to the classical definition and includes various textual idiosyncrasies within African American satire. I appropriate Frederick Kiley and J. M. Shuttleworth's definition here to provide the accepted goals of satirical discourse that are most pertinent to any study of African American satire. According to Kiley and Shuttleworth, satire is a "literary manner which blends a critical attitude with humor and wit to the end that institutions or humanity may be improved. The true satirist is conscious of the frailty of institutions of man's devising and attempts through laughter not so much to tear them down as to inspire a remodeling."[1] I must reemphasize, however, that no single definition of satire, including the one above, could possibly suffice to describe all forms of satiric discourse or satirists. Therefore, Guillermo Hernández's description of the satirist as "a subversive whose art represents an opposing incompatible, and overwhelming evaluative norm that challenges the legitimacy of cherished normative values and figures" is more appropriate for the satirists and satirical novels

1. Frederick Kiley and J. M. Shuttleworth, eds., *Satire from Aesop to Buchwald,* 479.

in my study.[2] I must add, though, that the "normative values and figures" Hernández writes of have not remained constant or consistent throughout the history of African American satire or satire in general. Each period in the history of African American culture and literature holds its own views as to what "normative" values should be and what should be ridiculed for falling outside a particular norm. These views frequently coincide with dramatic changes in social, economic, and political status of African Americans in general.

I would therefore argue that the African American satirical novel is not entirely consistent ideologically within the twentieth century, outside of a few essential characteristics: unremitting iconoclasm, criticism of the current status of African American political and cultural trends, and indictment of specifically American forms of racism. The *form* or *mode* of these criticisms, however, changes significantly over time. It is difficult to imagine Wallace Thurman writing a novel similar to Paul Beatty's *White Boy Shuffle* in the 1930s, despite some similarities in the authors' protagonists. On the other hand, we can detect a stylistic continuum and ideological genealogy running from George Schuyler's groundbreaking *Black No More* (1931) to Ishmael Reed's later novels, especially *Japanese by Spring*. What binds these novels together, besides the identity of these authors in the context of American racial categories and the fact that their novels combine indirection, "wit, and adverse criticism" for their critiques is their sense of purpose, one that transcends political and temporal boundaries.

This purpose, however, does not always fit the boundaries of Kiley and Shuttleworth's broad, traditional definition. Satire does not always offer a corrective for social ills; in fact, it often celebrates the "triumph of folly and vice."[3] When it does offer solutions, they are often doggedly unrealistic and impractical, if not completely absurd. Rita Bergenholtz is perhaps more accurate when she says that "the satirist's primary goal is not to 'teach' us moral lessons or to reform us, but to entertain us *and* give us food for thought."[4] This distinction requires that we avoid placing a broad definition of satire on a text or looking for the corrective "point" to satire. To seek such an easy

---

2. Guillermo Hernández, *Chicano Satire: A Study in Literary Culture*, 5.
3. John R. Clark, *The Modern Satiric Grotesque and Its Traditions*, 51.
4. Rita A. Bergenholtz, "Toni Morrison's *Sula:* A Satire on Binary Thinking," 90; italics in the original.

conclusion is to set an expectation for satire that hardly fits within the genre. John Clark correctly points out that "the satiric author will not permit us to continue to float securely upon a cloud of virtuous platitudes and grandiloquent delusions," including the notion that a novel should consist of a linear plot, fully developed characters, and a tidy ending.[5]

It would be more productive for the reader of satire to ask him- or herself instead which kind of satire he or she is encountering. The source of the traditional definitions of satire has often been Juvenalian formal verse satire, but that form is now relatively rare. Most common is Menippean satire comprising primarily prose narrative but frequently combining a number of distinct rhetorical and literary genres. Juvenalian satire, with its prescriptions for vice and folly, is part of the *generative* model of satire, which Steven Weisenburger defines as "a rhetoric of irony or ridicule used against exemplars of folly and vice, with an eye toward their correction, according to norms of ethical behavior and right thinking." Menippean satire may also be generative, but it is equally likely to adhere to the *degenerative* model, which is "a means of exposing modalities of terror and of *doing violence* to cultural forms that are overtly or covertly dedicated to terror."[6] Within the degenerative model, virtually all hegemonies are ridiculed, often through the use of appalling grotesqueries and exaggerations. Hegemony may take the form of actual characters or mere tropes that wield some sort of significant power over other characters or situations.

African American satire tends to follow the degenerative model in its iconoclasm, with the icons subverted ranging from oppressive individuals or systems to the very culture that allows for systematic racism to obtain. African American political discourse has frequently focused upon the following facts: (1) that African Americans have experienced oppression due to their "race" and class distinctions on both individual and systematic levels and must, therefore, struggle against this victimization; (2) that past and present victimization of African Americans cannot be looked at exclusive of the injuries African Americans have inflicted upon themselves. These two paths are relatively universal, with the difference that African American satire examines

5. Clark, *Modern Satiric Grotesque*, 51.
6. *Fables*, 1–2, 5.

its own set of historical circumstances. If African American culture is itself a product of the intercourse between sub-Saharan African and various European cultures, then African American satire also draws from both traditions. Its propensity for a more degenerative mode as Weisenburger defines the term, however, has at least some substantial grounding in African models that privilege an iconoclasm that need not be reconciled with a staid morality.

As a reader of African American satire, then, my task is to determine where issues dealing primarily with African American cultural politics diverge from the more traditional models of satire. Since satire appears throughout literary history, we must be aware of the components of traditional satire and of how African American culture converges with these components. In all satirical models and modes, many of the same rhetorical figures and strategies emerge for many of the same purposes. It is when African American satire utilizes the broad rhetorical trope of irony that it has the distinct advantage of being an excellent tool for those wishing to speak the otherwise unspeakable; it is the primary tool of the iconoclast. In African American literature the voice of the satirist is often sorely needed (though not always heeded) to provide the critiques of his or her community that might otherwise be elided. These critiques are especially useful when we consider the adverse conditions under which African Americans live now. Satire can expose the fallacies within popularly accepted schools of thought to push African Americans forward to improve their liminal, physical, and economic conditions.

Since, as I stated above, I do not argue that the African American satirical novel is immutably different from other satirical novels, few of the works studied here reveal anything that could readily be identified as representative of an African essence. In fact, a number of the authors and works studied deny the existence of such an essence and eschew any attempts to identify them with what others believe to be essentially "African." For that reason, my analysis cannot be called strictly or consistently Afrocentric, if an Afrocentric analysis focuses primarily upon the existence of cultural practices and tropes that originated in Africa in the text at hand, or seeks to analyze a text in a way that necessarily benefits African diasporic peoples.[7] This is not

7. Molefi Kete Asante, *Afrocentricity*, 86–87.

to say that such an analysis is not useful; I repeatedly contextualize portions of the texts discussed herein within African and African Diasporic cultural traditions. I do so, however, for the sake of clarity and to reify the satiric aspect of my subjects. I argue, in fact, that African American satire tends to cross discursive communities and rarely, if ever, confines itself to African-centered concepts and traditions. Such a restriction would, in fact, work against the ideological freedom that African American satirists often demand and might also suggest that African-centered concepts and traditions are somehow sacrosanct. In the African American satirical novel, few ideologies—if any—are sacred.

Thus, I follow instead at least three tracks:

(1) identifying tropes and rhetorical strategies that are commonly found in African American culture and literature then showing how African American authors transform some of these tropes and rhetorical strategies as they turn their attentions to the economic, political, and social situations of African American communities and individuals;

(2) noting and unpacking economic, historical, and cultural references that might be opaque to the layperson; and

(3) marking the ways in which African American satire often differentiates itself from critical and satirical projects within American literature as a whole.

I should point out that my pursuance of the first track does not exclude or ignore African origins of African American cultural tropes; in fact, they are highly important to my project. I remain convinced, though, that an African-centered focus on these works, however revelatory, would not allow for all the possible foci I wish to explore. George Schuyler would hardly qualify as Afrocentric—despite his deep interest in African cultures—nor would Wallace Thurman or Ralph Ellison. Yet all of these authors reveal a profound interest in exploring African American culture in all its complexity, a primary reason for my studying them.

In this chapter, then, I would like to follow the tracks outlined above as a means of laying some theoretical groundwork for discussing the African American satirical novel. My overarching purpose will be to show the links between African American satire and its cultural and material bases as well as larger rhetorical traditions. While not all black satirists foreground African American cultural traditions—especially folk culture—we may find culturally specific allusions to folk figures and practices within certain texts that differentiate African American satire from its more frequently studied European or Euro-American cousins. How, for example, does the irony found within the smaller discursive communities created within larger African American communities differ from that found within the larger society, if at all? Does it reflect a folk or proletarian sensibility? If satire is, as some theorists argue, the hallmark of any culture of folk humor, a serious study of African American satire requires that we consider the folk origins of African American literature. Without speaking to an African-based folk cultural matrix, how, for example, would we explain the inclusion of disparate references to African, Afro-Brazilian, Afro-Caribbean, and other tricksters of the black diaspora in Ishmael Reed's *Mumbo Jumbo*? It would require that we divest ourselves of any interest in exploring many rich interpretations of that novel, a deprivation we can ill afford, just as we cannot afford to focus solely on African-based forms.

In that light, we might begin by examining irony's central role in African American satire. Like satire, irony is one of the most widely contested terms in rhetoric, defined variously by innumerable critics and writers. The traditional definition of irony is perhaps most clearly understood as a rhetorical and literary mode wherein a speaker "has said P and meant not-P." In other words, a speaker has made a statement that is usually, but not always, *intended* to be understood as being improbable or ridiculous if taken at face value, inasmuch as the superficial statement violates a moral or philosophical code held by the speaker and (if the irony is to be understood properly in the first place) by his or her interlocutor. An ironic statement may, if read superficially, ask a reader to believe something that is physically impossible, not unlike metaphor.[8] Irony may be a muted expression of anger and aggression toward an authority and a sign of contempt for those unable or unwilling to pick up the clues the speaker/writer lays out for his irony to be understood.[9] Wayne C. Booth thus divides

8. See Wayne Booth's summary of the process through which we must pass to understand an ironic statement in *A Rhetoric of Irony;* it alludes to the difficulty in *defining* satire as well, 15 nn. 10, 13.
9. Kiley and Shuttleworth list a few useful, though reductive, indicators of satirical modes: "If the critic simply abuses he is writing invective; if he is personal

irony into two major subcategories: *stable* and *unstable*. The former is the sort of inference an author or speaker makes about a person, thing, or situation that may be understood by a reader or interlocutor via a series of normally unconscious cognitive steps. Ostensibly, these "four steps of reconstruction" are applied to any and all statements that a reader or interlocutor might have reason to suspect as being ironic.[10] They require the reader to reject a term's normal meaning in favor of one accepted by a select in-group. Stable irony thus depends upon the use of puns and metaphors shared with the speaker or author's audience that may be taken literally if one wishes.

As Linda Hutcheon discusses in her 1995 study of irony, though, the discursive community that is required for an ironic statement to be understood is a more complex entity than it would first appear to be. Whereas the most common theories of irony—including Booth's—assume correctly that an ironic statement may be comprehended only if the speaker and her or his interlocutor share a common discourse and context, these same theories also assume that the speaker is comprehensible only if the interlocutor is competent in a single cultural discourse. Hutcheon argues instead that a number of different discourses are in operation at all times in any larger culture; there is, therefore, no such thing as *one* immutable "American" irony that must somehow be learned and mastered. Thus the periodic "lamentations . . . that young people [are] losing what [is] claimed to be some sort of homogeneous, general cultural knowledge" that would facilitate the comprehension of one type of irony might have some foundation, but they are misdirected insofar as the discursive community and cultural knowledge of one generation is not necessarily the same as that of the prior or subsequent one. That is to say, if a listener does not understand an ironic statement, it does not necessarily mean that the interlocutor is somehow less competent in the discourse of his or her culture; it means that she or he is not part of the discursive community to which the person writing or uttering the statement belongs. As Hutcheon points out, though, the good news is that "we

---

and splenetic, he is writing sarcasm; if he is sad and morose over the state of society, he is writing irony or mere gloom. As a rule, modern satire spares the individual and follows Addison's self-imposed rule: to 'pass over a single foe to charge whole armies'" (*Aesop to Buchwald*, 479).

10. Booth, *Rhetoric of Irony*, 10–14.

can learn—and be taught—enough of each other's communal contexts to enable some comprehension, without the . . . privacy of those secret ironic in-jokes being totally lost" outside those contexts.[11]

It is not uncommon for the communal contexts of African American discursive communities to be derogated, declared insufficient, lacking, or incompetent. The assumption can extend from the level of grammar and linguistics to culture. For example, the idea that African Americans competent in Standard English are inherently endowed with higher intelligence and therefore superior in other cultural respects—educational, economic, social—is common but not always supported by the facts. The very assumption that competence in *one* linguistic and discursive community is in direct proportion to something called "intelligence" ignores the skills, intellectual and verbal, necessary to parse the discourse of another community. I should stress that I use the passive voice here because this assumption is not held by only one portion of American society; blacks commonly believe that Standard English is "the appropriate speech style for interaction with socially distant interlocutors and formal rather than informal situations where the prestige function of language is important," in much the same way that many whites might assume that Standard is the only "proper" form of discourse. Less acceptable among African Americans, however, might be the idea that Standard English and the culture whence it originated are *necessarily* superior. The notion that Black English and its cultural tropes as forms of communication are deficient does not always obtain; they may be considered the most appropriate forms within many African American communities. Claudia Mitchell-Kernan notes, for example, that the "inappropriate use of [Standard English] to an in-group member . . . may find the hearer interpreting this careful speech as an index of disidentification, an attempt to maintain social distance or trying to be superior. It is in this context that 'X tries to talk so proper' is used as an indictment against individuals."[12] Similarly, the use of one *type* of ironic discourse outside a particular context may easily be misread as an aspiration to superiority. Conversely, failure to use or comprehend another type of irony within a specific context may be read as an inferior grasp of

11. Linda Hutcheon, *Irony's Edge: The Theory and Politics of Irony*, 96, 97.
12. Claudia Mitchell-Kernan, "Language Behavior in a Black Urban Community," 80.

the context and therefore a marker of distance from the group. Put in Linda Hutcheon's terms, "in certain discursive communities . . . there is a positive valuing of irony; in others, there is not. If you are a member of the first, you are more likely to develop an 'ear' for irony or a 'sense' of irony" and therefore appreciate it within that context.[13]

In some African American discursive communities, comprehending and appreciating irony may depend upon the degree to which the individual understands that an adversarial relationship might exist between a great number of African Americans and the larger American society. At the level of the trope, it may be as simple as recognizing that the value the larger American society and/or whites place upon African American culture is problematic at best, or that a double standard exists for interpreting and evaluating African Americans. Therefore some African Americans may view Standard English definitions of the words *black* and *white* as emblematic of this double standard and thus as inherently ironic. One example of this sort of irony is within the discourse of Langston Hughes's character Jesse B. Semple, whom I will examine at greater length in the third chapter:

> What I want to know is, where do white folks get off calling everything bad *black*? If it is a dark night, they say it's *black* as hell. If you are mean and evil, they say you got a *black* heart. I would like to change all that around and say that the people who Jim Crow me have got a *white* heart. People who sell dope to children have got a *white* mark against them. And all the white gamblers who were behind the basketball fix are the *white* sheep of the sports world. God knows there was few, if any, Negroes selling stuff on the black market during [World War II], so why don't they call it the *white* market? No, they got to take me and my color and turn it into everything *bad*.[14]

To examine this passage in context, we must first admit that what Semple says about the signifieds underlying the signifier "black" in standard derivations is true. Simultaneously, though, we must reject the notion that Semple is seriously calling for an official revision of the English language. Such an effort would likely fail, but even if it were probable, it would not necessarily alter the material conditions of African Americans, a primary concern throughout Hughes's Semple

---

13. Hutcheon, *Irony's Edge*, 96.
14. *Best*, 209, italics in the original.

stories. Rather, Hughes, through Semple, is pointing out that language has been and is still frequently an essential part of racism's whole. The *codes* of racism, including the terms by which African Americans have been called, ranging from the derogatory to the supposedly neutral, have changed with the economic and social status of African Americans as a whole. How, Semple's argument proposes, can it be possible for African Americans to progress without the language undergoing some modification? Yet one trope—blackness as a sign of inferiority and evil—remains part of the Standard English lexicon, without taking into account the concerns of another discursive community. If a discursive community may be ignored, it stands to reason that social and economic communities may also be ignored. We may next conclude that those material conditions or the people who put them in place are the true objects of Semple's allusion. Our subsequent decision that these objects are the true ones is based upon not only knowledge of the usual subject matter of the Semple stories—social or racial injustices—but also a working knowledge of the material conditions of African Americans, of the popularly held, stereotypical views of African Americans, of the structure and composition of the "black markets," and of the perpetrators and intended victims of Jim Crow laws. We must also accept the premise that perhaps all the evils credited to African Americans are either not perpetrated by them or pale in comparison to those of the whites of whom Semple speaks. Furthermore, we must accept the notions that racial, ethnic, and cultural classifications (and the stereotypes associated with them), like linguistic signifiers and their signifieds, are arbitrarily assigned. This last understanding amounts to what Booth terms "general irony," inasmuch as we do not necessarily have to have a specific target to understand it.

If my reading of the example above indicates my confidence that its ironic sense is fairly stable, I wish to correct that impression. Hutcheon proposes convincingly that despite Booth's categorization of ironies as stable and unstable, it is possible that "no irony is ever really 'stable' " for the reason that irony and the "signals or markers that are encoded or decoded to establish" irony's presence are "culturally specific."[15] So if Booth defines unstable irony as texts or statements in which the

15. Hutcheon, *Irony's Edge*, 97–98.

interlocutor can never be entirely certain whether the speaker/author is being ironic, Hutcheon argues that the differences between and among cultures destabilize ironies that we might consider inarguably present. This does not mean that it is impossible for irony to exist; on the contrary, it simply means that irony can be (mis)recognized and (mis)read as discursive communities shift. To refer again to the Hughes/Semple example above, it was not uncommon for some of Hughes's readers to regard Semple, his language, and his ideological proposals as a sign of psychopathy and racial sycophancy rather than irony, especially after Hughes's audience for the columns shifted from one almost exclusively black to one including a number of whites.[16] A small but significant portion of African American readers were either not part of the discursive community Semple represented or refused to accept his discourse as unproblematically—stably—ironic. Part of the problem here is that Hughes did not always offer clear, consistent markers that his discourse was to be read ironically; he could shift from one discursive community to another several times within a single vignette. Thus "unstable" irony means that if the author *is* being ironic, it is nearly impossible to decide if he or she possesses an unambivalent view of the target of his or her irony. It is equally difficult to discern the number of different ironies present in the ironic passage. In other words, choosing one ironic meaning as we would do with a stable irony only leads to another choice of irony, and another, and so on, in an eternal, seemingly nihilistic pattern. Some forms of unstable irony may be said to be *deconstructive* rhetorical tropes, inasmuch as an unstably ironic text would continually call attention to the impossibility (and the irony) of its ever producing singular meanings; it therefore undermines its claim to simple, closed coherencies.

In the African American satirical novel, we are just as likely to find ourselves confronted by ironies that are stable within a number of African American discursive communal contexts but only if the reader has a substantial degree of knowledge about black diasporic cultural customs and social histories. On the other hand, some recent novels, such as Paul Beatty's *The White Boy Shuffle* or Darius James's *Negrophobia*, seem to defy even those stabilities, revealing a marked ambivalence toward numerous phenomena in African American culture. The instability of these works' ironies and what they reveal about

16. *NSS*, 191–94.

the status of African American politics at the end of the millennium shall be the subject of chapter 5, but their greater degree of instability is just that, a matter of degree.

The *rhetorical* force behind African American satire is frequently based upon the notion that if seemingly sound, decent ideas were cast in other contexts or considered from an entirely radical perspective, we would be forced to perceive them as blatantly fallacious. Thus *reductio ad absurdum*, literally translated as "reduction to the absurd," functions in both straight polemic and satirical discourse to show the foolishness of a concept or idea by taking it to its apparent logical—and most outrageous—conclusion. The device is the rhetorical linchpin of George Schuyler's "Our Greatest Gift to America," which argues that African Americans' greatest contribution to the American cultural scene has not been the many inventions emerging from black minds, support in times of war, or even jazz music, but instead "flattery."[17] For Schuyler, the tireless search for proof that people of African descent are hardly devoid of history undertaken by black historians and scholars, such as his friend J. A. Rogers, is indicative of a massive inferiority complex plaguing the black masses. In other words, African American scholars and "race leaders" are obsessed with proving that African Americans possess a sort of cultural equivalency by virtue of their contributing to rather than challenging Western culture.

Unfortunately, in many cases, reductio ad absurdum may also become a tool of demagoguery since, by definition, it necessarily avoids complexity in favor of elision. The point is to strip a complex situation of any contradictory information to score a rhetorical point by manipulating the reading audience's emotions and prejudices. In Schuyler's essay, for example, the possibility that complete cataloging of African Americans' achievements can counter and transform the larger society's perception of African Americans and contribute to the winning of civil and human rights is dismissed out of hand in favor of a critique of black cultural nationalism. If this particular feature of some satire is found throughout the history of the African American satirical novel—and it is—we have to maintain a healthy skepticism toward the satirist's claims. When, for example, Ishmael Reed critiques main-

17. George S. Schuyler, "Our Greatest Gift to America," in *Ebony and Topaz: A Collectanea*, ed. Charles S. Johnson, 123.

stream feminism in his novels of the 1980s and 1990s, especially 1985's *Reckless Eyeballing*, he frequently reduces feminism to a grotesquerie and focuses upon an individual feminist's ideological failings rather than considering the fact that "feminism"—if such a broad label may be used—has always been subject to conflicting, contradictory voices; there is no single voice of feminism. Schuyler and Reed, therefore, are guilty of creating precisely what African American satire tends to condemn: ideological positions that do not allow for the possibilities of diversity.

Nonetheless, reductio ad absurdum remains one of the central, if problematic, rhetorical elements in African American satiric discourse primarily because of satire's general tendency to avoid the specific and the detailed in favor of the general critique. This does not mean, however, that African American satire avoids the specific altogether. On the contrary, certain texts draw upon specific kinds of invective to name and condemn specific offenses, and provide, in some cases, corrective admonitions. Invective found within the African American satirical novel may range from the kind Harlem Renaissance authors used, which was heavily influenced by the political and cultural satire of American journalist and critic H. L. Mencken, to verbal and referential "signifying," which originated within African American culture. George Schuyler was often referred to, in fact, as the "Black Mencken" for both his style and wide-ranging commentary upon the American scene. If invective may best be described as openly hostile "name-calling and nose-thumbing" or insult, in literature it provides the means for a character and/or the author to shock another character and/or the reader with forceful, occasionally profane language expressing deep displeasure. According to David Worcester, we may divide invective into two categories: (1) gross invective, or abuse, which is characterized by "direct, intense sincerity of expression"; and (2) satiric invective, which "shows detachment, indirection, and complexity in the author's attitude."[18] The former category includes curses or epithets that reveal no ambivalence whatsoever on the speaker's part toward the target. Satiric invective, on the other hand, veers toward the ironic or sarcastic and may reveal some ambivalence on the speaker or author's part as to how despicable the target of the invective is.

18. David Worcester, *The Art of Satire*, 16, 19.

Selected African American satirical novels tend to combine both types of invective in African American culture and literature, where it commonly manifests itself as "signifying" and the Dozens, a verbal game arising from signifying practices. "Signifying" is a verbal behavior used in African American vernacular discursive communities for a number of purposes. It may describe a type of verbal jousting consisting of insults and trickery used to create a clever, often subtly devastating critique of a particular person, idea, or object. According to Roger D. Abrahams, signifying can mean several things, including "the propensity to talk around a subject, never quite coming to the point . . . ; making fun of a person or situation; . . . speaking with the hands and eyes," and so on.[19] Equally instructive is Claudia Mitchell-Kernan's suggestion that signifying is "a way of encoding messages or meanings which involves, in most cases, an element of indirection," which "might best be viewed as an alternative message form, selected for its artistic merit, and may occur embedded in a variety of discourse."[20] Not coincidentally, signifying's definitions, as outlined here, closely resemble those of irony above, to the extent that signifying enables a speaker to create a critique that, if taken on one level, seems less vicious than it actually is; it must be *decoded* for its full significance to be revealed. Abrahams goes on to add that "it is signifying to stir up a fight between neighbors by telling stories"; it "is a 'technique of indirect argument or persuasion,' 'a language of implication,'" comprehended only by those within a specific (African American) discursive community, one that, like other forms of irony, exists anterior to and helps produce the conditions for the discourse. Again, Mitchell-Kernan points out that signifying occurs when "implicit content" is "potentially obscured by the surface content or function," with the person or group being "signified upon" possibly never becoming aware of the aspersion cast upon her, his, or their character.[21] This is also a defining characteristic of irony. Where, then, do the two verbal/rhetorical forms differ?

Their differences lie in the history behind the practice of using such discourse to preserve one's life and one's community in slavery and

19. Roger D. Abrahams, *Deep Down in the Jungle: Negro Narrative Folklore from the Streets of Philadelphia*, 52.
20. Mitchell-Kernan, "Language," 87.
21. Abrahams, *Deep*, 52; Mitchell-Kernan, "Language," 94.

freedom in the United States and as a nearly definitive social skill within African American communities. Signifying, as a specifically *African American* verbal form, is rooted in African cultures, in which it consists of "a relation between two persons . . . in which one is by custom permitted, and in some instances required, to tease or make fun of the other, who in turn is required to take no offence." Frequently, however, signifying *does* offend and is *meant to* offend at least some interlocutors so that their behavior may be impugned and perhaps altered for the better. I would disagree with A. R. Radcliffe-Brown that "the behaviour is such that in any other social context it would express and arouse hostility; but it is not meant seriously and must not be taken seriously"; signifying is often taken quite seriously.[22]

In the African American satirical novel, signifying plays a number of different roles, but in this study, I focus upon only two major ones. The first consists simply of representations of joking relationships and dialogues between characters that allow for thinly veiled (if veiled at all) critiques of specific issues. A subtler form of signifying occurs intertextually. Ralph Ellison's *Invisible Man,* for example, is perhaps the most successful form of extended signifying upon previous narratives, novels, and ideologies, specifically those that seem to delimit the scope of African American critical and creative discourse. Decoding Ellison's signifying requires extensive knowledge of the following areas and authors: African American folklore / folk culture; the short stories and novels of Richard Wright; naturalism and realism; Freudian psychoanalysis; James Joyce; Fyodor Dostoevsky; Walt Whitman; and American history, especially the U.S. Declaration of Independence and Constitution, which are the defining documents in American political and cultural mythology. Perhaps most important, the reader of *Invisible Man* must be an adept in African American history, from slavery through World War II, especially the arc of black intellectual and political activity from Booker T. Washington to W. E. B. Du Bois, Marcus Garvey, and Richard Wright. Ellison's magnum opus duly satirizes or parodies all of the above in turn. One scene in which the protagonist escapes from a riot via snowy rooftops parodies the structure and rhythm of a similar scene in Wright's landmark novel *Native Son.* Similarly, Wallace Thurman's *Infants of the Spring,* John Oliver Killens's

22. Alfred R. Radcliffe-Brown, *Structure and Function in Primitive Society: Essays and Addresses,* 90, 91.

The Cotillion, Ishmael Reed's *Mumbo Jumbo,* and Paul Beatty's *White Boy Shuffle* all require that the reader be able to recognize sometimes obscure literary and pop culture references that are occasionally dated.

African American *literary* signifying as found in these novels is closely related to postmodernity to the extent that it is "a contradictory phenomenon, one that uses and abuses, installs and then subverts, the very concepts it challenges," to use Linda Hutcheon's most perfunctory definition of the postmodern.[23] Like its verbal form, literary signifying presumes that the reader is conversant with a vast repertoire of discourse and cultural knowledge, then immediately subverts that knowledge. Unlike its verbal form, though, literary signifying may demand continuous code-switching between African American and other discursive communities that may extend beyond national or generic borders. In addition, if verbal signifying is a trope used to create a semblance of communal cohesion in African American society, in literary texts it can be both inclusive and exclusive; in the case of Ellison's novel, for instance, the reader may enter into the text on any number of levels and without complete knowledge of many areas Ellison satirizes and parodies. It is quite possible to enjoy Ellison or Reed without possessing their wealth of knowledge, but the entertainment factor of their respective satires increases exponentially with increased knowledge. For this reason, Ishmael Reed concludes *Mumbo Jumbo* with a partial bibliography; Rudolph Fisher appends a glossary of Harlem slang to *The Walls of Jericho;* Zora Neale Hurston teaches her reader all about the Mosaic myth while writing about it, and so on. These texts still signify upon the reader, though, if or when they push and taunt her or him to expand an epistemological repertoire; it implies, arguably with some elitism, that the reader's knowledge base is somehow sufficient. The reader—presumably one steeped more deeply in mainstream, Western forms of knowledge—is thus simultaneously satirized in the process and brought into the crowded satiric scene.

This last feature is one that African American satirical novels commonly share with those of the larger history of satire itself. The primary components of satire include scenery and characters that reflect the frenetic and often chaotic manner in which the narratives signify upon

---

23. Linda Hutcheon, *A Poetics of Postmodernism: History, Theory, Fiction,* 3.

the objects of their critiques. Alvin P. Kernan describes the essential satiric scene as one that is

> always disorderly and crowded, packed to the very point of bursting. The deformed faces of depravity, stupidity, greed, venality, ignorance, and maliciousness . . . stare boldly out at us. . . . The scene is . . . choked with things: ostentatious buildings and statuary, . . . clothes, books, food, horses, dildoes, luxurious furnishings, gin bottles, wigs. Pick up any major satiric work and open it at random and the immediate effect is one of disorderly profusion. The sheer dirty weight, without reason or conscious purpose, of people and their vulgar possessions threatens to overwhelm the world.[24]

Kernan errs slightly, however, in averring that the crowdedness of the satiric scene is "without reason or conscious purpose." As John Clark demonstrates, "[a]ll this clutter and disarray results from the fact that the satiric artist renders an 'imitation' of the excessive, the imperfect, and the negative"; the satiric scene and plot are actually carefully planned, for the most part.[25] This grotesque, carnivalesque scene hints at an essential reason for satire's critical efficacy. Satire frequently fails or succeeds according to its ability to make the reader feel as if she or he has entered a world that is immensely disgusting and clearly mad, except for those corners of the text's universe where the sensible, albeit not infallible, satiric voice resides. The satiric scene acts as a means to transmit that feeling, inasmuch as it foregrounds the material and shuns the abstract and ephemeral, instilling a sense of an absurd, seemingly chaotic reality in the reader's mind.

This chaos appears in African American satire when the need arises to demonstrate how quickly and easily the accepted epistemological and ontological order of American and African American realities can be reversed or cast aside by absurdity. For example, in George S. Schuyler's *Black No More*, one of the primary characters, the picaresque Dr. Junius Crookman, throws American racial and sociopolitical order into virtual chaos through one fantastic act: enabling African Americans to become phenotypically Caucasian. This single event provides us a window into a world somewhat similar to the one Ralph Ellison might have had in mind when he wrote "What America Would Be

---

24. Alvin P. Kernan, "A Theory of Satire," 254.
25. Clark, *Modern Satiric Grotesque*, 51.

Like without Blacks," a world in which every cultural institution is thrown into disarray once the abstract "certainty" of black inferiority is subtracted from the American equation.[26] The black satiric novel frequently presents such absurd, obscene milieux that reveal racism as the rotten but definitive core of American cultural politics. The satiric novel repeatedly installs, subverts, then reinstalls racism as the agent of ideological and political irrationality and chaos, ending with a pessimism that suggests the permanency of racism in the absence of a transformation of the American body politic. The apparent chaos of the satiric novel's scenery is but a pale imitation of the senselessness of racism.

Racism is but one ideological system interrogated within the African American satiric novel, but it is dissected in one form or another as the synecdoche of America's failure to live up to its promise. To that extent, the African American satirist joins other American writers in scrutinizing the idealistic promises of American democracy, and often considers racism a sign that those promises are ultimately hollow. Yet African American satire spends less time upon *protesting* the existence and persistence of racism as a sociological phenomenon per se and more upon examining its effects, both direct and indirect, upon the African American. The effect examined most often, however, is frequently not the more obvious, such as legal segregation (Jim Crow), de facto segregation, the grotesque physical violations of lynching and slavery, and the fact that African Americans suffer disproportionately from the nation's economic and social ills. The more important effect black satire probes is the way American racism perverts African American intellectual discourse. If racism relies upon a stereotyped Other remaining in a position of inferiority, African American satire argues that some, if not most, blacks are more than willing to fulfill the stereotypes racism constructs as a means of getting ahead in an untenable economic situation. The problem is an inability to read the "code" of racism, which extends beyond the obvious actions listed above. Racism and racists are not stable, monolithic quantities any more than the black Other is. Racism may range from the individual and personal to the systemic, extending into all levels of American social and economic spheres. For this reason, it is altogether possible, even probable, that African Americans participate in their own

26. Ralph Ellison, *Going to the Territory*, 104–12.

oppression, with or without their conscious consent. A more chilling possibility that African American satire suggests is that even if some individuals are able to decipher racism's ubiquitous coding, they may not have the will to counter and destroy racism in whatever form it takes. To do so might require sacrifice of material comfort, and in the vision of the black satirist, blacks stand shoulder-to-shoulder with the rest of humanity in being venal, greedy, selfish, and self-sabotaging.

American racism thus encourages African Americans' seduction by materialism and ideological chaos as a substitute for the possibilities of true change. Colorism, or intraracial racism, is more important than intragroup alliances; political ideologies that were not conceived with African Americans in mind, ranging from Americanism/capitalism to communism, trump reliance upon either individual or group initiative; rationality falls to irrationality. To say that satire has a cynical view of humanity is a drastic understatement, but it occasionally proposes alternatives to unrelenting hopelessness. African American satire utilizes two closely related figures for simultaneously criticizing human venality and offering a possibility for transcending the "social death" within American society: the trickster and the picaro. Susan Evertsen Lundquist best summarizes and defines the former as "a being who continually exposes those behaviors and thinking processes that have been marginalized. [The t]rickster is continually deconstructing ideologies and calling attention to foolish human behavior."[27] Put simply, tricksters are the archetypal figures found in virtually all cultural mythologies whose purpose is to suggest how an iconic member of the culture in question is supposed to behave. Picaros, on the other hand, are more prominent in the tradition of African American satire; I shall discuss them at greater length below.

In saying that tricksters are found in virtually all cultural mythologies, I am not arguing that there are not differences between tricksters from Western cultures and those of Native American, African, or Aboriginal Australian cultures. Although the comparison is not always consistent, we may find some of the same purposes and characteristics in African tricksters as in, for example, the ancient Greek myth of the satyr or in the figure of the Fool in Shakespeare's *King Lear:* irreverence,

27. Susan Evertsen Lundquist, *The Trickster: A Transformation Archetype,* 89.

invective, irony, attack of foolish human behavior, and so on. Perhaps the primary difference between the figures from different cultures is that Western figures tend to operate in a linear continuum, while Native American, African, and Aboriginal trickster figures inhabit a circular universe. Indeed, trickster tales are frequently told in cycles in each of the latter cultures.

Moreover, trickster tales come in many different, occasionally complex patterns. One of the most familiar is that of a physically weak or impoverished character playing off the prejudices or vanity of a physically stronger and more dangerous character to obtain some sort of material gain, teach a moral lesson, or have the stronger character suffer at the hands of a third, even stronger character.[28] This particular plot does not encompass the entirety of trickster tales, nor does it describe fully the trickster. Lundquist differentiates between two general types of tricksters: the "Trickster," who "is continually polarized between truth and error" and the "Hero-Trickster," who, while "often making mistakes, solves problems for humanity."[29] The Hero-Trickster is analogous to divine mythical figures who help form humanity's consciousness and material status, such as Prometheus from ancient Greek mythology and Esu-Elegbara in Yoruban mythoi. West African tricksters, the antecedents to and ancestors of African American folk figures and tricksters, were often considered divine, and therefore Hero-Tricksters, but their descendants did not always fall into this pattern. As John W. Roberts notes, tricksters developed during American slavery were closer to Lundquist's Trickster in their polarization "between truth and error," an equivocal stance between doing what is moral and what is sensually pleasurable. "Confronted daily with chronic material shortages and dehumanizing physical conditions, and inhibited by the masters' power in the options available to compensate for them," Roberts writes, "enslaved Africans came to view their situation as one in which behaviors that circumvented the masters' power rather [than] directly challenging it, offered the greatest advantages in securing their interests."[30] This last stratagem of

28. Daryl C. Dance, *Shuckin' and Jivin': Folklore from Contemporary Black Americans*, 180–81.

29. Lundquist, *Trickster*, 23.

30. John W. Roberts, *From Trickster to Badman: The Black Folk Hero in Slavery and Freedom*, 32.

indirection is the modus operandi of the trickster, who makes frequent appearances in African American satire.

The pragmatic purpose of trickster tales remains a prominent point of debate between scholars of folklore. Alternately a "mechanism" of "psychic relief from arbitrary authority" in Lawrence Levine's estimation or a model of behavior in Roberts's, it would be best to view trickster tales as narratives representing varying gradations of power relationships and possibilities for social change.[31] In the African American context, the trickster has been filtered through the particular conditions African Americans have had to endure to reflect a material existence that is at once similar to that found in sub-Saharan Africa and yet altered considerably for the social situations found under slavery and other oppressive conditions. For this reason, the trickster may range from the selfish/self-centered to the altruistic, but she or he consistently reifies the potential for the witty and idealistic to effect an alteration of material conditions. Thus some African American satirical novels posit protagonists who, as tricksters, occasionally have strong didactic purposes even as they sow discord.

It would be erroneous to assert, though, that the trickster is always synonymous with the protagonist of the African American satirical novel. That role is more likely to be occupied by a picaro who, as a close relative to the trickster, acts as an incorrigible, albeit "clever, likeable [and] unprincipled," scoundrel driving the picaresque narrative.[32] The picaresque narrative is one in which "we are meant simply to enjoy the high spirits of the trickster, to be astonished at the ingenuity of his stratagems, and to be excited by the trials and dangers through which he chooses to pass." Not all picaresque stories are satiric, but most do create a commentary upon the social mores of the society in which the picaro lives. According to Highet, the author of a picaresque narrative "is ostensibly narrating the exploits of a brilliant rogue for the sake of our amusement and excitement; but in fact he is commenting on the corrupt state of society. He implies that his era produces, even encourages, rascals; and that in his corrupt world open rascality is really more admirable than villainy masquerading as

---

31. Lawrence W. Levine, *Black Culture and Black Consciousness: Afro-American Folk Thought from Slavery to Freedom*, 105–6.
32. Northrop Frye, *Anatomy of Criticism: Four Essays*, 45. The Spanish word *picaro* may be translated best as "rogue" or "scoundrel."

virtue."[33] The picaresque story, then, is frequently an ironic commentary upon the problematic acceptability of subversive or transgressive behavior at a time when the cultural politics of a society are in a state of flux or relative uncertainty. Northrop Frye accurately describes the picaresque novel as a text that has an "interest in the actual structure of society."[34] Unlike the trickster tale, the picaresque narrative's interest in societal structures is foregrounded; rather than relying solely on symbolic action to make its ironic commentary, it makes a conscious attempt to lay bare the normative constructions of positive social values as false and illusory via the picaro's encounters with all sorts of morally decrepit denizens of his society. Although it is accurate to say that the two narrative forms are not mutually exclusive, the picaro is hardly the conscious outsider. Rather, "he is, in fact, aspiring to become part of the social order with its security, comfort, and privileges" and is willing to use whatever trickery or knavery is necessary to obtain that end.[35] The trickster, on the other hand, is in open rebellion against social mores primarily for the gain of sensual pleasures.

We may argue, then, that the picaro, especially the black picaro, is the quintessential African American satiric figure insofar as he seeks the bridges between two worlds, the heroic and the ironic. The question of morality of materialism through trickery for one's physical survival informs not only trickster tales but most of black satire as well, inasmuch as satire is a powerful tool for demonstrating the insanity of racism and economic oppression and may help in opening the doors to fair conditions for African Americans. In the trickster's capacity as a quasi-political figure, he is contained within his close cousin, the picaro, who is frequently used for overtly political satirical purposes.

Each of the terms defined above plays a part in the discussions of some of the major works that make up the tradition of African American satire. Additionally, each term has manifestations in African American literature and culture that strongly reflect the historically grounded concerns and aspirations of African Americans, especially the need to determine the social, economic, and political paths African

33. Gilbert Highet, *The Anatomy of Satire*, 218.
34. Frye, *Anatomy*, 310.
35. Ronald Paulson, *The Fictions of Satire*, 25.

Americans must follow. The following chapter explores the appearance and practical uses of African American satire in a selection of texts from the wide variety of work dating from the early twentieth century through the Harlem Renaissance, which witnessed the most effulgent production of satirical works.

CHAPTER 2

✦

Precursors

Satire through the Harlem Renaissance, 1900–1940

> Like most men with a vision, a plan, a program or a remedy,
> he fondly imagined people to be intelligent enough to accept a
> good thing when it was offered to them, which was conclusive
> evidence that he knew little about the human race.
>
> —George Schuyler, *Black No More*

The tradition of humor and ironic critique in African and African American trickster tales themselves produced a legacy of satirical literature long before slavery's abolition. As I discussed in the introduction, selected speeches and writings by Frederick Douglass, David Walker, Frances E. W. Harper, William Wells Brown, and Charles Chesnutt indicted and satirized America's racial caste structure. Their works were, in turn, influenced by elements of African American folk culture, especially folk tales involving tricksters. The folklorists, teachers, and scholars who collected the tales of enslaved Africans and their free descendants after the Civil War managed to provide us with a rich record of the ironic and frequently satiric thoughts and narratives of African Americans. These tales constitute the backbone of African American satire and, combined with the rhetorical and literary efforts of black antebellum authors, the basis of the African American satirical novel.

Although these folklorists performed arduous and diligent work in collecting African American folktales, they did not always have the advancement of African American art and culture foremost in their minds. Lawrence W. Levine points out that the language in most nineteenth- and early twentieth-century folklore collections is made up of "representations of that language recorded by observers and folklorists, the great majority of whom were white and a substantial proportion of whom were southern." Generally, then, these recorders filtered stories through their own biases, creating a record that is a mix of flawed empathetic fantasy and demeaning racism.[1] Although Levine is correct in his assertion that some recorders of black folklore had no intention of portraying Black English inaccurately, such portrayals were commonly and easily accepted, primarily because of widespread beliefs in the inferiority of black people and concomitant beliefs in white supremacy. This pair of odious doctrines partially explains why stories by and about African Americans written in what was considered "Negro dialect" were popular in the latter part of the nineteenth century. Charles W. Chesnutt's "conjure woman" tales and Paul Laurence Dunbar's poetry were among the most successful of these dialect works, inasmuch as they not only revised popular folk and trickster tales, but they did so within narrative frameworks that appropriated racist stereotypes of the "happy darky" for subtle critiques of the exploitation of the South, and southern African Americans in particular by northern white capitalism.[2]

While Chesnutt, Dunbar, and other African American authors who wrote dialect works were *attempting* to subvert racial stereotypes via dialect, their decision to write in such modes stemmed largely from the racist editorial policies and public tastes of their times, which were geared decidedly against an evenhanded view of African Americans. In any case, at the turn of the century African American literature still lacked a coterie of creative writers whose narrative forms reflected a broader range of African American life. A few notable exceptions surfaced in the early twentieth century, most notably W. E. B. Du Bois, whose sociological and critical texts, most distinctly *The Souls of Black Folk* (1903), have been heralded as the early apex of African American intellectual thought. Du Bois's most impressive work has become a

1. Lawrence W. Levine, *Black Culture and Black Consciousness*, xiv.
2. Charles W. Chesnutt's *The Conjure Woman and Other Conjure Tales* collects many of the "conjure" tales published in literary and other magazines between 1887 and 1899. Duke University Press has published a complete collection of the tales incorporating those selections originally expurgated for their insinuations, however subtle, that contemporary race relations were unjust. See the bibliography for further information.

classic based upon his pointed criticisms of Booker T. Washington's accommodationist policies and his declaration that the "problem of the Twentieth Century is the problem of the color-line." The logical outgrowth of the color-line was Du Bois's argument of the existence of a "double-consciousness," a "veil" between the black and white worlds that ensures that the black individual is "always looking at one's self through the eyes of others" and "measuring one's soul by the tape of the world that looks on in amused contempt and pity." Du Bois goes on to say that double-consciousness splits the African American into just that, "an American, a Negro; two souls, two thoughts, two unreconciled strivings; two warring ideals in one dark body, whose dogged strength alone keeps it from being torn asunder." The goal of African Americans is to reconcile these two selves while achieving social and political equality in the United States and becoming "co-worker[s] in the kingdom of culture" by "husband[ing] and us[ing their] best powers and . . . latent genius."[3]

Du Bois's declaration of African Americans' dual cultural citizenship was not entirely new, but it was the opening volley in twentieth-century African American intellectual thought, one that hit its target deftly. Virtually every major African American intellectual has had to consider the ideas Du Bois packed into this volume, including his carefully wrought arguments for greater political activism. James Weldon Johnson's *Autobiography of an Ex-Coloured Man* (1912), for instance, pays both implicit and explicit homage to Du Bois. It stands as one of the finest early African American novels, one that had a profound influence on the Harlem Renaissance literature that followed it. Johnson's novel about an anonymous, biracial, picaresque narrator is one of the keenest explorations and unpackings of the intricacies of America's racial categories. The novel's underlying irony is that the narrator is forced by both morality and circumstance to choose between racial identities for the sake of convenience and comfort. To that extent, the novel occupies the same position as that of much African American satire; it takes a cynical view of at least some African Americans' willingness to struggle for social and economic change, arguing that individualistic, conspicuous materialism and comfort inevitably trump long-term sacrifice and struggle. But the

3. W. E. B. Du Bois, *The Souls of Black Folk*, 5, 9.

ex-coloured man's struggle with the color-line clearly does *not* lie in the reconciliation of his cultural identities but instead in his inability to accept the complexities of his social and material existence. When the ex-coloured man predicts the eventual rise of the African American serious intellectual and novelist in one digressive passage, he heralds *The Souls of Black Folk* as a harbinger of the future direction of African American letters and prophetically helps clear the way for the next major movement in African American literature. It echoes Du Bois's frequent demands for the "husband[ing] and use" of African Americans' skills and powers, including later periodic admonishments of the younger crowd of Harlem Renaissance authors.

The Harlem Renaissance of the 1910s through the early 1930s was the epoch that engendered the most prolific collection of literature by and about African Americans that the world had seen to that point. The Harlem Renaissance's importance in African American literary history is virtually unsurpassed, its only rival being the flowering of black literature and arts in the 1960s. Moreover, as with most other fertile literary periods, the Harlem Renaissance saw the publication of not only extensive discourses on the ontological and political status of African Americans but also occasional satiric novels that critiqued most of these discourses. The intellectual exchanges during the Harlem Renaissance resulted in a wider dissemination of the full scope of African American political thought, reaching well beyond Harlem and into mainstream American discourse, albeit to a highly limited degree.

In this chapter, I examine the development and focus of a small selection of satiric texts during the Harlem Renaissance. The authors and works I have chosen—Wallace Thurman's *Infants of the Spring*, Zora Neale Hurston's *Moses, Man of the Mountain*, George Schuyler's *Black No More*, Rudolph Fisher's *The Walls of Jericho*, and selections from Langston Hughes's *The Ways of White Folks*—constitute a body of work that, while not always artistically consistent, provides us with an invaluable glimpse into issues affecting African American politics both during the renaissance and in subsequent decades. Three overarching problems guide these authors' major works: constructions of "racial" or group identity; the problem of white patronage; and the crisis in black leadership and political ideology.

Like most literary flourishes, the period we presently call the Harlem Renaissance did not carry that name while it was occurring;

rather, it was called the "New Negro (or Black) Renaissance." Unlike in other, previous flourishes, however, the writers of the Harlem Renaissance were fully conscious of the cultural significance of their entrée into American letters. In his literary history of Harlem, *Vicious Modernism: Black Harlem and the Literary Imagination*, James de Jongh writes that Harlem occupied a singular place in the African American imagination in the early twentieth century, owing to its status as a black community in which housing was both affordable and at least tolerable; a place where employment and social opportunities for black residents abounded in comparison to the commonly brutal and nearly total disenfranchisement of black people in the rest of the country, particularly the South; a black community that had been created in an astonishingly short period; a locus that attracted to and contained within its borders many of the preeminent black institutions, such as the NAACP, Urban League, Marcus Garvey's Universal Negro Improvement Association (UNIA), Father Divine's Universal Peace Mission, and virtually every denomination of black churches. In addition, James De Jongh credits Harlem's growth and shift from "a formerly prosperous farming community with no particular connection to black life" to the almost completely black area it became to several factors: (1) the "phenomenal northward growth of New York City . . . in the 1880s, when most of the houses standing in Harlem today began to be built"; (2) the flight of post-Emancipation African Americans from the violent South; (3) the collapse of the real estate market in Harlem during the depression of 1904–1905, which forced reluctant whites to sell their property (at unfair prices) to black residents seeking better housing.[4]

The newfound consciousness mentioned above was not a product of the simple historical fact that black writers had been repeatedly excluded from the literary marketplace; rather, the Harlem writer's awareness was largely the product of an era in which black cultures, particularly those within Harlem, were undergoing sharp changes in their cultural makeup and economy that managed to sweep African Americans and a gaggle of curious white patrons into a new appreciation of certain embodiments of black life. Black satirists of the Harlem Renaissance found a wealth of material with which to build their satirical texts, given the inherent absurdity of American racial stratification

4. De Jongh, *Vicious Modernism: Black Harlem and the Literary Imagination*, 5–6.

systems. In pursuance of this opportunity, numerous young writers experimented with classical satirical forms in short pieces. Witness, for example, Arthur Huff Fauset's essay "Intelligentsia" in Wallace Thurman's magazine, *Fire!!*, or some of Rudolph Fisher's short stories (especially "High Yaller"). In addition, some of Zora Neale Hurston's lesser-known short stories reveal a cynical, satirical view of intraracial class struggles. Analyses of Wallace Thurman's, Rudolph Fisher's, Zora Neale Hurston's, and George S. Schuyler's satiric *novels,* however, best reveal the singular frustration with the inability of both the "New Negro" and contemporary whites to recognize the intricate and ultimately delimiting system of racial difference overpowering the United States and, moreover, to perceive and pursue the best means to destroy that system.

Destroying that system would involve a dramatic shift in the way all Americans perceived and interpreted African America as a whole. African Americans had occupied the role of entertainer in the popular imagination, due in no small part to the prevalence of minstrelsy as a major form of entertainment for much of the nineteenth century and the early part of the twentieth. In that sense, it is hardly surprising that that sensibility would be translated into a puerile fascination with African American culture. This fascination, of course, did not possess the reverence or desire for redefining the meaning of both African American and American culture that might have satisfied black satirists. Given their propensity to engage in shameless gawking, and even more shameless carnal abandon, many African Americans and their white patrons virtually begged the barbs of satire. Several Harlemites, most prominently the subjects of this chapter, were more than happy to comply with this unspoken request for lampoonery. In fact, both of Thurman's novels, *The Blacker the Berry . . .* and *Infants of the Spring,* reflect upon and satirize the predominant assumptions about racial categories held by African Americans and their curious onlookers. Furthermore, although Harlem's writers and graphic artists were profiled many times by reviewers and critics, none but Thurman dedicated his impressions to the medium of the satirical novel, one considered by at least one critic as "the only other important satire produced during the Harlem Renaissance" besides Schuyler's *Black No More.*[5] True to Thurman's reputation as a man of contradictions, *Infants of the Spring* poses numerous seemingly irresolvable

5. Norma R. Jones, "George Samuel Schuyler," 246.

questions about the directions African Americans, especially African American intellectuals, should take in view of their political and social ties to other racial and ethnic groups in the United States. Thurman's primary question revolves around the possibility of the formation of group and individual identities for African Americans that will simultaneously avoid being essentialist even as those identities carry the vast majority of African Americans forward.

In his autobiography, *The Big Sea*, Langston Hughes paints a portrait of Harlem that illustrates how whites frequently acted around and reacted to black culture:

> White people began to come to Harlem in droves. For several years they packed the expensive Cotton Club on Lenox Avenue. But. . . . [t]hey were not cordial to Negro patronage, unless you were a celebrity. . . . So Harlem Negroes did not like the Cotton Club and never appreciated its Jim Crow policy in the very heart of their dark community. Nor did ordinary Negroes like the growing influx of whites toward Harlem after sundown, flooding the little cabarets and bars where formerly only colored people laughed and sang, and where now the strangers were given the best ringside tables to sit and stare at the Negro customers— like amusing animals in a zoo.[6]

Like Hughes, writers of the Harlem Renaissance frequently questioned the motives of whites entering Harlem. A pressing issue vis-à-vis the white presence in Harlem was whether the interest and sympathy these white patrons held for Harlemites was indeed sincere and lasting. This suspicion was fueled in part by the reality that Harlem was, according to James de Jongh, *the* site that was "well-to-do" and relatively safe from racial violence of the sort commonly seen in the South and in the other black communities in New York City. Moreover, it was "a place for blacks to be themselves, as they saw fit. Harlem was host to a pantheon of colorful and freewheeling individualists and eccentrics, more akin to the vivid and self-expressive characters of African American folklore than to the severe personages of black history in America, who, in too many cases, had to be self-effacing to be acceptable to white mentors."[7] This defiance of circumscribed, "acceptable" black behavior also owed an enormous debt to the post–World War I feeling among African Americans that their worth as a

6. Langston Hughes, *The Big Sea*, 224–25.
7. De Jongh, *Vicious*, 7.

race had been proven via their impressive performance in the war and could not be denied, despite the racial violence that also followed the war. When, therefore, whites began to circulate heavily among the intellectuals and eccentrics of Harlem, their sincerity was inevitably questioned. Given the rapid abandonment of Harlem's clubs and people after the Great Depression hit the nation, the actions of whites fulfilled the cynical predictions of *Infants of the Spring*'s protagonist, Raymond Taylor. Eventually, Harlem Renaissance artists had to investigate their own culpability in allowing whites to dominate their circles, to find a framework that would reveal the stratifications along class and color lines that separated black people from each other socially, economically, and often physically.

Alain Locke's literary and critical anthology *The New Negro* (1925) was one of the first Harlem Renaissance texts to attempt to navigate the complicated terrain of African America and Harlem's location upon its map. In his essay "The New Negro," Locke posits the audaciously powerful argument that a greater consciousness spurred by racial progress is supplanting previous thoughts and images about African Americans. In the same volume, Charles S. Johnson describes the transformation in African American culture as an evolutionary process in which the new form of life is "a city Negro" who is "being evolved out of those strangely divergent elements of the general [that is, rural] background."[8] The racial admixture of Harlem helped introduce black artists to the marketplace and, simultaneously, pushed understanding of inter- and intraracial politics forward. In spite of this progress, a barrier still stood between and within the races; that barrier was the series of basic assumptions about essentialist racial differences and what constituted race. Both blacks and whites were guilty of perpetuating these reductive assumptions, a fact that *Infants of the Spring* amplifies.

The novel's satiric thrust is directed primarily toward those African Americans, and their allies or sycophants, who allow themselves to be deluded by ideals and dreams based upon an unquestioned belief in an all-encompassing collective identity. More specifically, the novel questions whether the artistry emerging from Harlem will have any lasting ideological or epistemological impact upon African Americans. Furthermore, the novel argues that the black artist cannot ever

8. Charles S. Johnson, "The New Frontage on American Life," 285.

be a "leader of the race" when she or he is consumed by the type of idealistic, bohemian atmosphere found among the renaissance's writers and artists; she or he must pursue a political life and artistry beyond the bohemian, one that inspires other black people to completely alter existing sociopolitical structures rather than work from a privileged position within them.

Most of *Infants of the Spring*'s plot transpires within the milieu of "Niggeratti Manor" (the name is a portmanteau "coined by Thurman and Zora Neale Hurston from 'nigger' and 'literati' ")[9], where several young black and white writers, activists, and artists reside and produce a highly frivolous, carnivalesque atmosphere through seemingly endless gin parties. Insofar as the manor's inhabitants live a decadent lifestyle and are sequestered away from other people and activities, preferring to dwell among their own, the manor acts both as a sign of an escapist bohemia and as a metaphor for Harlem itself. James de Jongh's description of Harlem in the 1920s virtually matches that of Niggeratti Manor: "Its creation corresponded, in dramatic ways, to historical alterations in the lives of black and white Americans in the early decades of this century; its mystique was intoxicating; it symbolized the very quality of black life," to the extent that the new concentration of blacks in a cosmopolitan city, in a space removed from, yet conversant with other cultures allowed unprecedented production of art and culture.[10] The irony of the parallels between the symbols of the renaissance and those of Niggeratti Manor, however, is that neither environment succeeded fully in producing cultural riches and changes to the degree its leading lights had hoped. The behavior of Niggeratti Manor's inhabitants produces more heat than light; they become so captivated by the newness of their society that they indulge excessively in its excrescences.

In fact, the satire begins with the protagonist, Raymond Taylor (who is, to all appearances, a close replica of Wallace Thurman), discussing his alleged "decadence" with his companions Stephen Jorgenson and Samuel Carter. The latter finds Raymond's apartment (according to Raymond), " 'all rather flamboyant and vulgar. He can't forget that he's a Nordic and that I'm a Negro, and according to all the sociology books, my taste is naturally crass and vulgar. I must not

9. Amritjit Singh, foreword to *Infants of the Spring*, by Wallace Thurman, xiv.
10. De Jongh, *Vicious*, 12.

go in for loud colors. It's a confession of my inferior race heritage' "
(*Infants,* 11–12). Within this short passage we find the satire operating
at multiple levels, though those levels only become visible as we
learn more about Sam later in the novel. First, Raymond is speaking
ironically about the credence Sam should give to sociological analyses
of black culture. In Raymond's view, it is ludicrous to allow (white)
sociologists, who have had little, if any, direct contact with the realities
and diversities of black existence, to circumscribe "acceptable" black
culture. Second, Raymond questions notions of a syncretic, "natural"
black culture, widely accepted at the time ("my taste is naturally
crass and vulgar"), notions that ignore the continuous construction of
cultural differences. Finally, Sam is satirized for being presumptuous
and arrogant enough to judge black culture according to his own
culturally biased standards, despite his claims to be an ally of African
Americans.

The novel pursues this last satirical point with distinct ferocity.
The second chapter is devoted almost entirely to a sharply sardonic
account of Sam's personal history, a history that maps the problem
of liberal whites and their patronage of black Harlem. Sam is a former elite college student who comes to New York City (specifically
Greenwich Village) "intent upon becoming a figure in the radical
movement. He had been seduced into radicalism by a Jekyll and Hyde
professor of economics, who mouthed platitudes in the class room,
and preached socialism in private seances to a few chosen students.
As a rule, these students were carefully chosen. Samuel was one of the
professor's mistakes" (*Infants,* 27). The professor's "mistake" (and the
key to the irony surrounding Sam) is that "nature had stamped [Sam]
an indelible conservative . . . obsessed . . . with the idea of becoming
a martyr" (*Infants,* 28). What Sam does become in the novel is the
classic sycophant and the stereotypical, hypocritical "white liberal."
In his quest for martyrdom, Sam "ultimately allied himself with every
existing organization which had the reputation of being red or pink,
no matter how disparate their aims and policies. He was thus able
to be in sympathy both with anarchists and pacifists, socialists and
communists. He went to the aid of any who called, and was unable to understand his universal unpopularity" (*Infants,* 28). Via this
description, Thurman places Sam firmly within the tradition of the
satirical naïf, which includes Voltaire's Candide and Fielding's Joseph
Andrews. The difference between Sam and the sort of naïf represented

by Candide, however, lies in the motives for each character's quest. Whereas the traditional naïf may become a hanger-on in different groups either against his will or in the absence of deterring knowledge, thus making him a tragicomic character who often reflects satirically upon his associates, Sam is a captious joiner intent upon satisfying his own desires. "[C]oncurrent with the realization that he was and probably would remain a mere nobody in the radical movement, [Sam] also became aware of a duality in his nature, a clash between his professed beliefs and his personal sympathies. More often than not he considered his capitalistic opponents in a more favorable light than he did his radical allies. . . . In short, his natural conservatism began to assert itself" (*Infants,* 29). Sam's realization leads him to "an arena in which his mediocrity was overlooked because he had a pale face," and he soon becomes a "white hope, battling for the cause of the American Negro" (*Infants,* 30).

At this point, the satire begins to shift its focus from Sam's imbecility to the blindness of the "American Negro" to those working among African Americans who hardly have their interests at heart. Sam receives, alternately, wide praise and condemnation for this dedication to African Americans. The praise comes from blacks obsessed with the notion of a single white man willing to aid them; the condemnation emerges from whites horrified at Sam's willingness to be associated with the nation's pariah class. This attention makes Sam a "martyr," without any sort of material sacrifice on his part (*Infants,* 30–31). Again, the novel's satire operates on several levels: first, and most obviously, we are presented with the irony of Sam's obtaining his cherished goal of martyrdom through mediocrity; second, Sam achieves his goal with the aid of people who should regard him as, at best, a buffoon; third, black political and social leaders waste no time conferring their highest honors upon someone who is not only a buffoon, but who shares the beliefs of and is unconsciously in league with oppressive whites. In fact, the one black person who pleases Sam is Niggeratti Manor's Pelham Gaylord, who "was servile, deferential, and quite impressed by Samuel's noisy if ineffectual crusade" (*Infants,* 31); in other words, only a stereotypical black dupe should be satisfied with Samuel's acts. The two characters who consistently find Samuel annoying are Raymond and Paul Arbian, a flamboyant artist; both are also the most consistently irreverent characters. Raymond, as the character that best embodies Thurman's political and social ideas, criticizes Samuel most often as symbolic of the degree to which African Americans unintentionally display slavish loyalty to popular notions of racial inferiority. Samuel repeatedly insinuates himself into discussions about race and racial categories, arrogantly assuming that he can speak for African Americans due to his alleged radicalism. His confidence in his abilities to translate African American experiences as a radical is no less dismaying than that of the southerner who argues that whites necessarily have superior abilities to speak for people they consider cognitive, racial, and cultural inferiors.

Yet Thurman is not creating a blanket indictment of whites per se. Stephen, a Danish immigrant and Raymond's friend, criticizes Samuel's hypocrisy from the point of view of a white foreigner, pointing out that he likes Ray and his African American friends, but "none of [his] likes are based on color" (*Infants*, 52). Instead, he "knows nothing about your damn American prejudices, except what [he's] read in books and been told. A person is a person" (*Infants*, 52). Stephen's recognition that the construction and maintenance of discrete racial categories that cast one "race" below another occur primarily within the confines of the United States, and that they are not universal, was a key focal point of Harlem Renaissance–era discussions of race. For Thurman, in particular, it was a bitter topic, given his own take on the function of African American art at the time. Thurman's position was remarkably similar to that of George Schuyler in his controversial June 1926 essay, "The Negro-Art Hokum." In his 1927 essay, "Nephews of Uncle Remus," Thurman presents the "constant controversy" over the possibility of there being a "negro literature" in America at all between, on the one hand, the school believing in "inherent differences between whites and blacks" and, on the other, those who argue that "the Afro-American is different from the white American in only one respect, namely, skin color, and that when he writes he will observe the same stylistic conventions and literary traditions." Thurman comes down on the side of the latter position, declaring that it "seems to have the better of the argument" since the "negro" is a myth foisted upon the public by anthropologists. Thurman then sings the praises of Jean Toomer, whose first book, *Cane,* and subsequent poems are allowing him to free "himself from restrictive racial bonds and letting the artist in him take flight where it will." Thurman asserts that artists such as his friend Langston Hughes do a fine job of representing cultural phenomena and concerns many African Americans have but publish without enough "restraint" due to being "[u]rged on by a faddishistic interest in the unusual" or the primitive.[11]

Thurman was, as Langston Hughes asserts in *The Big Sea*, very "pessimistic" "[a]bout the future of Negro literature" because of his feeling that the younger crowd of black artists—the same ones who had quietly left him holding the bag when the bills for *Fire!!* were due—were "all too conscious of [themselves]" and "flattered and spoiled" by gin parties and patronage.[12] Thurman explores this idea throughout the novel by establishing a pattern of characters allying themselves with specific categories' positions but finding that those stances make sense within only one locale or moment, then become obsolete or limiting. We are treated to numerous instances in which Niggeratti Manor's tightly knit bohemian atmosphere becomes too confining and tense for its inhabitants, especially Raymond, who is seeking a solution to his racial conundra within the manor's creative milieu, ironically finding Stephen, the foreigner and outsider, the only other manor dweller able to share fully his musings on the compound's absurdities and their similarities to the problems of African America. In what acts as perhaps the novel's most telling trope, Raymond outlines his view of African Americans' intrinsic problems in the United States in answer to Stephen's uncertainty about the two friends' respective futures. Raymond avers that

> I'm going to write, probably a series of books which will cause talk but won't sell, and will be criticized severely, then forgotten. Negroes won't like me because they'll swear I have no race pride, and white people won't like me because I won't recognize their stereotypes. Do you know, Steve, that I'm sick of both whites and blacks? I'm sick of discussing the Negro problem, of having it thrust at me. . . . I'm sick of whites who think I can't talk about anything else, and of Negroes who think I shouldn't talk about anything else. I refuse to wail and lament. My problem is a personal one, although I most certainly do not blind myself to what it means to be a Negro. . . . I have a sense of humor. That's all that saves me from becoming like most of the Negroes I know. Things amuse me. They don't make me bitter. (*Infants*, 214–15)

Significantly, this conversation occurs after the carnivalesque party during which Raymond rejects Samuel's patronizing view of black

---

11. Wallace Thurman, "Nephews of Uncle Remus," 296, 297.
12. Hughes, *Big Sea*, 238.

culture, and the inhabitants of Niggeratti Manor engage in a donnybrook over white women, convincing Raymond that "ninety-nine and ninety-nine hundredths per cent of the Negro race is patiently possessed and motivated by an inferiority complex" (*Infants*, 140). This complex is the primary explanation for Samuel's acceptance and popularity among Harlemites and an illustration of Thurman's assertion in the *New Republic* that the African American "insists on selling every vestige of his birthright for a mess of pottage."[13]

Inscribed into Raymond's position is Thurman's resistance against circumscriptions of African Americans' personal, cultural, and intellectual pursuits. This resistance is, in one sense, comfortably within the tradition of black intellectual thought that eschews the status of black victimhood, whether that status be foisted by well-meaning whites or progressive African Americans. Booker T. Washington, James Weldon Johnson, and Thurman's contemporary George Schuyler all criticized this position as at least partially dishonest or inadequate to enact change for and within African American communities. Raymond goes on to posit a version of individualism as his solution to the problem of black disenfranchisement. After making a plea for the basic humanity of all Americans, Raymond notes that a

> few years ago it was the thing for all Negroes who could get an education to be professional men, doctors, lawyers dentists, et cetera. Now, they are all trying to be artists. Negroes love to talk, love to tell the stories of their lives. They all feel that they are so different from the rest of humanity, so besieged by problems peculiar only to themselves. And since it is the fashion now to be articulate either in words, music or paint brush, every Negro . . . is tempted to act according to the current fad. . . . [The individualist] is the only type of Negro who will ever escape from the shroud of color . . . who [will] go on about [his] business, and do what [he] can in the best way [he] can, whether it be in business or art. . . . The rest [of the Negroes] must wait until the inevitable day of complete assimilation. (*Infants*, 216–17)

In his articulation and apparent endorsement of an assimilationist individualism, Raymond completes a political program for African Americans that is remarkable for its opposition to the popular progressivism and group identity politics widely accepted at the time by

13. Wallace Thurman, "Negro Artists and the Negro," 38.

Harlemites, especially the intellectuals of the renaissance. This political posturing further qualifies Raymond (and, by extension, Thurman) as a satirical figure, insofar as the satirist is occasionally conservative in his taste for a more rational outlook by those within his social group.

This is not to say, however, that Thurman, via Raymond, is positing an entirely conservative political position. Immediately following his articulation of his individualism, Raymond reveals that he'd like to spread dissent among black people with the aid of communistic and leftist rhetoric " '[j]ust to see if their resentment is near enough the surface to be inflamed. I'd like to see them retaliate against the whites in their own sphere. For every lynching, I'd like to see Negroes take their toll in whites' " (*Infants*, 218). When Stephen questions Raymond's conflicting views, wondering how he "can . . . fight both for the masses and for the individual," Raymond answers, "you have to improve the status of the masses to develop your individuals. It is mass movements which bring forth individuals. I don't care about stray darkies getting lynched, but I do care about people who will fight for a principle. And if out of a wholesale allegiance to Communism, the Negro could develop just a half dozen men who were really and truly outstanding, the result would be worth the effort" (*Infants*, 218–19).

Our problem here is deciding which of these positions best represents the novel's satiric thrust. Thurman is clearly engaging in some degree of reductio ad absurdum in these passages; Raymond's lack of compassion for "stray darkies getting lynched" is obviously intended to be shocking. It is less certain, however, whether Raymond's advocacy of complete assimilation of African Americans is to be equally startling. As George Hutchinson points out in *The Harlem Renaissance in Black and White*, those who believed in the inevitable assimilation of the races during the Harlem Renaissance did not necessarily mean "accepting the contemporary civilization of the United States as the 'American' norm." Instead, cultural assimilationists such as Charles S. Johnson argued that assimilation "entailed the 'blackening' of the national culture, a process it recognized as having begun before the founding of the nation itself and apparently accelerating in the early twentieth century, despite a simultaneous intensification of racism."[14] Raymond's clear distrust of white attitudes, therefore, does not clash with his assimilationist beliefs as much as it might appear.

14. *B&W*, 145.

Raymond's (and Thurman's) goal, then, is to embody the role of the satirist, playing the eternal role of devil's advocate no matter who his target is, to push African Americans away from a cultural separatism and toward a position of cultural leadership for the nation that requires perspicacity rather than strict categorization. It is ultimately a pragmatic position that requires a sensually and ideologically inclusive aesthetic. As Raymond tells Stephen he is "bound to thrive on antagonism" since he'd be "bored to death" unless he spent his "life doing things just to make people angry" (*Infants,* 221). African Americans, he says, "are a curiosity . . . even to [themselves]. It will be some years before the more forward will be accepted as human beings and allowed to associate with giants. The pygmies have taken us over now, and I doubt if any of us has the strength to use them for a step-ladder to a higher plane" (*Infants,* 221). Raymond thus acknowledges the urgency of pushing African American culture and politics forward, of criticizing them to improve it, which is, of course, one of the satirist's central missions. The growth of African American culture depends precariously on its ability to continuously investigate and question itself and recognize when, precisely, its greatest leaders and ideas are at hand.

This view later informs Raymond's reaction to a meeting of Harlem's African American writers called by one "Dr. A. L. Parkes," Thurman's pseudonym for Alain Locke. This meeting draws together most of the major black voices of the Harlem Renaissance, as well as some of the minor ones, "for the purpose of exchanging ideas and expressing and criticizing individual theories," with the possibility of bringing "into active being a concerted movement which would establish the younger Negro talent once and for all as a vital artistic force" (*Infants,* 228). This meeting is based both upon meetings that various Harlem Renaissance writers had with Locke and upon Thurman's general attitude toward the sort of political mission that Locke, as the editor of the *New Negro,* represented to him. Thurman and other renaissance artists started the periodical *Fire!!* as a direct response to the *New Negro.* As such, *Fire!!* "represented the esthetic frustration of [Harlem writers]; their revolt against bourgeois subject matter had been easily co-opted in *The New Negro*" by "racial propagandists."[15]

15. *ZNH,* 45.

Fire!! was intended to allow the renaissance artists to express their artistic ambitions without the fear of censure that Locke's patronage might have wrought. Unfortunately, without such funding, *Fire!!* did not live past its first issue (of which most copies were destroyed, ironically, in a fire) and, moreover, was roundly castigated in the black press.[16]

Each of the characters present at Parkes's meeting represents a major artistic or intellectual figure of the Harlem Renaissance hidden beneath a pseudonym that plays on either the initials, rhythm or other characteristics of the historical figure's name. Amritjit Singh notes, for example, that "Sweetie May Carr" is Zora Neale Hurston; "Doris Westmore" is Dorothy West; "Tony Crews" is Langston Hughes; "Dr. Manfred Trout" is Rudolph Fisher.[17] Unfortunately, Parkes's/Locke's discourse at the actual meeting is not as lucid; he "perorate[s]" numerous disapproving allusions to the "decadent strain" running through the artists' work and cajoles them to cultivate "a healthy paganism based on African traditions" (*Infants,* 233–35). Given Parkes's purported openness to the artists' ideas, Raymond and others find Parkes's exhortations patronizing, if they can comprehend them at all. When "DeWitt Clinton" (a pseudonym for Countee Cullen, who attended De Witt Clinton High School) agrees with Parkes, Raymond imagines "that poet's creative hours—eyes on a page of Keats, fingers on a typewriter, mind frantically conjuring African scenes. And there would of course be a Bible nearby" (*Infants,* 236).[18] Raymond and Paul then ask Parkes and Clinton if " 'there really [is] any reason why *all* Negro artists should consciously and deliberately dig into African soil for inspiration and material unless they actually wish to do so,' " and " '[h]ow can I go back to African ancestors when their blood is so diluted and their country and times so far away,' " respectively (*Infants,* 237).

Raymond and Paul are, for all intents and purposes, simultaneously raising questions Harlem Renaissance artists commonly asked about

16. Phyllis R. Klotman, "Wallace Henry Thurman," 262–63.

17. Singh, foreword to *Infants,* xv; Bernard W. Bell, *The Afro-American Novel and Its Tradition,* 133.

18. A reference to Cullen's "ambivalence that vacillates between African ancestralism and Western classicism" in addition to Cullen's skeptical view of religion and superstition in his only novel, *One Way to Heaven* (Bell, *Afro-American Novel,* 134).

black identity and predating the questions asked by the intellectuals of the Black Arts movement of the 1960s: What does it mean to be black? What does it mean to be a black artist? What should a black artist or intellectual identify with to have an affirmative effect upon black culture? How far will this effect extend? Pursuant to these questions, Parkes's literary troupe, egged on by Raymond and Paul, begins arguing heatedly over whether African influences and elements in black literature and culture would have any sort of effect over the black middle class, which is arguably unable to "laugh and sing and dance spontaneously" like black people of other classes due to its tendency to espouse individualism (*Infants*, 240–42). Raymond and Paul thus consider the idea of a syncretic black culture and literature as a myth, at best. The discussion goes on heatedly until Sweetie May Carr calls Cedric Williams "a polysyllabic expletive," and the intellectual discourse devolves into a carnivalesque state of "pandemonium." The meeting's attendants subsequently disperse, with no consensus attained as to what the responsibilities, goals, and obligations of black artists might be (*Infants*, 242–45).

Parkes's literary summit thus becomes a metaphor for the state of black art in the renaissance. Raymond reflects soon thereafter that "[i]t was amazing how in such a short time his group of friends had become separate entities, wrenched apart, scattered" by its interest in matters both within and outside of Niggeratti Manor. Not unlike the pragmatic endings found in much satire, the latter portion of *Infants* finds the various Niggeratti pursuing careers that put their talents to more profitable uses than those found within the manor's confines. The manor itself follows this rubric, inasmuch as its landlady, Euphoria Blake, decides to convert it from, in Thurman's euphemisms, "a congenial home for Negro artists to a congenial dormitory for bachelor girls" (*Infants*, 277). Soon thereafter, Paul, the novel's quintessential symbol of flamboyant bohemianism, commits suicide, prompting Raymond to ask if "Paul the debonair, Paul the poseur, Paul the irresponsible romanticist, finally faced reality and seen himself and the world as they actually were? Or was this merely another act, the final stanza in his drama of beautiful gestures," his final means "to make himself stand out from the mob" (*Infants*, 280). Raymond's ponderings frame Paul's death as a synecdoche for the disintegration of Niggeratti Manor; in life, he "[w]ooed the unusual, cultivated artificiality, defied all conventions of dress and conduct," and consequently had "nothing left to do except execute self-murder in some bizarre manner" (*Infants,* 280–81), not unlike the Niggeratti's heavy flirtation with the flamboyant and subsequent dissolution in the cascade of economic necessity that overwhelmed any aspirations to a unique society within both Harlem and American culture in general.

Paul leaves behind a manuscript of a novel, but it is accidentally destroyed in the process of his suicide, except for one page that includes a drawing of "a distorted, inky black skyscraper, modeled after Niggeratti Manor, and on which were focused an array of blindingly white beams of light. The foundation of this building was composed of crumbling stone. At first glance it could be ascertained that the skyscraper would soon crumple and fall, leaving the dominating white lights in full possession of the sky" (*Infants,* 284). The combined images of Paul's death and his drawing function as the novel's final metaphors for its satiric purpose. The high aspirations of the Niggeratti, and, by extension, black Harlem in general, are built upon a foundation of bohemian, carnal desires and excess that, while amusing in and of themselves, will contribute little or nothing toward solving African American problems. Under the pressure of white racism, which would consciously seek to destroy African Americans and their culture or unconsciously patronize it until its resources have been exhausted (an action symbolized by Samuel), black bohemias will end up consuming themselves, leaving no structure upon which to ensure the future of African America. A group identity based upon respect for individuality, as Raymond espouses to Stephen, is the most credible means of concretizing black culture.

Infants of the Spring, then, asks us to reconcile what is normally considered an oxymoron, at least in the United States: an individualistic group consciousness. Raymond's struggle with this apparent dichotomy might tempt us to dismiss his ideological underpinnings as inherently unrealistic. What Raymond (and, by extension, Thurman) demands, however, is actually a precursor to the conundra that Ralph Ellison would propose in his widely acclaimed *Invisible Man.* Raymond argues that principles upheld by masses of African Americans are the ultimate linchpins to African Americans' cultural and political progress, not unlike the narrator of *Invisible Man,* who argues that African Americans "were to affirm the principle on which the country was built" despite the reality of staunch, violent opposition, lest the nation, and therefore African Americans, be lost forever.[19] It is precisely this fear of total loss, of an African American community swallowed up because it wastes its energies on frivolities instead of a fight for principles, that drives *Infants of the Spring*'s satire.

Although *Infants of the Spring*'s satire of the Harlem Renaissance occupies a unique place among the works that emerged from the period as the only novel primarily about the artistic goals of the movement, its greatest failing was, ironically, artistic. Thurman's observations of the movement were incisive, but he consistently failed to become the writer of the "Great American Novel" he so desperately wished to be. David Levering Lewis's judgment that "[t]he novel is so poorly done it hardly seems possible that the best-read, most brilliant, and most uncompromising of the Harlem artists could have read it" is rather harsh but not too far from the mark.[20] While there are insightful passages, some of which I have quoted here, the novel's plot is minimal and slow, a far cry from the artistic ambitions Thurman set for himself. As a further irony, many of Thurman's friends commented after his death that both his art and his health had been victims of his own slide into decadence. The novel evinces a cynicism toward the renaissance shared by Thurman and his voice, Raymond.

This is not to say, however, that Thurman was the only major author of the movement to hold the politics of the period in some contempt, nor was *Infants of the Spring* remotely close to being its best satirical novel. That particular honor goes to its predecessor, George S. Schuyler's *Black No More* (1931), which stands as a double milestone in African American literature. It is simultaneously the first completely satirical novel written by and about African Americans and the first extended work of science fiction by a black author. It was also the culmination of many years of journalistic work that enabled Schuyler to obtain a perspective on racial matters that was not only more comprehensive than Thurman's, but also more easily translatable into crisp, deadly satirical jabbing.

These laurels notwithstanding, *Black No More*, like most of Schuyler's work, remained in relative obscurity even as scholars of the Harlem Renaissance were recovering many other works and authors. Only in the last decade has interest in Schuyler grown, owing in part

19. *IM*, 574.
20. David Levering Lewis, *When Harlem Was in Vogue*, 277.

to increasing interest in the Harlem Renaissance and perhaps to the advent of black neoconservatism. In fact, Jeffrey Tucker reminds us that the "claims of [black neoconservatives Thomas] Sowell, [Randall] Kennedy, [Clarence] Thomas, [Shelby] Steele, and others merely echo those of" Schuyler.[21] John C. Gruesser points out that until recently,

> critical attention to Schuyler consisted of brief discussions of the author in critical surveys of African American literature, a handful of articles on and interviews with the writer, and a Twayne series book by Michael Peplow. Given not only the popularity Schuyler enjoyed in his four decades as an outspoken journalist, critic, and editorial writer for the largest black weekly newspaper, the *Pittsburgh Courier,* but also his unprecedented access to mainstream publications . . . the dearth of critical interest in Schuyler prior to 1991 is striking, though not wholly inexplicable. It may result in part from the fact that he published only three literary works in book form during his lifetime.

Gruesser goes on to say that Schuyler's "frequent role as a gadfly within the African American intellectual community," the perception that he was an assimilationist trying to escape his "blackness," and his rather rancorous criticisms of the major figures in the Civil Rights movement have made dismissal of Schuyler an easy proposition for many African American critics.[22] Finally, Schuyler's sharp anticommunist stance taken after a hard swing to the extreme Right in the 1940s put him at odds with most factions within African American politics. Schuyler was one of very few African Americans, for example, willing to support Sen. Joseph McCarthy's hunt for Communists in the federal government or conservative Republican Barry Goldwater's run for the presidency in 1964.[23]

Born in 1895 to a family extremely proud of its apparently slaveless genealogy, Schuyler enjoyed a seven-year stint in the army before

21. Jeffrey Tucker, " 'Can Science Succeed Where the Civil War Failed?': George S. Schuyler and Race," In *Race Consciousness: African American Studies for the New Century,* ed. Judith Jackson Fossett and Jeffrey A. Tucker, 137. Tucker continues by showing how all of these commentators' views on race are ultimately inadequate since they follow the same flawed pattern Schuyler helped to establish in *Black No More* and many other works.

22. John C. Gruesser, review of *Black Empire,* by George S. Schuyler, 681.

23. For further discussion and analysis of Schuyler's politics, see Jeffrey Tucker's essay, cited above. The best resource, of course, would be Schuyler's own autobiography, *Black and Conservative.*

moving to New York City. After enduring a period of itinerant work, Schuyler joined the Socialist Party of America, through which he met A. Philip Randolph, later of the Brotherhood of Sleeping Car Porters, who subsequently hired Schuyler to work at his magazine, the *Messenger,* which boasted of being "the only magazine of scientific radicalism in the world published by Negroes." It was at the *Messenger,* with its socialist creed and well-cultivated iconoclasm, that Schuyler developed many of the critiques and the satirical style that formed the body of *Black No More.* If Schuyler's later archconservative views do not seem to jibe with his earlier identity as a socialist, there are two likely explanations for this split. First, it is hardly unusual for leftist radicals to disavow their radicalism after becoming disillusioned and moving quickly to the Right. This was the case with one of Schuyler's former employers, Chandler Owen, and Harlem Renaissance poet Claude McKay.[24] Second, Schuyler's membership in the Socialist Party and position at the *Messenger* were apparently far less opportunities to advocate socialism than they were chances to gain invaluable experience as a journalist and editor:

> The *Messenger* was a good place for a tireless, versatile young fellow to get plenty of activity and exercise. I swept and mopped the office when necessary, was first to arrive and last to leave, opened the mail and answered much of it, read manuscripts and proofs, corrected copy.... In between these chores I would take Randolph's dictation directly on the typewriter.
> Many a time we would stop and laugh over some Socialist cliché or dubious generalization, and at such times I realized Randolph was wiser than I had imagined.[25]

Schuyler's minimizing of his role, however, cannot be taken entirely at face value; his articles and columns for the *Messenger* were mostly filled with rhetoric that would have done any socialist proud, though the *Messenger* had lost some of its radical fire months before Schuyler joined the masthead. It is also worth noting that Schuyler wrote his autobiography, *Black and Conservative,* over a quarter century after he'd thoroughly rejected radicalism. The book is therefore rife with

24. George S. Schuyler, *Black and Conservative: The Autobiography of George S. Schuyler,* 137. See also McKay's *A Long Way from Home,* 1937.
25. Schuyler, *Black and Conservative,* 136.

Schuyler's obsession with the so-called communist threat, skewing his views appreciably.

In any case, Schuyler's work at the *Messenger* was not his sole outlet for satiric invective. Schuyler became a correspondent for the *Pittsburgh Courier* in 1924 and spent the early part of his forty-year career with the paper writing many columns similar to those in the *Messenger*. Most satirized a number of the figures prominent in contemporary mainstream American and African American politics. In addition, Schuyler's most famous essay, "The Negro-Art Hokum," published in the *Nation* in 1926, argued against a syncretic African American artistic sensibility. This particular column was followed by Langston Hughes's "The Negro Artist and the Racial Mountain," which disagreed with Schuyler's argument at certain points. Both columns had a significant influence on Harlem Renaissance intellectual politics.

The critiques Schuyler created in his columns and articles for these and other publications bear strong resemblances to the satire in *Black No More*. In his early journalistic career, Schuyler tended to "quote a news story that had absurd ramifications, then comment, bitingly and punningly, on its significance for the average black man," which was frequently shame upon and potential or actual harm for black people as a whole.[26] Several months after Schuyler started writing his regular *Messenger* column, "Shafts and Darts: A Page of Calumny and Satire," he and *Messenger* drama critic Theophilus Lewis drew up a topical philosophy for the column, one that placed them in the classic role of the satirist:

> [Our] intention is . . . to slur, lampoon, damn and occasionally praise anybody or anything in the known universe, not excepting the President of the immortals. . . . Furthermore [we] make no effort to conceal the fact that [our] dominant motive is a malicious one and that our paragraphs of praise shall be few and far between, while [we] go to greater lengths to discover and expose the imbecilities, knavery and pathological virtues of [our] fellowman. . . . If any considerable body of Americans were intelligent in the human sense, or even civilized, . . . their manly and dignified behavior would be copied. . . . It pains this pair of *misanthropes* even to think of such a state of affairs, and they fervently hope their excursions into morbid humor will not be confused with the crusade of benevolent killjoys to change America.[27]

26. *GSS*, 22.
27. George S. Schuyler and Theophilus Lewis, "Shafts and Darts: A Page of Calumny and Satire," 108. Emphasis mine.

Through their use of the word *misanthrope*, Schuyler and Lewis give some indication of their joint affection for the satire of H. L. Mencken, whom both authors, but especially Schuyler, emulated. Schuyler in particular contributed a number of essays to Mencken's journal *American Mercury*, which "concerned itself intensively with investigations into the total nature of American civilization."[28] Mencken and Schuyler were so closely allied ideologically, in fact, that Schuyler soon earned a reputation as the "black Mencken." On matters of race, Schuyler and *American Mercury*'s publisher were remarkably consistent in their inconsistency. Both were inarguably antiracist in their general outlook and philosophy but repeatedly scoffed at the possibility of black cultural nationalism or group identity being a viable avenue for opposition to racism. Beyond his arguments in "The Negro-Art Hokum," Schuyler delighted in lampooning anyone who argued in favor of Black Nationalism in any form. Schuyler caricatured Marcus Garvey and his Universal Negro Improvement Association many times in "Shafts and Darts" and in his columns for the *Pittsburgh Courier*, with the focus often on Garvey's most recent embarrassing legal incident or rhetorical gaffe. Simultaneously, though, Schuyler supported black economic cooperatives in Harlem and wrote predominantly in black publications such as the *Courier* for most of his career, with the focus almost always on "racial" issues—this, despite the fact that Schuyler considered race a scientific fiction, just as Thurman did.[29] While Schuyler was certainly inconsistent in his beliefs about race, I agree with Jeffrey Tucker that his work is not simply an example of double-consciousness writ large. It would be more accurate to say, as Tucker does, that Schuyler's view of race was "flawed" in that he allowed the fact that race is a scientific myth to overshadow his awareness that race, as a social construction, still carries social *weight*, and that group identity can be a useful tool for liberation.[30]

Nonetheless, the rhetorical pattern established in "Shafts and Darts" provides the guideline for *Black No More*. Schuyler prefaces the novel with a narrative meant to resemble an actual news bulletin that

---

28. *B&W*, 313.
29. Schuyler, *Black and Conservative*, 195. One of the most intriguing products of Schuyler's tenure at the *Courier* was *Black Empire*, his novel written under the nom de plume Samuel I. Brooks and serialized between 1936 and 1938. The novel seems to favor a pan-Africanist ideology not unlike those supported by W. E. B. Du Bois and Marcus Garvey, both of whom Schuyler caricatures in *Black No More*.
30. Tucker, "Science," 140–41.

sneers at common beliefs among black people of white phenotypical (and, by extension, cultural) superiority. The preface tells us first of the actual invention of the "Kink-No-More" hair process used to straighten kinky black hair, then proceeds to catalog the subsequent profitability of similar cosmetic hair and skin processes that only reify "Americans' constant reiteration of the superiority of whiteness" (*BNM*, 13). We are then informed that several contemporary scientists have come close to fulfilling the rather outrageous, if unconscious, wish of many black people to become phenotypically white, which sets the stage for the satire and posits its central, fantastic premise: What would ensue if science provided all African Americans with access to the ultimate privilege of American society, whiteness?

In his literary biography of Schuyler, Michael Peplow reveals that the underlying irony of Schuyler's preface is that the articles he cites to record the scientists' experiments are based upon historical events. In the preface, Schuyler tells us that a Dr. Yusaburo Noguchi claimed in October 1929 that he had discovered the means to "change a Negro into a white man by using a treatment involving glandular control and electrical nutrition" (*BNM*, 13–14). Peplow reports that in the *Pittsburgh Courier* of November 2, 1929, "a front page article about a Dr. Yusaburo Noguchi was headlined: 'Racial Metamorphosis Claimed by Scientist: Japanese Says He Can Change Black Skin Into White. . . .' The article claims that Noguchi's treatments 'include the use of sun rays, ultra-violet rays, special diets and glandular treatments.' "[31] Through this particular obscure reference we witness Shuyler's penchant for basing his satire upon significant historical events that point toward the sickness of essentialist obsessions if they were subjected to reductio ad absurdum.

Indeed, *Black No More*'s very framework ironically posits this confrontation between science and America's racial situation via its subtitle, *Being an Account of the Strange and Wonderful Workings of Science in the Land of the Free, A.D. 1933–1940*, which is made doubly ironic by the facts that the novel was written in 1930 and millions of African Americans, subject to lynchings and the gross inequalities of sharecropping and other forms of economic exploitation, could hardly be considered "free." In Schuyler's terms, as we shall see, true freedom

---

31. Peplow, *GSS*, 57, 123 n. 6.

for African Americans means both liberation from exploitation and abuse and the evisceration of constructions of racial identity and meaning in America.

The novel opens with the black protagonist, Max Disher, attending a Harlem nightclub and mourning his inability to impress the "yallah" women he prefers with his friend Bunny. Each man "had in common a weakness rather prevalent among Aframerican bucks: they preferred yellow women. Both swore there were three things essential to the happiness of a colored gentleman: yellow money, yellow women and yellow taxis. They had little difficulty in getting the first and none at all in getting the third but the yellow women they found flighty and fickle. . . . They were so sought after that one almost required a million dollars to keep them out of the clutches of one's rivals" (*BNM*, 19). The disproportionate premium Max and Bunny place upon "yellow," or light-skinned black, women simultaneously recalls the problem of the intraracial color-caste system, which was highly pronounced, strict, and overt in the early twentieth century, and acts as one signifier of the pervasiveness of essentialist racial constructions. Schuyler emphasizes early in the narrative that African Americans are generally obsessed with race. After Max and Bunny pontificate on the supposed vices of "yallah" women, Max attempts to court a southern white woman who summarily rejects and slurs him, yet he remains intrigued and thunderstruck, fantasizing about "dancing . . . , dining . . . , motoring with her, sitting beside her on a golden throne while millions of manacled white slaves prostrated themselves before him" (*BNM*, 24). This dream gives way to a nightmare of a lynching, of which Max is the victim, for daring to desire a white woman. Bunny then tells Max that a "Dr. Junius Crookman" has just "announced a sure way to turn darkies white" (*BNM*, 24–25). Max subsequently volunteers to be one of the first to subject himself to Crookman's process, and is transformed into a Caucasian; Bunny later follows suit.

From this point, the novel enters the realm of the picaresque, with Max and Bunny as the most obvious picaros. Michael W. Peplow posits that via the role Max plays in exploiting a fantastic America virtually bereft of black people, Schuyler is creating "a black *picaro*" in which "both European and black folklore traditions" are merged; Max is "an archetypal black trickster who dons a white mask to 'put on Ole Massa'" (*GSS*, 67; italics in the original). The correctness of Peplow's assertion may be easily observed if we apply his definitions of the picaro as "a lovable rogue . . . who makes his way 'more through his wits and his industry' " (*GSS*, 67). Furthermore, the picaro never develops as a realistic character but "starts as a picaro and ends as a picaro, manifesting the same attitudes and qualities throughout." He can be a trickster, for "tricks are essential to survival in chaos". . . . Finally, "the *picaro* is a protean figure who can not only serve many masters but play different roles," wear different masks (*GSS*, 67; italics in the original). In Max's case, his masks begin to accumulate once he undergoes his physical transformation. He changes his name to Matthew Fisher, decides to "play around, enjoy life and laugh at the white folks" (*BNM*, 48) and eventually, by playing the role of a staunch racist, infiltrates the Ku Klux Klan clone "Knights of Nordica" and becomes its "Grand Exalted Giraw" (*BNM*, 111). Through this role, Max helps incite the xenophobia of whites watching a country built on racial stratifications crumble as millions of African Americans undergo Crookman's process, causing the nation's most despised race essentially to disappear.

The disappearance of African Americans is the vehicle carrying Schuyler's critique of America's obsession with race. When faced with having no one to exploit for various purposes, the economy and social structure of the nation falls into chaos. The satire exposes officials and ordinary citizens at every level of American society as, essentially, advocates of the beliefs that "a white skin was a sure indication of the possession of superior intellectual and moral qualities; that all Negroes were inferior to [whites]; that God had intended for the United States to be a white man's country and that with His help [whites] could keep it so; that their sons and brothers might inadvertently marry Negresses or, worse, their sisters and daughters might marry Negroes, if Black-No-More, Incorporated [Crookman's company], was permitted to continue its dangerous activities" (*BNM*, 78). Although Max, as Matthew, inculcates these traditional racist beliefs into a Knights of Nordica audience, we observe that groups and individuals of all races accept coded variants of these dogma.

The National Social Equality League, for instance, headed by the Du Boisian Dr. Shakespeare Agamemnon Beard finds that

> [n]o dues had been collected in months and subscriptions to the national
> mouthpiece, *The Dilemma* [equivalent to the NAACP's the *Crisis*], had
> dwindled to almost nothing. Officials. . . . began to envision the time

when they would no longer be able for the sake of the Negro race to suffer the hardships of lunching on canvasback duck at the Urban Club surrounded by the white dilettante . . . or undergo the excruciating torture of rolling back and forth across the United States in drawing-rooms to hear each lecture on the Negro problem. . . . And now they saw the work of a lifetime being rapidly destroyed. (*BNM*, 89)

Schuyler's satire is directed not only toward a thinly disguised NAACP, but also toward all civil rights or other African American–centered organizations that, while supposedly working on behalf of African Americans, enjoy enormous profits and luxury at the expense of their constituencies and seem to yield scant results in the form of actual progress toward equality. Schuyler's satire thus becomes a thinly veiled roman à clef using comical pseudonyms for the most prominent characters, especially those characters who shall be subjected to the most bilious satirical treatments. Crookman's surname, for example, signifies his obvious willingness to make obscene amounts of money fulfilling African America's greatest, if most pathetic, wish of becoming white. Again, Dr. W. E. B. Du Bois appears as Dr. Shakespeare Agamemnon Beard, whose name is a reference to Du Bois's background in Western letters, his abilities as a "warrior . . . for equal rights" and his trademark Van Dyke beard; "Dr. Napoleon Wellington Jackson," president of the N.S.E.L., represents James Weldon Johnson.[32] "Santop Licorice," leader of the "Back-to-Africa Society," is Marcus Garvey, and the UNIA; the surname "Licorice" refers to Garvey's dark skin color. Significantly, Schuyler is not content to lampoon only the NAACP; the "Back-to-Africa Society" also watches the contents of their coffers evaporate and their apparently useless nationalist plans fail (*BNM*, 101–5).

In his satires of both the integrationist and nationalist branches of black politics, Schuyler points out that messianic programs and leaders are virtually as problematic as white racist organizations who would destroy African Americans altogether. Each end of the political spectrum uses African Americans for its own enrichment and would not in fact exist without the continued presence and suffering of black people. The only difference between the two, and the text's clearest irony, is that the former is enriched by attempting to save

32. Ibid., 61–62.

black people, the latter, by trying to destroy them. Moreover, Schuyler demonstrates the value of foregrounding race in the political arena. Labor unions and both the Democratic and Republican Parties find themselves warring between and among themselves as to the best way to exploit common fears of black social equality and, implicitly, of miscegenation. In the first case, Max is able to break a mill workers' strike in Paradise, South Carolina, by simply planting rumors that the strike leader is of African heritage. When "liberal" and "radical" labor leaders travel from New York City to investigate the situation, the former is persecuted because he lives in Harlem and is therefore guilty by association of being a "nigger"; the latter is "prevented from holding a street meeting when someone start[ed] a rumor that he believed in dividing up property, nationalizing women, and was in addition an atheist. He freely admitted the first, laughed at the second and proudly proclaimed the third. That was sufficient to inflame the mill hands, although God had been strangely deaf to their prayers, they owned no property to divide and most of their women were so ugly that they need have had no fears that any outsiders would want to nationalize them" (*BNM*, 127–28). Thus the "radical," like the "liberal," is driven out of town and the labor dispute killed, with the "erstwhile class conscious workers . . . terror-stricken by the specter of black blood," thereby fulfilling the prophecy that "unorganized labor meant cheap labor; . . . that so long as the ignorant white masses could be kept thinking of the menace of the Negro to Caucasian race purity and political control, they would give little thought to labor organization. . . . [The] Black-No-More treatment was [therefore] more of a menace to white business than to white labor" (*BNM*, 127, 65).

Under Schuyler's absurdist rubric, each major political party can and will always rely on xenophobia as a rallying point in an election. In the 1936 election,

[f]or the first time in American history it seemed that money was not going to decide an election. The propagandists and publicity men of the Democrats had so played upon the fears and prejudices of the public that even the bulk of Jews and Catholics were wavering and many had been won over to the support of a candidate who had denounced them but a few months before. In this they were but running true to form, however, as they had usually been on the side of white supremacy in the old days when there was a Negro population observable to the eye. (*BNM*, 175)

It is this set of fears that Max, as the trickster, utilizes for his amusement and considerable enrichment, including, ironically, marriage to the daughter of Henry Givens, head of the Knights of Nordica, thus perpetuating miscegenation (*BNM*, 222).

In addition to using Max as the picaro/trickster exploiting the irony of racial obsession, Schuyler draws upon common satirical rhetoric. Michael Peplow lists Schuyler's rhetorical devices as *"reductio ad absurdum,* projection, caricature, parody, . . . a picaresque hero. . . . [and an] ability to walk that fine line between Horatian lightheartedness and Juvenalian despair."[33] In the latter category, Schuyler displays extraordinary skill. While *Black No More* certainly follows in the footsteps of Swift's *Gulliver's Travels* in its implicit belief in misanthropy, in the inevitability of human failure, it simultaneously finds this failure comical, insofar as humankind, especially its American genus, professes a curious hatred for those things it unconsciously longs to be or should be, or vice versa.[34] In Schuyler's milieu, we find Dr. Shakespeare Agamemnon Beard, who "wrote scholarly and biting editorials . . . denouncing the Caucasians whom he secretly admired and lauding the greatness of the Negroes whom he alternately pitied and despised" (*BNM*, 90); we witness numerous people describing themselves as staunch "Christians" even though they violate every principle of the Christian religion regularly, including one Rev. Mc-Phule (pronounced "Mc*fuel*," which McPhule and his flock consider all black people to be for lynching purposes), who bases his calling upon sexual orgies and frequent lynchings. In addition, McPhule's sexual appetites allow Schuyler to engage in substantial punning and double entendre. As part and parcel of his message of Christ's "love," McPhule fulfills the stereotype of the immoral preacher: "Every latch-string hung out for him. As usual with gentlemen of the cloth, he was especially popular with the ladies. When the men were at work in the fields, the Man of God would visit house after house and comfort the

33. Ibid., 72.
34. This is perfectly in keeping with Frank Stringfellow's psychoanalytic theory of irony, which argues that "human beings develop a limitless variety of ways of expressing at one and the same time (or in rapid succession) contradictory wishes, impulses, desires, and meanings—at least one of which is curiously unconscious. . . . Certainly irony would qualify as a compromise formation of this kind. For irony allows the ironist to express two or more conflicting ideas at once and to mean both or all of them" (28).

womenfolk with his Christian message. Being a bachelor, he made these professional calls with great frequency" (*BNM*, 207). Furthermore, McPhule *"erects"* an altar upon which Happy Hill's loneliest or most deranged women would supposedly make "confessions and requests," an exercise from which "[n]one departed unsatisfied" (*BNM*, 207; emphasis mine).

One McPhule-led lynching in particular provides the novel with its climax and an opportunity for Schuyler to engage in his strongest and most effective parody. Presidential candidates Snobbcraft and Dr. Buggerie are forced, due to a plane crash, into McPhule's parish in Happy Hill, Mississippi, disguised as African Americans. The lynching-hungry inhabitants of the hamlet interpret the men's appearance as a religious omen and subsequently proceed to lynch them in the village square. Michael Peplow describes the lynching as a "horrible parody of a true religious celebration" (*GSS*, 75), since Rev. McPhule convinces the lynch mob to "proceed according to time-honored custom," with grotesque, carnivalistic "preliminaries" such as emasculation, tortuous "surgery," and a brief chase of the maimed men through the woods that ends with a burning at the stake, which the village "gaily" and "proud[ly]" conducts (*BNM*, 216–18). The underlying irony of the occasion, of course, is that such rituals and tortures were commonly inflicted upon black lynching victims throughout the South at the time.[35]

The novel concludes by returning to circumstances similar to those at its beginning. Dr. Junius Crookman, now surgeon general of the United States, publishes findings

> that in practically every instance [of black people made white by the Black-No-More process] the new Caucasians were from two to three shades lighter than the old Caucasians, and that approximately one-sixth of the population were in the first group. . . . To a society that had been taught to venerate whiteness for over three hundred years, this announcement was rather staggering. What was the world coming to, if the blacks were whiter than the whites. (*BNM*, 218–19)

Subsequently, white people begin seeking out processes to tan and darken themselves and begin persecuting all of the country's palest

---

35. See for example, Ralph Ginzburg's *100 Years of Lynchings* (Baltimore: Black Classics Press, 1988), a partial record of lynchings in the United States.

citizens in precisely the same ways blacks were persecuted. The same figures who led black civil rights organizations before Black-No-More, such as Dr. Shakespeare Agamemnon Beard (now Karl von Beerde), become leaders of "The Down-With-White-Prejudice-League" and similar associations; history is rewritten to demonstrate that civilization came from people with less pale skin, and various companies arise to exploit these hatreds to enormous profit. Meanwhile, Max Disher has fled to France with his family and considerable fortune, both gained from taking advantage of racial phobias (*BNM*, 220–22).

Thus Schuyler's satire effectively becomes complete. The United States is completely unable to break free of its long history of policies, laws, and social rituals upholding white supremacy for the simple reason that racial equality is inherently unprofitable. The rise in financial and social stature of Max and Crookman demonstrates, to an absurd degree, precisely how much can be gained from racial essentialisms and, furthermore, how many Americans are eager to exploit those same essentialisms.

While interest in Thurman and Schuyler has grown in the last decade, it has become no less difficult to glean information about the life of Dr. Rudolph "Bud" Fisher, despite the fact that his two novels, *The Conjure-Man Dies* (1932) and *The Walls of Jericho* (1928), are among the finest of the Harlem Renaissance's output. Although both novels are noteworthy for their fairly accurate representations of everyday life in Harlem, the former novel, like Schuyler's *Black No More*, stands as a milestone in the history of African American literature, being the first detective novel ever published by an African American. For our purposes, however, *The Conjure-Man Dies* is far less relevant than *The Walls of Jericho*, to which it is a sequel of sorts. Although the latter novel might legitimately be called the first satirical novel by an African American, I argue that the satirical tone is less pervasive and consistent than in other works. Fisher is more determined to re-create a feel for Harlem in the 1920s, and his work, while often funny, ironic, and disturbing, does not always veer into the sort of bitter satire prevalent in Schuyler's and Thurman's novels. Fisher's roman à clef does, however, contain plotlines that are continuous, thinly veiled attacks upon the decadent atmosphere and some major figures of the renaissance. Perhaps more important, Fisher engages in one of the more salient criticisms of class differences based on color. These were differences that Fisher witnessed firsthand as a medical doctor and therefore a member of the so-called "Talented Tenth" that W. E. B. Du Bois argued would be responsible for uplifting the race. *The Walls of Jericho* certainly qualifies as one of the few novels by a member of Harlem's black bourgeoisie that openly criticizes that caste's ambitions. In that respect, it is an important forerunner of novels such as John Oliver Killens's *The Cotillion* (1971) or Ishmael Reed's *Reckless Eyeballing* (1986), both of which question the racial commitment and sincerity of the black bourgeoisie.

Immediately dividing Harlem in the opening pages into a community of "dickties," represented by the very fair-skinned African American lawyer, Fred Merrit, and "shines" or "rats," personified in the comic pair of piano movers, Jinx Jenkins and Bubber Brown, Fisher maps out a city within a city that is in the process of converting into the black Mecca of legend.[36] When Merrit purchases a house on Court Street in an upscale, predominantly white section of Harlem, the African American community begins to split over whether Merrit's civil rights should be protected, allowing him to move into his dream home, or it is more important not to raise racial tensions by acquiescing to the established definitions between the races. Using their own form of "signifying," Jinx and Bubber debate whether it is worth the time and effort of any "rat" to defend the aspirations of "dickties," who "prefer to ignore [their] existence" (*WOJ*, 3):

> "Ef he move in that neighborhood, [Bubber argues], fays'll start sump'm sho'—and sho' as they start it, d' boogies'll finish it. Won't make no difference 'bout this Merrit man—he'll jes' be d' excuse. . . ."
> "Yea," said Jinx. "I've head 'bout that, too. But I don't think no shine's got no business bustin' into no fay neighborhood."
> "He got business bustin' in any place he want to go. Only way for him to get any where is to bust in—ain' nobody gon' *invite* him in."
> "Aw, man, whut you talkin' 'bout? Hyeh's a dickty tryin' his damnedest to be fay—like all d' dickties. When they git in hot water they all come cryin' to you and me fo' help."
> . . . "Fays don' see no difference 'tween dickty shines and any other kind o' shines. One jig in danger is ev'y jig in danger. They'd lick *them* and come on down on *us*. Then we'd have to fight anyhow. What's use o' waitin'?" (*WOJ*, 7–8)

---

36. "Dickties" were the light-skinned, bourgeois African American professional class; "shines" were working-class African Americans.

Of critical importance in this passage is a question that ran beneath the surface of the entire Harlem Renaissance. As Harlem underwent the slow transformation from a largely white suburb of New York City to a predominantly black city within a city, and as African Americans themselves became more prosperous, the rift between different classes of African Americans, which had existed since slavery, began to widen, exacerbated by prevalent notions of the superiority of light skin and ancestral proximity to whites.[37] A certain degree of white privilege was reserved for those African Americans who were light-skinned, and many of those individuals—the so-called "dickties"—delighted in exploiting those same privileges.

This delight, however, frequently came at the expense of the black underclass. It also revealed an acceptance of the basic premises of American racism, thus expanding an already disturbingly large rift. Bubber and Jinx's ambivalence toward Merrit's situation is but a reflection of their culture's ambivalence and, as the novel progresses, a sign of Fisher's sympathies for the class to which they belong.

This sympathy is reinforced as the novel provides us with a deeper look at the cowardice and hypocrisy of the "dickties" themselves when the "Litter Rats Club," a group of dickties with members resembling the "Niggeratti" and their mentors, meets to discuss Merrit's case.[38] The club's concern, as its president, J. Pennington Potter, proclaims, is to make certain that " '[t]his colony . . . should extend itself naturally and gradually—not by violence and bloodshed' " (WOJ, 36). Merrit, arguably the text's representation of Fisher's voice, responds

37. Numerous historians of Harlem, such as Nathan Irvin Huggins, David Levering Lewis, and James de Jongh, have pointed out that Harlem "was not identified with African American life in the city of New York until the early decades of the twentieth century" (De Jongh, Vicious, 5). Several factors contributed to a rapid influx of African Americans into Harlem during the century's opening decades, including collapse of the Harlem real estate market, the beginning of the Great Migration of African Americans from the oppression of the Deep South to the relative bounty of opportunities in the North, and the potential for black independence. Still, in the mid-1920s, black Harlem was still surrounded—and controlled—by a larger white majority in the city.

38. Members include "Tod Bruce," whose personality resembles that of Richard Bruce Nugent and Wallace Thurman, and the Langston Hughes-esque "Langdon, an innocent looking youngster who was at heart a prime rascal and who compensated by writing poetry" (WOJ, 36). Potter is arguably an amalgamation of renaissance midwives James Weldon Johnson, W. E. B. Du Bois, Jessie Redmon Fauset, and Alain Locke.

militantly, arguing that " '[t]he extension of territory by violence and bloodshed strikes me as natural enough. . . . I haven't much of a memory, but I seem to recall one or two instances,' " from American history in which the nation expanded its boundaries through murder and deception. Potter's fear is a direct reflection of the views held by the more conservative element among the black bourgeoisie, reminiscent of Booker T. Washington, who support slow, natural progression of the race, rather than militant protest. As Litter Rat Tod Bruce observes,

> Nowadays . . . we grow by—well—a sort of passive conquest. The fays move out, and the jigs are so close no more fays will move in. So the landlord has to rent to jigs and the colony keeps extending. But if Fred wants to return to the older method, I don't think it will do any great harm to the rest of us. He's taking all the risk. And even though he claims a racial interest, he has admitted that the chief motive is personal after all. It's his business. (*WOJ*, 43)

By attempting to integrate white Harlem, then, Merrit is reaching beyond the boundaries set for African Americans via the example of Booker T. Washington, boundaries still held sacred by the genteel bourgeoisie.

Fisher's novel, like so many others emerging from the renaissance, exhibits the influence of H. L. Mencken, whose railings against the "booboisie," the genteel, Victorian-influenced American middle- to upper-class circles, were well loved by many among the Niggeratti, including Fisher. It is with Mencken in mind that Fisher later satirizes one figure in particular as a metonym for the white patronage that Wallace Thurman would retrospectively blame as one of the reasons for the renaissance's demise. The dowdy, stuffy Miss Agatha Cramp, a rich, white philanthropist and patron of the arts, is inarguably meant to represent Charlotte Osgood Mason, the patron responsible for financing the early careers of Langston Hughes, Zora Neale Hurston, Alain Locke, and other major figures of the Harlem Renaissance. Boasting of Cramp's "sufficiently large store of wealth and . . . sufficiently small store of imagination," Fisher creates a portrait of a hypocritically racist woman who has "been devoting her life to the service of mankind. Not until now had the startling possibility occurred to her that Negroes might be mankind, too" (*WOJ*, 58, 61). As David Levering Lewis has noted, Mason, known affectionately as "Godmother" by her beneficiaries, was a dowager obsessed with "primitives," whether they were of Negroid or Native American stock. She continually sought out the elements in African American culture that seemed to be "pure"; that is to say, she sought the last traces of unadulterated Africanisms in black culture, and usually failed to notice the rich amalgam before her eyes.

Thus, for Agatha Cramp, "Negroes to her [have] been rather ugly but serviceable fixtures, devices that [happen] to be alive, dull instruments of drudgery" until a conversation with her maid, Linda, reveals that some "primitives" may actually be worthy of social work and improvement (*WOJ*, 61–69). Fisher quickly compares Cramp to other whites who come to Harlem and head its civil rights and improvement associations (embodied in the "General Improvement Association," a composite of the NAACP and Marcus Garvey, UNIA) out of paternalistic rather than altruistic impulses, and those who come to gawk shamelessly at Negro life with "gasps, grunts, and ill-concealed squirms, or sighs and astonished smiles" (*WOJ*, 73). Cramp eventually meets Merrit and, mistaking him for a white man, is delighted to hear that the apartment he has purchased is next to hers. Much of the plot's remainder revolves around Merrit's sardonic attempts to expose Cramp for the fool she is by concealing his heritage, thereby drawing out the witless dowager's prejudices.

The novel eventually incorporates the metaphor of the biblical story of Joshua, who defeated the city of Jericho by forcing its walls down with God's aid, just as Merrit defeats the likes of Agatha Cramp by tearing down the walls of prejudice—whether based on race or class—and segregation. His victory in this regard is later negated, however, when, ironically, the black pool hall owner Henry Patmore burns down Merrit's residence and attempts to rape Linda, with whom Merrit had been involved, as vengeance for a past offense. Given that Merrit was expecting one of the white residents of his neighborhood to attempt to chase him out of the area, the novel thus comes full circle to show that intraracial tensions and problems can actually be more dangerous than interracial ones. It illustrates Fisher's ambivalence regarding racial issues. In his 1927 essay "The Caucasian Storms Harlem," Fisher questions the motives behind the rapid influx of whites into Harlem, but he also wonders whether whites, in taking a strong interest in African Americans, "at last have tuned in on our wavelength. Maybe they are at last learning to speak our language" (*WOJ*, 82). This possibility might have inspired Fisher to include a glossary of Harlem slang at the end of *Walls of Jericho* to help his predominantly white audience translate Harlem lingo and therefore enter Harlem's discourse. Fisher implicitly posits the possibility for black and white America to begin communicating on equal terms, using the same lexicon.

To that extent, Fisher's *The Walls of Jericho* maintains the cultural introspection found throughout the novels of the Harlem Renaissance and adds the ironic critique found later within Schuyler's and Thurman's columns and novels. As the Harlem Renaissance eventually withered away beneath the pressures of the Great Depression and the entire period's decadence, these ironic introspectives would prove to be the most cogent views of the renaissance extant. While they certainly did not lack Harlem Renaissance contemporaries who were willing to criticize the movement either as it occurred or in retrospect, Fisher and Thurman were the only former members of the "Niggeratti" who wrote novels explicitly devoted to satirizing the period.

Hughes and Zora Neale Hurston also offered their satirical and allegorical takes on the racial politics at the time. Discussing Hughes and Hurston in the context of *African American Satire*, though, is somewhat problematic. Hughes's satirical view of race relations emerged in his *The Ways of White Folks* (1934), a collection of short stories that, while brilliant and almost universally praised by his contemporaries, is still not a novel in the strictest sense. The stories are connected by one overarching problematic: the condescension, paternalism, and hypocrisy of whites nationwide. Not all are satirical, though, despite Sherwood Anderson's mostly accurate assertion that Hughes turned his white characters into "caricatures."[39] Hurston's 1939 novel, *Moses, Man of the Mountain,* presents a thornier problem: only select passages are explicitly satirical and therefore fit squarely in the genre. Hurston's novel instead combines a revision of one of the biblical tales historically most popular among African Americans with passages that hint ambiguously that Hurston might have tried to write a roman à clef lampooning portions of the contemporary African American leadership. I cannot comfortably claim that Hurston's novel should be read primarily as a satire, but examination of the aforementioned passages will reveal how her folk humor embodies a critique of the crisis in

39. *LLH,* 1:289–90.

black leadership. I shall turn first to a brief analysis of selections from Hughes's work and conclude by aligning Hurston's novel with other satirical Harlem Renaissance works.

Although Hughes's contribution to the Harlem Renaissance's satiric oeuvre was published in 1934, it is perhaps best discussed in the same breath as Fisher's *Walls of Jericho*. Both works contain passages or stories that satirize old white female patrons of the arts. In both cases, these patrons resemble Charlotte Osgood Mason, who kept Fisher on her payroll for young artists. Fisher and Hughes both eventually became disillusioned with Mason's condescending view of African Americans as "America's great link with the primitive" and translated that resentment into satire. In Hughes's case, the impetus for writing the vignettes in *The Ways of White Folks* stemmed from the extremely close relationship he had with Mason and its bitter ending in 1930. As Hughes stated bluntly in *The Big Sea*, "She wanted me to be primitive and know and feel the intuitions of the primitive. But, unfortunately, I did not feel the rhythms of the primitive surging through me, and so I could not live and write as though I did." Hughes was also becoming troubled by the comfort he enjoyed as the Great Depression was settling in; it "became hard [to eat] dinner on Park Avenue [with Mason] while the snow fell outside" and black Americans were becoming poorer and finding it even more difficult to survive from day to day.[40] In addition, Hughes was not as prolific as before, and this meant an end to the $150 personal stipend Hughes had received from Mason every month, to say nothing of the occasional $50 to $200 clothes, dinners, and other perquisites she gave him (*LLH*, 1:185).[41]

On the other hand, the break between Hughes and Mason made absolutely clear to him what Thurman had been saying for years about the Harlem literati. He best distanced himself from Mason's call for primitivism through the catharsis of his writing. In Rampersad's terms, Hughes "set a new standard of excellence for black writers" even as he "emphasiz[ed] the folly of liberal whites, or whites who involve themselves with black mainly to exploit them."[42] This allowed him to "exorciz[e] the fiercest demon in his own past; the entire venture had started with his recognition of Mrs. Mason's terrifying

40. Hughes, *The Big Sea*, 316, 325, 318, 324, 318.
41. In today's dollars, his stipend would be approximately $1,800.
42. *LLH*, 1:290.

white face in a story by D. H. Lawrence, and with Hughes's immediate recognition that he could lash back at her behind the disguise of fiction" (*LLH*, 1:290). Hughes added another level of irony to his exorcism by parodying the title of Du Bois's landmark text *The Souls of Black Folk*, indicating that Hughes was casting yet another baleful look across the veil.

One story in *The Ways of White Folks*, "Slave on the Block," best embodies Hughes's cynicism toward the exploitative white liberal. It opens with Michael and Anne Carraway, an artistic (musician and painter, respectively) white couple who "went in for Negroes," but, we are told, "not in the social-service, philanthropic sort of way, no. They saw no use in helping a race that was already too charming and naïve and lovely for words. Leave them unspoiled and just enjoy them" (*Ways*, 19). That the Carraways exploit a fetish for all things African American should be clear by the sarcastic "no" at the end of the first sentence in this passage, but it is reinforced by the unrelentingly ironic tone throughout the story. For example, the Carraways "owned some [Miguel] Covarrubias originals. Of course Covarrubias wasn't a Negro, but how he caught the darky spirit! They owned all the [Paul] Robeson records and all the Bessie Smith. . . . Of course they knew Harlem like their own backyard, that is, all the speakeasies and night clubs and dances halls. . . . They were acquainted with lots of Negroes, too—but somehow the Negroes didn't seem to like them very much" (*Ways*, 19–20).[43] One reason for African Americans' dislike of the pair is their paternalism. It allows them to consider Luther, a dark-skinned young black man, a "boy" and, because of his skin, "so utterly Negro" and the exemplar of "the jungle," thoroughly stereotypical associations (*Ways*, 21–22). The pair become obsessed with painting and interpreting Luther as a slave on the auction block in New Orleans, the most notorious of all American slave markets. Their obsession extends to posing him nearly nude, thereby eroticizing an already fetishistic image (*Ways*, 24–25). Luther plays along with the Carraways' ambitions, taking full advantage of their stupendous

---

43. Covarrubias was a Cuban-born painter and one of the leading graphic artists of the Harlem Renaissance. Paul Robeson (1898–1976) was an internationally renowned actor, singer, and radical political activist. Blues singer Bessie Smith (1898–1937) first earned the title of "Queen of the Blues" during the Harlem Renaissance.

guile by consuming all of their tobacco and wine and disparaging them behind their backs in much the same way that Zora Neale Hurston would lampoon Mason while she was still on her payroll. The relationship begins to dissolve when the Carraways discover Luther in bed with their black maid, Mattie. Although Anne condones the relationship—" 'It's so simple and natural for Negroes to make love,' " after all—Michael grows tired of "the same Negro always in the way," and after Luther insults his mother, Michael fires him and Mattie, after they have extracted their pay.

While no evidence exists that Hughes viewed Mason cynically while he was in her employ, Luther and Mattie's cynical manipulation of the caricatured Carraways is clearly a stab at Mason. It suggests that if Mason had paid attention to Hughes's work at the point of publication, she would have seen that Hughes and other African Americans benefiting from white patronage were playing the role of trickster. George Hutchinson's arguments suggest, however, that Hughes's characterization is equal parts posture and reality; while whites obsessed with the "primitive" African American—one allegedly free of (white) "civilization"—certainly existed, they do not represent the sum total of whites. Hughes certainly recognized this, inasmuch as one of his closest friends was Carl Van Vechten from the 1920s until Van Vechten's death in 1964. Hughes assiduously defended Van Vechten during the firestorm of controversy over his novel *Nigger Heaven* (1928)—supposedly the low point of white "primitivism"— and Van Vechten was one of the first two people to read the manuscript of *The Ways of White Folks,* so it is highly unlikely that Hughes was making a blanket statement about whites.[44] Moreover, the volume is dedicated to white playwright Noël Sullivan and has as its epigraph a quotation from the story "Berry": "The ways of white folk, I mean *some* white folks" (*Ways,* 181). Therefore, like most satire, Hughes's text is shooting for a broad target at the expense of a balanced critique. In fact, whites *qua* whites are not Hughes's satiric target at all; it is simply those obsessed with primitivism. Like Fisher, Hughes was well aware that whites could not be blamed en masse for African Americans' problems; any criticism of white racism must be balanced with an internal critique.

44. *LLH,* 1:282–83. The other person was Blanche Knopf, also known as Mrs. Alfred A. Knopf, founder of the publishing firm.

Although Zora Neale Hurston is often recognized for her skillful defense of and desire to celebrate African American folk culture, she was as skilled at creating internal critiques of this culture as her Harlem Renaissance contemporaries. That Hurston should possess this skill is not surprising, given the amount of criticism she received once her career as a novelist was well under way. Robert Hemenway has already documented Hurston's struggles with her critics, especially figures such as Richard Wright and Alain Locke, in great detail; I shall not attempt to repeat his work here. Hemenway notes at several points, though, that Hurston's critics frequently misunderstood her technique of combining the folk/vernacular voice with more formal narrative discourse in her short stories and novels as either a sign of artistic inconsistency or an imposition of folklore upon reality, rather than an attempt to represent reality itself. In other words, Hurston was often accused of writing her novels as glib expanded folktales, failing to comprehend that her "fiction represented the process of folkloric transmission, emphasizing the ways of thinking and speaking which grow from the folk environment." Moreover, in her efforts to represent African American realities, Hurston doggedly refused to write the naturalistic "social document fiction" that replaced the experimentalism of the early Harlem Renaissance in the 1930s.[45] Hurston chose instead to use folklore to write about African American lives through indirection. Nor was she above offering sharp criticisms of African America in her novels. I argue that *Moses, Man of the Mountain* stands as an allegory that sometimes satirizes the problem of African American leadership.

In *Moses*, Hurston draws upon the Mosaic legend "not so much to debunk a Judeo-Christian prophet as to remove him from scripture in order to relocate him in Afro-American tradition." The novel is a revision of Hurston's short story "The Fire and the Cloud" (1934), which posited Moses as "half man, half god," a figure standing midway between the divine and the earthly.[46] This role is identical to Moses' place in the Vodun (Voodoo) practices that Hurston had studied in *Tell My Horse*, her 1938 anthropological study of Haitian and Jamaican syncretic religious practices. *Moses* remains Hurston's least-studied novel; whereas her 1937 masterpiece *Their Eyes Were Watching God* has

45. *ZNH*, 242.
46. Ibid., 258, 256.

received virtually immeasurable critical attention and posthumous classic status, articles and book chapters on *Moses* remain scarce. The reasons are diverse, but perhaps the most important is that *Moses* is easily the most ambitious work Hurston published in her lifetime. It also flits between the satiric mode, folklore, romance, and the picaresque; it is therefore difficult to classify.

Equally important is the radical move Hurston attempts by suggesting that Moses and the Israelites in bondage in Egypt are analogous to African Americans; they speak in Black English and contemporary slang, are kept in slavery, must withstand various forms of overt racist oppression, and are more deeply tied culturally to the land of their oppression than they would like to admit. Invariably, racism is portrayed as utterly irrational, yet possessing absolute hegemony over the Israelite body. "The Hebrew womb," for example, "had fallen under the heel of Pharaoh. A ruler great in his newness and new in his greatness had arisen in Egypt and he had said, 'This is law. Hebrew boys shall not be born. All offenders against this law shall suffer death by drowning'" (*Moses*, 1). Hebrew women consequently begin shuddering with "terror at the indifference of their wombs to the Egyptian law" (*Moses*, 1). Hurston's spoofing of the contingent nature of chattel slavery—whether of the Egyptian or American kind—sets a tone of absurdity for the novel, however, that is not meant to be maintained throughout the text. While the pharaoh and his Egyptian slaveholders are repeatedly lampooned as imperious, arrogant buffoons, Hurston relies more upon the dramatic irony written into the original biblical account to drive that portion of the narrative. That is to say, the original account of the Hebrews' escape from bondage in Egypt is wrought with an unspoken irony; those who read or hear how God—through Moses—led the Hebrews to the Promised Land surely understand that the pharaoh is doomed to failure for defying the supreme God of the oppressed. Any dramatic tension is leached out of this archetypal story of the triumph of good over evil.

Hurston's text, though, inserts both dramatic tension and greater irony into the legend by making two crucial moves: (1) minimizing the role of God, and (2) raising Moses from the role as a mere prophet for God to that of a true leader and messianic figure. Hemenway asserts correctly that Hurston recognizes the power of the Mosaic myth in African American culture; it undergirds narratives as diverse as folktales such as "When the People Could Fly," which tells of an African

American griot who teaches other slaves how to fly to freedom, or the spiritual "Go Down, Moses."[47] Slave narrators such as Frederick Douglass frequently compared themselves to biblical prophets; it is no accident that Underground Railroad conductor Harriet Tubman was known as "the Moses of her people." If African Americans in slavery and freedom believed that God would provide a messianic figure to lead them to complete freedom from oppression, then Hurston had an extensive cultural base whence to posit Moses as a human imbued with great powers. I should emphasize that Moses' *humanity* as a leader is Hurston's focus; his adopted siblings, Aaron and Miriam, frequently chide him for his arrogance, which they believe to be a product of his mysterious heritage, which could be either Hebrew or Egyptian. As Hemenway recounts, "In 1937, two years before *Moses* appeared, [Sigmund] Freud had published two controversial essays . . . which drew from sketchy historical evidence to assert not only that Moses was Egyptian, but also that the monotheistic religion he brought to the Hebrews originated with a heretical ruler of Egyptian antiquity."[48] Hurston uses this evidence as another basis to argue that Moses must be considered a great prophet, both a hero and an antihero, inasmuch as he is a decidedly flawed leader of an even more flawed people who admire and revile him at turns. She calls him "a two-headed man"—a nod to Moses' status as a Vodun trickster—and an outcast.

Moses' greatest struggle in the novel, in fact, is not to conquer the pharaoh; it is to find a way to lead the Hebrews, who are obsessed with skin color—they resent having a leader whose wife, Zipporah, is dark-skinned—and with wresting power from Moses, doubting whether he was ever called to lead them in the first place (*Moses*, 242–44). In casting the Hebrews, especially Aaron and Miriam, as overly ambitious, Hurston suggests a crisis in black leadership that Schuyler also recognized. That is to say, the Hebrews, like African Americans, have been beset with leaders who "are much too sensitive to the wishes of the people but [that are] too unconscious of their needs" and have "a big idea of [their] own importance" (*Moses*, 245). This portrait of Aaron reflects Hurston's opinions of leaders ranging

47. Toni Morrison later used this tale as the basis for her novel *Song of Solomon* (1977).
48. *ZNH*, 257. Ishmael Reed later exploited this concept in his novel *Mumbo Jumbo*. See chapter 4.

from Marcus Garvey to Du Bois and Locke, all of whom struck her as arrogant and self-important.[49] While Moses exhibits these same flaws, though, Hurston does not necessarily posit him as the object of satire. Rather, she satirizes the unrealistic expectations the Hebrews and, by extension, African Americans, have of their leaders.

This last idea, which, as we have seen, finds its grounding within the satirical novels of the Harlem Renaissance, recurs innumerable times in subsequent decades. Although critical debates about the failures and successes of the Harlem Renaissance rage on, the period's satirical authors inarguably provided a healthy skepticism toward the grandiose claims of the New Negroes, including themselves. In the process, they opened the field of African American literature for similar critiques in the decades that followed. As I will discuss in subsequent chapters, Hurston and Schuyler's doubts about the qualifications of African American leadership find a new voice in *Invisible Man* and Beatty's *The White Boy Shuffle* (1996), while Ishmael Reed adopts Thurman's sneer toward the advocates of new artistic horizons, calling for a more inclusive aesthetic.

49. *ZNH*, 37–38.

CHAPTER 3

⬚

Channeling the Lower Frequencies

African American Satire from World War II through the Postwar Era

Who knows but that, on the lower frequencies, I speak for you?
—Ralph Ellison, *Invisible Man*

Although the Great Depression effectively ended the high times of the Harlem Renaissance, African American satire continued to flourish after the movement's zenith. In fact, some of the best work of the Harlem Renaissance was published well *after* the movement's heyday. If we recall that *Black No More* was published in 1931, while *Infants of the Spring* saw print in 1934, it becomes clear that the Harlem Renaissance was not immediately cut short by the economic horrors engendered by the stock market crash of October 24, 1929. A cursory glance at the highly influential poetry, short stories, and novels of such authors as Zora Neale Hurston, Langston Hughes, Sterling Brown, and Claude McKay published after 1929 reveals that the authors popular in the 1920s continued writing steadily. Hurston, for example, published her first novel, *Jonah's Gourd Vine*, in 1934, her great anthropological work, *Mules and Men*, in 1935, her masterpiece, *Their Eyes Were Watching God*, in 1937, and one of her least-studied novels, *Moses, Man of the Mountain*, in 1939, a decade after Black Friday. Steven Watson reminds us that the stock market crash "ushered in a period in which white patrons attended to more immediately pressing financial matters than their support of Negro writers," while Harlem continued to act as a cultural and social mecca for African Americans and white Manhattanites until the 1933 repeal of the Volstead Act.[1] Yet the curious assumption that the Harlem Renaissance ended in 1929 persists in the popular mind, due in part to assertions such as Langston Hughes's that the crash "sent Negroes, white folks and all rolling down the hill toward the Works Progress Administration" and away from Harlem.[2] As George Hutchinson argues, though, principal Harlem Renaissance authors like Hughes "rang the death knell of interest in African American writing . . . [p]erhaps because the blossoming of the 1920s had seemed so miraculous, and perhaps the number of *parties* declined."[3] While African American writers no longer enjoyed the vogue in the mind of the American public, a combination of funding from odd writing jobs, continued patronage, and the Federal Writers' Project kept most of the Harlem literati from starving.[4] The myth of the Harlem Renaissance being summarily eliminated by Wall Street's woes is just that.

What is certainly true, however, is that a substantial portion of one generation of African American writers found itself distracted by either an economy that did not lend itself to the sort of bohemian extravagance that the 1920s had afforded or by new careers and interests. In some assessments of African American literature, this change has been cast as a positive development. In his retrospective of the time, George S. Schuyler points out that the term *Harlem Renaissance* is a misnomer, since many of the artists of the renaissance either did not live in Harlem or spent much of their time outside the city within a city.[5] To Schuyler, the renaissance was ultimately an "unscientific and unsound" "sort of racket" by which many people made money, rather than great art. Schuyler was far from alone in his assessment and opinion of the Harlem Renaissance's efficacy as a literary and social

1. Steven Watson, *The Harlem Renaissance: Hub of African-American Culture, 1920–1930*, 157–58.
2. Hughes, *The Big Sea*, 223.
3. *B&W*, 385; italics in the original.
4. In his biography of Hughes, Arnold Rampersad points out that the stock market crash did not immediately affect Charlotte Osgood Mason's protégés—Hughes, Zora Neale Hurston, and Wallace Thurman's future wife, Louise Thompson, *LLH*, 1:174.
5. Ishmael Reed and Steve Cannon, "George S. Schuyler, Writer," 205.

movement; as I discussed in the previous chapter, many of the participants in the renaissance, especially Wallace Thurman, predicted the movement's self-destruction. As Steven Watson has surmised, "[t]he New Negro movement was also torn apart by internal contradictions (the "Niggerati" versus the Harlem intelligentsia, politics versus art, race-building versus literary merit) and its external dependence on Harlemania and white Negrotarians for support. As had the Greenwich Village rebels a generation ago, the New Negroes mistook art for power."[6] The demise of the Harlem Renaissance, then, may prove to be one of the steps that African American literature needed to take to free itself from the paternalism that was a frequent component of outside patronage.

At the very least, our own retrospective of African American writing from the late 1930s through the 1950s quickly reveals a collection that has surpassed the works of the Harlem Renaissance in artistic success. Since Richard Wright's groundbreaking and stunning novel *Native Son* (1940), African American literature has spawned a pantheon of writers whose accomplishments range from the social protest Wright championed or the ideological analyses of Chester Himes to the lyricism of Gwendolyn Brooks or the intellectual precision of James Baldwin. Each of these authors explored inter- and intraracial discourse, perhaps a crucial catalyst for critical debate on race in the twentieth century. Satire by African Americans did not die out completely; as I discussed in the previous chapter, Zora Neale Hurston's later novel *Moses, Man of the Mountain* (1939), even attempts to continue the sort of satirical impulse sprung from the Harlem Renaissance with an opening that simultaneously reinterprets and parodies the Mosaic myth in a way that is intended to parallel the situation of African Americans in America. But this particular novel, like others before it, does not sustain the satiric scene for its entirety, choosing instead to provide an extended morality play for understanding African American politics and the politics of oppression.

In the decade preceding World War II, the radical political notions found within socialism, Marxism, and communism gained new acceptance and popularity among African American intellectuals and,

6. George S. Schuyler, "The Reminiscences of George S. Schuyler," 77, 159.

to a far lesser extent, the African American masses. Radicalism's newfound popularity was fueled partially by the promises of jobs and political organization different radical groups offered. By the early 1930s, the Great Depression had only made African Americans' status more tenuous. Throughout the nation, African Americans accounted for as much as three-quarters of the unemployed, which was double to quadruple the percentage of blacks in a particular area.[7] The Communist Party's radical economic theories, open advocacy of African Americans' civil rights, and continuous publishing opportunities were attractive to the Harlem Renaissance's former stars as well as to future lights such as Langston Hughes, Ralph Ellison, Margaret Walker, Richard Wright, and Chester Himes. At the level of the greater black masses, radicalism as an official affiliation was far less popular, given the often arcane language and content of radical theories. More popular, however, was a sense that America would have to undergo some sort of drastic change if violent social revolution were to be averted. Given that acts of desperation by members of the growing jobless population were becoming commonplace, such a revolution seemed possible and not likely to be cooled. Even the idealism and social programming of the New Deal were ineffective for most of President Roosevelt's first four years in office and were not directed to the needs of African Americans at all in that period.[8] Given the lack of assistance combined with an increase in annual lynching rates after the rapid drops of the 1920s, the outlook for African Americans was grim indeed. It wasn't until Roosevelt's second term and pre–World War II events that African Americans were able to raise some scant hope that social justice waited in the wings. As the New Deal helped to ease the depression's effects, if ever so slightly, African Americans found a national friend and advocate in the person of Eleanor Roosevelt. Her open criticism of her husband's inaction on racial issues resurrected previous hopes that the United States government would offer opportunities for the black worker. When war broke out in Europe in 1939, there were new demands for labor, but they did not touch most African Americans at first; it took Executive Order Number 8802 of June 25, 1941, to end discrimination against blacks in the war industries.[9]

7. *LLH*, 1:214.
8. Robert S. McElvaine, *The Great Depression: America, 1929–1941*, 92, 188.
9. *NSS*, 26–27.

The excellent performance of African Americans in the military during the war revived the hope that had bloomed in many African Americans' minds after World War I, another war in which black servicemen and laborers had performed well. These successes emboldened both those African Americans on the home front and those returning from military service to demand protection of suffrage and other civil rights long denied, especially in the South. Unfortunately, the voicing of these demands met a response similar to that following World War I: increased discrimination and horrific racial violence. Unlike in the post–World War I era, however, African Americans maintained a solid and relatively consistent struggle for civil rights that led to the dramatic legal gains of the 1950s and 1960s. Underlying the hue and cry for equality, though, were the literary efforts of African America's intelligentsia. With the publication of his earth-shattering novel *Native Son* in January 1940, Richard Wright had become the de facto dean of African American letters, almost singlehandedly sweeping in a new era in which gritty social realism, naturalism, and overt political agendas would dominate black literature. Wright was directly responsible for starting or boosting the careers of many prominent young black authors, including Margaret Walker, James Baldwin, and Ralph Ellison. He also bore some responsibility for eclipsing or diminishing the careers of those who had come before him, including Langston Hughes—despite their personal friendship—and Zora Neale Hurston, whose novels Wright attacked viciously for their emphases upon the spirit of humor and irony within black life and marked lack of social realism.[10]

While Wright's role as a major force—perhaps *the* key player—in twentieth-century African American literature is indisputable, his attack upon literary depictions of black life that did not fit the politics of his seminal essay "Blueprint for Negro Writing" did not leave much place for satire and its rhetoric in the future of African American authorship. Wright accused writers of the Harlem Renaissance of entering "the Court of American Public Opinion dressed in the knee-

10. Wright's attacks upon Hurston's fiction are well documented in virtually every account of her literary career, but especially insightful is Robert Hemenway's *Zora Neale Hurston: A Literary Biography*. Less known, perhaps, is the slow eclipsing of Langston Hughes as a leading black author, but Arnold Rampersad's *Life of Langston Hughes* documents the period thoroughly.

pants of servility, curtsying to show that the Negro was not inferior, that he was human, and that he had a life comparable to that of other people." Literature that "crept in through the kitchen in the form of jokes" or that was the product of patronage incensed Wright for what he perceived as its "simplicity" and continuance of "the minstrel technique that makes the 'white folks' laugh."[11] Wright's dismissal of Harlem Renaissance authors—particularly Zora Neale Hurston—for their supposed avoidance of political statements and a black audience in "Blueprint," however, seems curious given the number of black authors of the period who openly condemned racism.

Despite Wright's heated condemnation of writing that apparently avoided direct confrontations of black realities, African American satire and irony hardly evaporated. George Schuyler continued on his particular iconoclastic path, although his politics had begun a rightward turn by the early 1940s.[12] Concomitantly, Chester Himes published two semiautobiographical novels on the political and social conditions in Los Angeles and its factories during World War II: *If He Hollers Let Him Go* (1945) and *Lonely Crusade* (1947). They stand as two of the most richly detailed and poignant accounts of the black worker's life in the war years. Himes also observes the ironies of the new economic opportunities for African Americans during that time, most notably that none of these opportunities are given for purely altruistic reasons; war is the primary catalyst. Himes's critique of whites' (mis)understanding of black culture (especially in *Lonely Crusade*) is startlingly similar to Ralph Ellison's, although Himes's novels predate *Invisible Man* by about five years:

> Lee [Gordon, the novel's protagonist] could not find the words to say how ironical he thought this [liberal whites' purported trust of black people] was. Because by the very statement, Smitty was insisting that he, Lee Gordon, mug, and did not even know it—in fact, would not have believed it if Lee had tried to explain. For like many other white people whom Lee had met, Smitty mistook the mugging of a Negro for integrity. And if he, Lee Gordon, had any sense, Lee said to himself, he should have learned, as had the great Negro leaders who always

11. Richard Wright, "Blueprint for Negro Writing," 53, 54; Richard Wright, Review of *Their Eyes Were Watching God*, 17.

12. See the previous chapter and Kathryn Talalay's *Composition in Black and White: The Life of Phillipa Schuyler* for a more detailed discussion of Schuyler's political transformation.

mugged, that white people preferred the mugging to the honesty. (*Lonely Crusade*, 142)

Himes also includes bits of black folk culture in his novels as metaphors for the intricacies of black intra- and interracial relationships. In *Lonely Crusade*, for example, Himes includes a version of the "Signifyin' Monkey" toast (*Lonely Crusade*, 202–4); in *If He Hollers Let Him Go*, Himes includes several scenes of black people playing the dozens and signifyin(g) upon each other.

Himes's landmark novels, however, could not reasonably qualify as satire so much as social document fiction; he is closer to Richard Wright than to Rudolph Fisher, even if his later, popular detective novels crib from Fisher's work. An inevitable result of the hegemony maintained by the Wright school of social document fiction was a backlash against its form and content. Almost as soon as Wright published *Native Son* and staggered the literary world, some of his African American literary peers expressed some reservations—often private—about the implications of focusing upon the violence and pathological effects of racism. Langston Hughes considered the novel "a disheartening challenge . . . in that he found the black world it described both familiar and utterly repugnant. The raw, phallic realism and naturalism . . . the unrelieved sordidness of [Wright's] depiction of black life" repelled Hughes, who saw deeper nuances in black life.[13] Similarly, Ralph Ellison's 1963 essay "The World and the Jug" argues that Wright could "imagine [*Native Son* protagonist] Bigger [Thomas], but Bigger could not possibly imagine Richard Wright. Wright saw to that" by presenting Bigger Thomas as a "near-subhuman indictment of white oppression," one illustrating Wright's "ideological proposition that what whites think of the Negro's reality is more important than what Negroes themselves know it to be."[14] Ellison offered this criticism as part of his direct response to Irving Howe's attempt to place Wright in the role of literary father figure for Ellison and James Baldwin, thereby belittling the sophistication of the latter authors' novels. Ellison both denies that Wright served as a literary father and points out that Howe missed much of *Invisible Man*'s irony because he was unaware of the complexities of African American folk culture. Through the folk

13. *LLH*, 1:383.
14. Ralph Ellison, "The World and the Jug," 114.

element informing *Invisible Man*, Ellison offers a satiric assessment of America's failure to uphold the ideals of democracy. Consequently, both Hughes and Ellison used their major fictional creations of the 1940s and 1950s to distance themselves from the explicit protest of Wright's naturalistic fiction, choosing instead to use the folk, whether northern or southern, as signs of infinite possibilities. Both critiqued and indicted America's failure to live up to its promised social contract in the racial arena, yet they did so with a distinct sense of irony and satire that is exceedingly difficult to find in protest/social document fiction. In this chapter, then, I will examine the satirical mode within Hughes's and Ellison's midcentury work as a means for creating cultural and political critiques. I will focus first on the history, topical breadth, and ideological content of Hughes's "Jesse B. Semple" story cycle, then Ellison's *Invisible Man* (1952). In both cases, I will show how Hughes and Ellison expand and alter the discourse surrounding "race" in America to reflect its shifting content during and after World War II and into the Civil Rights era.

Hughes's "Jesse B. Semple" stories are among the most notable, artistically successful examples of progressive debate on black issues in a satirical context to emerge from the 1940s and 1950s, their depth, breadth, and consistency equaled only in George Schuyler's columns. For over twenty years, Langston Hughes wrote a column for the *Chicago Defender*'s opinion page; it eventually featured one of his most famous creations. "Here to Yonder" began as one of several new columns in the *Defender*, arguably African America's most important nationally distributed newspaper, on November 21, 1942.[15] Hughes's column was the only one expressly focused on working-class African Americans and their everyday concerns. Donna A. S. Harper notes that the very first "Here to Yonder" columns used the same humorous tone as the later Simple columns and even some characters and situations that were clear precedents of the "Simple Minded Friend."[16] It wasn't until almost two months after the column's premiere that

15. This is not to slight the prominence and popularity of the *Pittsburgh Courier* or Harlem's *Amsterdam News* at the height of their powers. Both played essential roles in disseminating information to African American communities. The *Defender*, however, received special praise, including Hughes's own, for its unflinching, consistent attention to and protests against lynching, segregation, and other forms of discrimination.

16. *NSS*, 47–48.

Hughes introduced his "Simple Minded Friend," a regular at the neighborhood bar, who was "barely literate but highly opinionated and possessed of a powerful, sometimes even bizarre, racial pride."[17] At first Hughes kept the man anonymous and posited himself as the character's foil. Hughes eventually distanced himself from the foil, first making him anonymous as well, then renaming him Boyd. By 1949, the "Simple Minded Friend" had, in turn, been given the name Jesse B. Semple.[18]

The exchanges between Boyd and Jesse B. Semple—whose name is an ironic pun deceptively glossing his rather complex worldview—constitute some of the most scathing and perceptive, as well as the most frequently published, satire by an African American to appear between the Harlem Renaissance through the 1960s.[19] The same may be said of the "Here to Yonder" columns in general, but those devoted solely to Simple's exploits—the most highly anticipated of all—allowed Hughes to employ many of the devices that are common in satire by African Americans. I briefly discussed one example of the Simple stories in chapter 1. In the portion of this chapter devoted to the Simple cycle I shall examine two additional stories as exemplars of black folk and political discourse and conventional satirical rhetoric.

As Donna A. S. Harper points out, the milieu in which Boyd and Simple converse, a neighborhood bar posing as a "poor man's club," "equalizes them" by suspending their class and education distinctions, normally clear indicators of the sort of intraracial tensions and interracial issues Hughes examines.[20] It is no accident that Simple, as a working-class black man, functions as the voice of the "race man" who takes a strong, frequently uncompromising, and occasionally irrational stance on racial issues. Boyd, on the other hand, takes a more moderate, even liberal position, one informed by his middle-class status and education. In the vast majority of the Simple stories, Boyd acts as the narrator and therefore the persona mediating and interpreting the exchanges through his perspective. This narrative strategy has the potential to cast Simple in a primarily negative light,

17. Rampersad, "Langston Hughes," 169.
18. *NSS*, 91.
19. For the sake of simplicity—no pun intended—and clarity, I shall hereafter refer to Jesse B. Semple by the shorter name Hughes used most often in his columns: Simple.
20. *NSS*, 6.

but his dynamism in the face of Boyd's eternal temperance at least partially compensates for such biases. Most of the pair's discussions take place in their favorite tavern, symbolically the common ground between their two classes and worldviews.

Although Simple acts as the primary satirical voice, critiquing blacks and whites with occasionally vicious ire, Boyd frequently interrupts him to point out fallacies in his arguments, lending a degree of realism to Simple's almost invariably fantastic yet incisive homilies. This particular pattern exemplifies Leon Guilhamet's definition of the deliberative form of satire. In the deliberative form, two or more characters engage in frequently contentious dialogue over an issue. The dialogue's essential purpose is to motivate an unconvinced character to pursue a particular course of action. At all times, though, the implicit goal of these interrogations is to inspire the reader to consider future options available regarding an issue.[21] The rhetorical practices of the characters in a dialogue may range from the hyperrational to completely irrational; through the characters' deliberations, the issues at hand are reduced to their most ridiculous levels and exposed for their logical and strategic fallacies. In the earliest Simple columns, Simple and his foil debated the precarious position of African Americans during World War II. To be specific, their debates focused on whether African Americans were truly better off under American democracy than they would be under German fascism; America's armed forces were segregated, and African Americans suffered severe discrimination, both at home and in the armed forces, and did not seem poised to end such conditions. Since these columns were written during the war, it would have been impolitic for Hughes, through Simple, to suggest any subversive activities. Moreover, Hughes had no detectable desire to inspire subversion, despite his own radical past; he believed that Jim Crow, as bad as it was, was inherently better than fascism.[22] Thus, although Simple questioned the irony of African Americans in a Jim Crow army fighting fascism, the foil's position in favor of a problematic America as the rational choice was affirmed.

Similarly, in one column late in the war, "Simple on Military Integration," Hughes reifies unequivocally the deliberative form's imperative to urge a course of action as Simple decries the continued segregation

---

21. Leon Guilhamet, *Satire and the Transformation of Genre*, 33.
22. Langston Hughes, "Conversation at Midnight," 15; *NSS*, 68.

of the U.S. armed forces.[23] The opening follows the rhetorical pattern typical of Hughes's mature columns: an exordium and narration in which Simple baits Boyd, Boyd's rhetorical questions and/or refutations in response, then Simple and Boyd's respective proofs regarding the question at hand. In this case, Simple ponders the principles of the Declaration of Independence and the Constitution. He points out that both documents state clearly "that all men are borned equal and everybody is entitled to life and liberty while pursuing happiness," so he does not "see why it has to be resolved all over again."[24] In this case, Simple highlights a white church's resolution at its convention to affirm these principles and treat African Americans fairly, citing the Golden Rule, then he argues that "white folks better stop resolving and get to *doing*. They have resolved enough. *Resolving ain't solving.*"[25] Simple urges whites to "[treat] us like humans," drawing Boyd to point out that "[t]hey don't treat each other like human beings . . . so how do you expect them to treat you that way?"[26] Simple argues that even though whites are at war with each other—hence the charge of dehumanization—they "do not Jim Crow each other," thereby allowing a shred of dignity for one group on the "right" side of the racial divide.[27] Of course, Simple elides the fact of Germany's concentration camps, whose existence was well known long before the end of the European segment of the war, nor does he seem to be aware of the many other cases in history in which people now considered "white" segregated each other. The point, however, is both rhetorical and satirical; it is a deliberate distortion of the historical record not meant at all to be entirely accurate, even if Boyd tends to correct Simple's claims. In this case, though, Boyd takes a view of the situation that is both defeatist and optimistic insofar as he points out the lack of humanity on the part of whites but suggests that their resolutions indicate not only their capacity for humane action, but also the likelihood of concrete

---

23. This column was first published in the February 17, 1945, *Chicago Defender* under the title "Simple Pins on Medals." Like many "Here to Yonder" Simple columns, it was retitled for reprinting in one of Hughes's six Simple collections. This column, for instance, was reprinted in *The Best of Simple* (1961). As a general rule, I use the title of the reprinted version if it differs from the original.

24. Langston Hughes, *The Best of Simple*, 80.

25. Hughes, *Best*, 80; italics in the original.

26. Ibid., 81.

27. Ibid.

action toward integration. Simple then presses the issue by arguing that action must proceed immediately, implying that a racial crisis will ensue. This implicit argumentum ad baculum—an appeal to force— is characteristic of Hughes's tone within the Simple columns. Since Hughes could not very well write that violence was inevitable, he had to use indirection through Simple's play on language; he *signifies* upon the words *resolve* and *solve,* tracing their etymology while making a deictic gesture toward a desired action—integration.

Although Simple apparently plays the role of the *eiron* here, with Boyd as the simultaneous cynic and optimist, Hughes manipulates and alters these positions within his primary characters' deliberations to satirize a wide variety of situations endemic to African Americans' experiences and concerns accordingly. In the overwhelming majority of Simple narratives, Boyd and Simple's debate is a tug-of-war between Boyd's moderation and Simple's radicalism on racial issues. Hughes constantly alternates, however, between casting Boyd or Simple in the position of the (ir)rational. In doing so, he purposely avoids privileging one class or ideological position. Boyd's moderation is as likely as Simple's extreme approach to provide the solution to a pressing problem; conversely, Simple may become the voice of common sense even when Boyd attempts to deconstruct his interlocutor's position. For instance, in the story entitled "Simple Stashes Back," Simple boasts, " 'When I stash back on my hind legs and really speak my mind . . . white folks better beware of what they are liable to hear,' " to which Boyd responds, " 'But most of the sounding off you do is done in Harlem with not a white man in earshot, unless it is some Italian bar owner who has been selling you liquor for years— and bar owners are so used to Negroes sounding off that they pay you no mind.' " In this case, however, Simple deftly sidesteps Boyd's satirical jab by foregrounding the absence of African Americans and their interests in the international scene: " 'I wish I was in the United Nations . . . so the world could hear what I have to say.' " Simple then proceeds to unpack contemporary African American views of anti-black violence in Mississippi by attaching invective condemnations to the letters of the word *Mississippi* as if he were presenting before the United Nations: "[T]he word *Mississippi* starts with an *M* which stands for *Murder,* which is what they have done there to Negroes for years just for being colored. . . . It goes way back to slavery days when they whipped Negroes to death, and freedom days when the Klan drug us behind horses till we died, and on up to now when they shoot you for belonging to the N.A.A.C.P." Simple clearly alludes to several crucial events in black history: slavery, Reconstruction-era terrorism committed by the Ku Klux Klan, and the murder of civil rights workers in Mississippi. Each event, as part of Mississippi's horrific history of racism, is in continual danger of being forgotten or erased. It is only the sort of close study and analysis of history, similar to Simple's meticulous deconstruction of the word *Mississippi* before the United Nations, that will place the concerns and struggles of African Americans at the forefront of the world's consciousness. Simple's proud role as a "race man" is based upon such foregrounding and his desire to change the common perception of racial matters. Thus in another column, "For the Sake of Argument," Simple argues that "[t]here are sometimes more than two sides . . . except to the race question. For white folks that don't have but one side." Boyd's scornful response notes that Simple and African Americans in general "can never get together without discussing the race question." Simple's rejoinder is that Boyd is correct, but the reason for this state of affairs is that "it is not even a question"; it is "a hammer over our heads and at any time it may fall."[28] To Simple, then, discussion of racial issues is a matter of prime importance; to stop the discourse is to risk annihilation.

The rest of Simple's critique in "Simple Stashes Back" simultaneously utilizes two common components of African American satire: scatological references and black folklore. Simple points out later in his diatribe, "S . . . stands for several things. Mississippi ain't from none of them, neither from double *S*, which is followed by an *I* meaning *imps*—imps of Satan—which is what Mississippians is. In spite of the fact that they claim to be Christians, they is devils." Simple then declares, "I hope all you translators setting here at the United Nations . . . has got an *S* in your language to spell what I mean that Mississippi ain't from," a thinly veiled reference to certain types of fecal matter. Further in his critique, Simple refers to and alters a well-known black folktale for his purposes, telling his imagined audience "[n]ow I will go on to the *P*—which is what I plan to do as soon as I reach heaven, attach my wings, and learn to fly. As soon as I get to be an angel, that *very* first day, I will fly over Mississippi and I

28. Langston Hughes, ed., *The Langston Hughes Reader*, 231, 189; italics in the original.

will *P* all over the state. After which I will double the *P*, as it is in the spelling. Excuse the expression, but right over Jackson, which is the state capital, I will *P-P*. As I fly, I hope none of them Dixiecrats has time to get their umbrellas up."[29] Simple's allusion to "get[ting] to be an angel" is more than a reference to Christian visions of the afterlife; the image of the black angel wreaking havoc in heaven was common in early black folklore and other myths. Susan L. Blake points out that in black folklore, "the ability to fly [acts] as a metaphor for freedom and manhood"; moreover, "[f]lying is a predominant motif in black American folklore as well as in Western myth; its meanings vary from one tradition to another. . . . In a folk context the aspiration to fly recalls Harriet Tubman's dream of flying over a great wall, the numerous references in the spirituals to flying to freedom in Jesus . . . and the humorous folktale of the Colored Man who went to heaven and flew around with such abandon that he had to be grounded but who boasted that he was 'a flying black bastard' while he had his wings."[30] We could safely argue, then, that "Simple Stashes Back" rests squarely in the traditions of black folklore, even as it engages in a devastating, scatological debasement of the satiric target not unlike that found in *Gulliver's Travels*, in which authority figures are subjected to urination, defecation, and detailed catalogs of institutional and societal evils.

Hughes reserved some of his most brilliant satire for one societal evil in particular: the absence of consistent leadership for African American communities. In "Dear Dr. Butts," Simple comments upon the prevalence, ideological hegemony, and lack of fortitude of contemporary "Negro leaders." The narrative begins with Simple relating his anger to Boyd about his recent firing and the mystery of "Negro leaders, and how they're talking about how great democracy is—and me out of a job. Also how there is so many leaders I don't know that white folks know about, because they are always in the white papers. Yet *I'm* the one they are supposed to be leading." Simple has picked out one leader, "Dr. Butts," and written a letter to him about his

---

29. Dixiecrats were southern white Democrats, responsible for creating many of the Jim Crow laws accepted in southern states until the changes wrought by the Civil Rights movement. Hughes, *Reader*, 232; italics in the original.
30. Susan L. Blake, "Ritual and Rationalization: Black Folklore in the Works of Ralph Ellison," 124.

complaints. Dr. Butts is, of course, a trope for those prominent black leaders who attempt to speak for all African Americans but who have, ironically, little or no contact with their purported constituencies. Simple quotes Butts in his letter as saying, "America is the greatest country in the world for the Negro race and Democracy the greatest kind of government for all, but it would be better if there was equal education for colored folks in the South, and if everybody could vote, and if there were not Jim Crow in the army, also if the churches was not divided up into white churches and colored churches, and if Negroes did not have to ride on the back seats of busses South of Washington." The remainder of the letter and narrative is an ingenious exercise in punning and double entendre concentrated primarily on the word *but* and Dr. Butts's surname. The satire targets those black leaders who, in exchange for acceptance by whites, often attempt to minimize the pressing concerns and frustrations of the masses of African Americans. To this end, Simple creates a nuanced analysis of the process of marginalization of black concerns exemplified by Dr. Butts:

> [N]ow, all this later part of your article is hanging onto your but. You start off talking about how great American democracy is, then you but it all over the place. In fact, the but end of your see-saw is so far down on the ground I do not believe the other end can ever pull it up. So me myself, I would not write no article for no New York Times if I had to put in so many buts. I reckon maybe you come by it naturally, though, that being your name, dear Dr. Butts.
>
> I hear tell that you are a race leader, but I do not know who you lead because I have not heard tell of you before. . . . But since you are my leader, lead on, and see if I will follow behind your but—because there is more behind that but than there is in front of it.

In this passage the word *but* takes on several nuanced meanings. As a pun on one name for a part of the human anatomy, "but" takes on a grotesque significance in the Bakhtinian sense. That is, Hughes raises a lowly part of the body, which is "far down on the ground" to identify Dr. Butts (whose name takes on the same significance) as a base human being, one who is clearly abusing his role as a leader by attempting to fool African Americans into accepting inherently unacceptable conditions. Later, Simple warns, "*To put a* but *after all this Jim Crow fly-papering around our feet is just like. . . . telling a joker with no overcoat in the winter time, 'But you will be hot next summer.' The fellow is liable to haul off and say, 'I am hot now!' And bop you over your* head."[31] Simple's simile is not unlike those used in the black church to teach the urgency of doctrinal lessons; moreover, it is the same sort of simile found in the mouths of Harlem street preachers, who could and can be heard teaching and castigating Harlemites from street corner soapboxes, ladders, and other public pulpits.

"But" is also used as a verb to point out the degree to which Butts and black leaders force on the public both untenable ideas and glaringly faulty logic; their points seem strained and make no sense in and of themselves. Thus, in a later passage, Simple writes,

> *From the way you write, a man would think my race problem was made out of nothing but buts. But this, but that, and yes, there is Jim Crow in Georgia but—. America admits they bomb folks in Florida—but Hitler gassed the Jews. Mississippi is bad—but Russia is worse. Detroit slums are awful—but compared to the slums in India, Detroit's Paradise Valley is Paradise.*
>
> *Dear Dr. Butts, Hitler is dead. I don't live in Russia. India is across the Pacific Ocean. And I do not hope to see Paradise no time soon. I am nowhere near some of them foreign countries you are talking about being so bad. I am here! And you know as well as I do Mississippi is hell. There ain't no but in the world can make it any different.*[32]

The issue at stake here is the power of rhetoric: the power it can hold over the uninformed; its ability to hold a population enthralled by discursively erasing or at least minimizing a problem in the public mind, thereby allowing it to be ignored and subsequently fester. In addition, this particular portion of Simple's diatribe offers a serious rebuttal to the assurances of black conservatives and assimilationists. We may even argue that Hughes is positing a rebuttal—no pun intended—to such former adversaries as George S. Schuyler, against whom Hughes wrote his famous "The Negro Artist and the Racial Mountain" essay at the height of the Harlem Renaissance. Moreover, the fact that Butts's discourse does not reach the constituents he purportedly serves is highly problematic. At one point, Simple allows, "I am glad to read that you writ an article in The New York Times, but also sometime I wish you would write one in the colored papers. . . . Because we have too many colored leaders now that nobody knows until they get from the white papers to the colored papers and from the colored papers

31. Hughes, *Reader*, 210–11, 212; italics in the original.
32. Ibid., 212; italics in the original.

to me who has never seen hair nor hide of you."[33] Hughes, therefore, is not merely targeting African American leaders and intellectuals for obstructing or failing to solve racial problems; he is simultaneously creating a more subtle critique of black leaders' co-optation by white organizations and powerful individuals, whether those leaders are conscious of their co-optation or not.

Thus, Hughes revisits the problem of the black intellectual and his cultural role. "Dear Dr. Butts" posits the notion that the sincerity and pragmatic use of black leadership has waned and is in desperate need of repair due to its reliance upon outdated ideological and strategic models. It was an argument repeated ad infinitum at the dawn of the Civil Rights era, most notably in novels such as *Invisible Man*, which interrogates the fallacies of racial, ideological, and cultural essentialism. Its comic sensibility resembles Schuyler's in its antipathy toward the normal American understanding of race. It stands as one of the most important American novels of the twentieth century, and perhaps the entire history of American literature, because of its ency-clopedic analysis of African Americans' diversity. The rich complexity through which Ellison delineates and colors this diversity has helped the novel's stature immensely, inspiring many volumes of critical thought. The bases upon which these critiques rest vary widely, with many of them pointing out the novel's comic qualities. Less common, however, are focuses upon its *satiric* qualities, many of which are directly based upon African American folklore, as mentioned briefly in chapter 1. I will have occasion here to focus upon Ellison's satiric use of folk elements within the novel, thereby revealing some of Elli-son's sociopolitical agendas. *Invisible Man* subverts the entire idea of a stable African American identity while parodying Ellison's literary antecedents. If Ellison wrote the novel in part as a response to Wright's *Native Son*, he did so to suggest that African American identity cannot be reduced to a sociological phenomenon, a pathological and violent reaction to racism, or meekness and obsequiousness in the face of oppression. It is a combination of all these positions and more, a loose aggregate containing the multitudinous array of positions and masks African Americans continuously adopt, discard, and manipulate. To contain all of these identities, though, frequently requires that African

33. Ibid., 211–12.

Americans become *picaros* who alternate between naive and cynical views of the American landscape, past and present.

In *Invisible Man*'s oft-studied chapter 11, the Liberty Paints Factory doctors torture the Invisible Man while he is in their care. Under this torture, the Invisible Man is asked, "BOY, WHO WAS BRER RABBIT?"; directly preceding this question, the Invisible Man tells his torturers "I don't play the dozens," when they ask about his mother (*IM*, 241–42; emphasis in the original). The doctors' question about Brer Rabbit and the Invisible Man's mention of "the dozens" are two of the more obvious instances wherein Ellison foregrounds African American folk cultural figures. In the complicated process of reading *Invisible Man*, it becomes necessary at some point to highlight and consider its cultural context, which Ellison considered essential to understanding the text's ideological premises. *Invisible Man* is "packed full of folktales and tellers, trinkets, toasts, songs, sermons, jazz, jive and jokes" that, in his words, show "what Negro experience really is."[34] "We back away from the chaos of experience and from ourselves, and we depict the *humor* as well as the *horror* of our living. We project Negro life in a metaphysical perspective and we have seen it with a complexity of vision that seldom gets into our writing." The combination of "humor" and "horror" Ellison mentions demonstrates the degree to which he is ensconced within the traditions of satirical narrative. A cathartic, simultaneous realization of existence's horrific humor is satire's primary impetus. Via *Invisible Man*, Ellison eschews and parodies "all condescending, narrowly paternalistic interpretations of Negro American life and personality from whatever quarters they come, whether white or Negro," because they insufficiently portray the complexity of African American life. Ellison specifically disavows the urban realism and naturalism of his friend Richard Wright, not because it is of no value but because Wright's naturalism sticks too closely to sociology, especially the Chicago School of Sociology, and ignores the " 'something else' which makes for [African Americans'] strength . . . endurance and . . . promise."[35] For that reason, Ellison foregrounds African American folklore in a novel that partially parodies the plot structure and premise of Wright's *Native Son*. If parody involves, as Linda Hutcheon asserts, an "ironic reversal" of an original

34. Blake, "Ritual," 121.
35. Ralph Ellison, " 'A Very Stern Discipline,' " 283, 288, 276; emphasis mine.

text, Ellison parodies Wright by including one element noticeably missing from Wright's portrait of African American life: a complete, balanced evaluation of folklore, one relatively free of political dogma. Ellison reinserts the folk into that portrait, thereby highlighting the one major failure of Wright's landmark. In the process, Ellison creates a roman à clef that is both comic and satiric, with the satire aimed primarily at totalizing ideologies to which African Americans have subscribed.

Although *Invisible Man* draws upon several traditions, cultures, and philosophies, it is at least partially the product of some of the most fascinating traditions of African American folklore, specifically the trickster tale cycles. *Invisible Man* follows the typical pattern, combining these stories with a parodied structure of urban realism and the cyclical plot of the satiric novel to enter the picaresque and the satirical. Two of the novel's central questions are whether the Invisible Man ever achieves the level of transcendence that his fellow picaros often do or whether he remains in a cyclical world of trickery, continually shifting between the roles of the trickster and the tricked; where does he stand (or fail to stand) in the novel's satire? These questions have a particular significance for the text's efficacy, for they determine what, if any, degree of affirmation remains at the novel's contested, inconclusive end. The answer, however, can be ascertained only if we first consider some of the complexities of the cultural references abounding within the text; the forms of these references arguably hold the key to a more satisfying and enriching reading.

Invisible Man is marked by instances in which the characters, legends, and terms of black folk and vernacular discourse become integral parts of the narrative. These instances provide the crucial link between Ellison's comic and satiric sensibility and the traditions of black folk culture. At the moment when Brother Tarp, a member of the "Brotherhood"—analogous to the Communist Party, U.S.A.—gives the Invisible Man a chain link, for example, we witness a transfer of the primary mode of empowerment in this novel: " 'I'd like to pass it on to you, son. There,' he said, handing it to me. 'Funny thing to give somebody, but I think it's got a heap of signifying wrapped up in it and it might help you remember what we're really fighting against. I don't think of it in terms of but two words, *yes* and *no;* but it signifies a heap more . . .' "(*IM*, 388; italics in the original). Ellison's use of the words *signifying* and *signifies* here is not accidental. In African

American cultural traditions, those who possess the power to engage in signifying (as defined in chapter 1), or who have mastered the art of signifying, are frequently considered clever and insightful, even sage in their total worldview. It is they who, through a humorous and ironic outlook, are best able to tolerate and overcome the burdens of society. Signifying, moreover, is occasionally the African or African American trickster's means of obtaining power previously denied him because of his already weakened position. In this example, then, dissembling, heavily coded language and discourse are the primary media through which knowledge and power are transferred to strengthen one's social position. Both tricksters and characters in *Invisible Man* who possess the ability to decode encrypted language demonstrate the centrality of that language to understanding black culture. Those who fail to do so, including the novel's protagonist, suffer.

One prominent example of the ubiquity of folk allusions is the frequency of references to a "bear" either as a noun or a verb. In Ellison's prologue, for example, the Invisible Man says, "Call me Jack-the-Bear, for I am in a state of hibernation" (*IM*, 6); soon thereafter, he establishes that "[a] hibernation is a covert preparation for a more overt action" (*IM*, 13); at the end of the prologue, he asks his audience, "Bear with me" (*IM*, 14). What becomes apparent in these instances is that the Invisible Man himself identifies and can be identified by the reader with the bear in African American trickster tales, a character who, through his strength and occasional wit, is able to endure or reverse the mischief of other, clever or trickster figures. Thus the "bear" and the act of "bearing" social difficulties make up an extended metaphor for the positions in which the Invisible Man finds himself throughout the text. Furthermore, this metaphor applies to African Americans as a group due to the Invisible Man's status as a picaresque Everyman for African Americans.

We should recall three notable elements of the bear and the lion in some trickster story cycles: first, they usually learn from their mistakes and get a chance to take revenge on the trickster; second, even after taking their revenge, they fall back into the role of the tricked; third, they may also serve as neutral figures in some stories (for example, Brer Bear serves as a referee in one version of "The Signifyin' Monkey").[36]

---

36. Roger D. Abrahams, ed. *Afro-American Folktales: Stories from Black Traditions in the New World*, 104.

As we examine different characters in *Invisible Man*, we find the thematic and ideological counterparts for both the trickster and the tricked in many of the more prominent characters. The protagonist's recounting of his grandfather's dying words, for instance, serves as the seminal event that provides some of the overarching metaphors for the remainder of the text:

> On his death-bed he called my father to him and said, "Son, after I'm gone I want you to keep up the good fight. I never told you, but our life is a war and I have been a traitor all my born days, a spy in the enemy's country ever since I give up my gun back in the Reconstruction. Live with your head in the lion's mouth. I want you to overcome 'em with yeses, undermine 'em with grins, agree 'em to death and destruction, let 'em swoller you till they vomit or bust wide open." They thought the old man had gone out of his mind. He had been the meekest of men. . . . "Learn it to the younguns," he whispered fiercely; then he died. (*IM*, 16)

Note that the grandfather is speaking of being subversive through speech, that he says that his son should "[l]ive with your head in the lion's mouth," that he is described as the meekest of men, and that further down the page, the Invisible Man says, "I could never be sure of what he meant." In addition, in the novel's epilogue, the Invisible Man confesses that his grandfather's dying words haunted him: "I'm still plagued by his deathbed advice. . . . Perhaps he hid his meaning deeper than I thought, perhaps his anger threw me off—I can't decide" (*IM*, 574). In several ways, the grandfather is the quintessential trickster. Houston Baker, for instance, says that Brer Rabbit is "a cunning figure who wins contests against much larger and stronger animals. In the general American scheme of things, to say that he is a subversive figure is not to engage in overstatement. We can, in fact, see Brer Rabbit as one of the first black American figures to repudiate the culture theorizing of whites."[37] Recall that trickster figures are frequently weak and subtle ("[The grandfather] had been the meekest of men."). Furthermore, a portion of the trickster's power is derived from the tricked figure's inability to understand the nature of the game the trickster is playing, or the subtleties of the language he uses. Or, as Henry Louis Gates describes the Signifying Monkey stories, "the

---

37. Houston A. Baker, Jr., *Long Black Song: Essays in Black American Literature and Culture*, 12.

Signifying Monkey is able to signify upon the Lion only because the Lion does not understand the nature of the monkey's discourse. . . . The monkey speaks figuratively, in a symbolic code; the lion interprets or reads literally and suffers the consequences of his folly, which is a reversal of his status as King of the Jungle."[38] With his final words, therefore, the grandfather signifies upon the Invisible Man, testing his ability to crack the folk-based code, an ability that the Invisible Man lacks, unfortunately. The Invisible Man thus spends the remainder of the novel struggling to interpret the grandfather's words, trying to discover what he meant by " 'overcome 'em with yeses.' "

The Invisible Man's quest to translate the grandfather's words leads him into other encounters with tricksters. The first, and perhaps most crucial, encounter occurs when the Invisible Man meets Jim Trueblood, a poor black "sharecropper who had brought disgrace upon the black community" near the Invisible Man's college for not only being sycophantic toward whites but committing incest with his daughter, thus satisfying white prejudices (*IM*, 46). The Invisible Man relates that "all of us at the college hated the black-belt people, the 'peasants,' during those days! We were trying to lift them up and they, like Trueblood, did everything it seemed to pull us down" (*IM*, 47). Trueblood thus functions as both a carnivalesque, "lowly" figure, and as the traditional trickster figure through his shameful act and roundabout manner of telling his story, playing upon the prejudices of the white philanthropist Norton, the black college folk, and the white town dwellers for his material gain. Both before and after the revelation of his transgression, Trueblood's storytelling ability and musical skills bring shame money from whites like Norton, a benefit he acts quickly and frequently to exploit. The fact that he is able to do so is an indirect satire upon the foolishness of the self-righteous, white "liberal" represented by Norton. The moral repulsiveness of Trueblood is of such a magnitude that he is essentially paid for resisting change or progress, thus providing "proof" that blacks are inherently inferior. The irony is that liberal whites are unable to recognize their own desire for, and complicity in, the perpetuation of Trueblood's class.

Simultaneously, however, Trueblood is an idealized figure inasmuch as he defies both the oppression of the white townsfolk and the

38. Henry Louis Gates, Jr., *Figures in Black: Words, Signs, and the "Racial" Self*, 241.

petty-bourgeois insults of the college administration without overt
punishment. Hence the punning, ironic name of TRUE BLOOD, or
the "true" black man, one without pretension, undiluted by the same
sort of compromises engaged in by the college crowd.[39] Trueblood,
on the other hand, also fulfills an especially unsavory stereotype;
if he plays the part of the trickster, he does so by simultaneously
playing the part of the old "Sambo" figure, who continually caters
to popular white conceptions of the docile, immoral black man via his
speech, mannerisms, and the unspeakable act he has committed with
his daughter. This last act, however, highlights the degree to which
Trueblood fulfills the role of trickster, whose morality, especially in
sexual matters, often runs contradistinctively to accepted mores.

After Trueblood's story, we are taken into the Golden Day Cafe,
where the Invisible Man encounters the "insane" vet, who criticizes
the narrator's inability to comprehend: " 'You see,' he said turning
to Mr. Norton, 'he has eyes and ears and a good distended African
nose, but he fails to understand the simple facts of life. *Understand.*
Understand? It's worse than that. He registers with his senses but
short-circuits his brain. Nothing has meaning' " (*IM*, 94). In a later,
retrospective moment, the narrator reacts angrily to the vet's words,
saying that with his taunts against Mr. Norton, he "had tried to turn
the world inside out, goddamn him! He had made Mr. Norton angry.
He had no right to talk to a white man as he had, not with me to
take the punishment" (*IM*, 106). The Invisible Man objects to the fact
that he has just been signified upon. But this critique of the Invisible
Man's cognizance continues when Bledsoe calls the narrator into his
office and chastises him for taking Norton to the Golden Day. Part of
Bledsoe's ire results from his consternation over the Invisible Man's
apparent inability to signify, to "lie" to Bledsoe, a more powerful figure
politically and socially: " 'My God, boy! You're black and living in the
South—did you forget how to lie? Why, the dumbest black bastard
in the cotton patches knows that the only way to please a white
man is to tell him a lie!' " (*IM*, 139). The problem here is that the
Invisible Man has yet to learn the power of language and gesture or
signifying as Bledsoe has, with his ingenious (though objectionable)
form of bowing and scraping: " 'I's big and black and I say "Yes, suh"

39. Houston A. Baker, Jr., *Blues, Ideology and Afro-American Literature: A Vernacular Theory,* 180.

as loudly as any burrhead when it's convenient, but I'm still the king down here. I don't care how much it appears otherwise. Power doesn't have to show off. Power is confident, self-assuring, self-starting and self-stopping, self-warming and self-justifying. When you have it, you know it'" (*IM*, 142). At this point, we should note that though just as much a part of their society as any of the other characters in the trickster stories, the trickster sets himself apart from any peers, both through the distinguishing power of signifying and through physical removal or other forms of distinction; the trickster is the ultimate confidence man.

The chain link the Invisible Man received from Brother Tarp is refigured as a trope signifying several important themes. The Invisible Man says that the link "had been twisted open and forced partly back into place, on which I saw marks that might have been made by the blade of a hatchet. It was such a link as I had seen on Bledsoe's desk, only while that one had been smooth, Tarp's bore the marks of haste and violence, looking as though it had been attacked and conquered before it stubbornly yielded" (*IM*, 389), and slightly further on, he says he "felt that Brother Tarp's gesture in offering it was of some deeply felt significance which I was compelled to respect . . . because of the overtones of unstated seriousness and solemnity of the paternal gesture which at once joined him with his ancestors, marked a high point of his present, and promised a concreteness to his nebulous and chaotic future" (*IM*, 389–90). In view of the Invisible Man's inability to understand how others (especially the Brotherhood) are manipulating him, through language and other means, it seems crucial that he find some way to counter the influence of the trickster. If he is truly the embodiment of Brer Bear, he must look for a chance to take his revenge. In this instance, the link symbolizes both the power of signifying and the power of confidence needed to overcome the wily trickster, to be able to say both "*yes* and *no*," to have the option of denying the trickster his will. Furthermore, the link had been "twisted open and forced partly back into place," and looked "as though it had been attacked and conquered before it stubbornly yielded." The Invisible Man demonstrates the first characteristic of the link when he appears before the committee of the Brotherhood, with Brother Wrestrum standing as his accuser. Wrestrum's actions in this scene closely resemble the signifyin' monkey's role. Wrestrum accuses the Invisible Man of being the most pernicious villain in the Brotherhood's eyes; he calls him a "double-dealer," an "opportunist," and "a *dictator*." By playing off the prejudices of the committee for his own self-aggrandizement, his own reward, Wrestrum is signifying, or as the Invisible Man describes his opponent's actions, "He was the plotter and from the serious looks on the committee's faces he was getting away with it" (*IM*, 400–401). Here the narrator sees through Wrestrum's language, recognizes the game he is playing and his motives. For this reason, he counters, " 'You're a liar and a fat-mouthed scoundrel. You're a liar and no brother of mine' " (*IM*, 402). But even after verbally jousting with the committee, the narrator yields at the end of this scene; he explains that he "felt suddenly empty; there was a logic in what he said which I felt compelled to accept. They were wrong, but they had the obligation to discover their mistake" (*IM*, 405). By deferring to the committee's decision, then, the Invisible Man is "forced partly back into place," in full understanding of both parties' moral position and correctness yet allowing his opponents the opportunity to find some degree of enlightenment that (supposedly) they did not possess previously. The narrator is showing signs of becoming more like the trickster: he is attempting to teach a moral lesson to the stronger figure. When the narrator again goes in front of the committee, to be accused by Brother Tobitt in much the same way as he was attacked by Wrestrum, the depowering nature of its accusations finally begin to sink in, forcing the narrator to assume a new, more assertive role: "My hand was in my pocket now, Brother Tarp's leg chain around my knuckles. I looked at each of them individually, trying to hold myself back and yet feeling it getting away from me" (*IM*, 473). Immediately afterward, the narrator begins to come back sharply, cross-examining the committee with a great deal of success; he's overcoming the trickster figure, upsetting the Master: " 'Who are you, anyway, the great white father? . . . Wouldn't it be better if they called you Marse Jack [another name for the slavemaster in the "John" trickster tales]?' " (*IM*, 473). The narrator has entered a crisis, wherein he has been forced to reinterpret the words of the primary trickster, his grandfather. Here he learns to use language to his benefit, to signify. Yet he yields at the end of this scene as well; hence, the narrator again embodies the second characteristic of the link: it is broken and looks "as though it had been attacked and conquered before it stubbornly yielded."

The narrator, then, continuously shifts between the roles of the tricked and the learning trickster as he attempts to reinterpret his grandfather's words. This cycle could easily be refigured as a form of trial and error in which problematic discourse is opened up with each successive trick suffered or played. We need to ascertain, however, the degree to which the narrator progresses beyond this cyclical shifting to become a picaresque figure.

From the episode in which the Invisible Man takes on the role of con man Reverend B. P. Rinehart through the final expositions of the epilogue, the Invisible Man becomes increasingly aware of the roles he plays as both a trickster and a tricked figure and the incidence of such figures in his society. This realization moves the narrator's mode of thought closer to that of the picaresque figure frequently found in African American literature (especially the slave narratives), and the narrative itself begins to resemble the picaresque form.[40] Charles H. Nichols's definition of the picaresque figure, or picaro, is especially cogent here:

> In each account the writer presents a welter of realistic detail designed to drive home the brutality and inhumanity of his experience as a victim, a commodity, a rootless, alienated soul without hope or future. His origin is obscure, his masters heartless and treacherous. [The narrative's] . . . frequent use of coincidence and chance dramatize the chaos and decadence of the world here depicted. With bitter irony the picaro . . . underlines his contempt for the illusions, the chivalric pretensions and the folly of the master class.[41]

The suffering the Invisible Man endures at the hands of Bledsoe, the Brotherhood, the Liberty Paints doctors, and other characters, as well as the frequency of apparently random or chaotic events need not be detailed here; his contempt, however, requires some discussion, for it is indeed with "bitter irony" that he evaluates his experience with those who have succeeded in using and controlling him. This

---

40. Although Ellison went on record as objecting to insinuations that he made any *conscious* effort to emulate the form and function of the slave narratives, it has been strongly argued that these forms had some degree of influence (whether direct or indirect) on *Invisible Man*'s narrative structure, since the experiences detailed in the slave narratives coincide with a great deal of general African American experiences. See Davis and Gates's "Introduction" to *The Slave's Narrative*, xviii–xxi.

41. Charles H. Nichols, "The Slave Narrators and the Picaresque Mode: Archetypes for Modern Black Personae," 283.

evaluation is a direct result of the narrator's brief experience of Rinehart's life, a life of considerable power, for Rinehart "was a broad man, a man of parts who got around. Rinehart the Rounder. . . . His world was possibility and he knew it. He was years ahead of me and I was a fool. . . . Jack wouldn't dream of such a possibility, nor Tobitt, who thinks he's so close. . . . freedom was not only the recognition of necessity, it was the recognition of possibility. And sitting there trembling I caught a brief glimpse of the possibilities posed by Rinehart's multiple personalities" (*IM*, 498–99). The commonalities among these multiple personalities allow the Invisible Man to see Rinehart as a trickster figure who embodies and who may exploit all the desires within African American communities, particularly the lowest sort of vices. In addition, however, Rinehart (and later the narrator himself) represents an "ironic withdrawal from the white world," which allows for a degree of successful functioning both within the dominant society's confines ("pandering") and apart from them, a sort of "healthy" cynicism in the face of a social order that has the ability to destroy those who do not know how to "signify" upon it.[42]

Neither the picaro nor the trickster figure, however, is content with merely signifying upon his environment for its own sake; the key element common to both figures is a nearly obsessive desire for survival manifested in their respective propensities for trickery; the trickster figure succeeds through his manipulation of the level of discourse; "the picaroon . . . survive[s] by trickery and deceit, by out-smarting others, by 'hustling' his way through a vicious *underground* existence." The "underground existence" of the picaro often represents the final stage of his being, even though the *form* of this existence may shift over time, for he "can never escape the iron ring of his caste status . . . [h]is world conspires to oppress and unsettle him. The maxim of the society is summed up in the directive: 'Keep this nigger running.' The instability of his emotional life leads him into the agony and conflict of a damaged ego." Hence the underlying bitterness as the narrator cries that "I've been trying to look through myself, and there's a risk in it. I was never more hated than when I tried to be honest. . . . No one was satisfied—not even I" (*IM*, 572–73). The Invisible Man's final disquisition concerning the meaning of his grandfather's

---

42. Blake, "Ritual," 129.

dying words, however, demonstrates that this bitterness is not the final form his "underground existence" must take, despite the "hole" he claims his invisibility has placed him in (*IM*, 572). The picaro is characteristically a figure "whose search out of poverty, deprivation and despair leads him through dreams of liberation to a transcendent sense of community."[43] In fact, we may argue, in view of the Invisible Man's earlier assertion that "[a] hibernation is a covert preparation for a more overt action" (*IM*, 13), that an "underground existence" is actually conducive to the process of dreaming of liberation. For it is from the Invisible Man's "hole" that he asks concerning his grandfather's words, "Or was it, did he mean that we should affirm the principle because we, through no fault of our own, were linked to all the others in the loud, clamoring semi-visible world, that world seen only as a fertile field for exploitation by Jack and his kind, and with condescension by Norton and his, who were tired of being the mere pawns in the futile game of 'making history?' Had he seen that for these too we had to say 'yes' to the principle, lest they turn upon us to destroy both it and us?" (*IM*, 574–75). The Invisible Man asks here the most difficult question of his career (and of the text itself): does saying "yes" to an "othered" figure, one that has the power to castigate or destroy the self, place the self within the role of the tricked or the trickster?

The answer, predictably, is "yes": the self at all times mediates between both roles; the narrator concludes that "the world is just as concrete, ornery, vile and sublimely wonderful as before, only now I better understand my relation to it and it to me" (*IM*, 576). This relation is a tacit recognition of the pitfalls, the other "holes" that arise in a society that seeks to deconstruct selfhood, to elide the individual's being and right to social empowerment. For "[i]n going underground, [the narrator] whipped it all except the mind, the *mind*. And the mind that has conceived a plan of living must never lose sight of the chaos against which that pattern was conceived. That goes for societies as well as for individuals. Thus, having tried to give pattern to the chaos which lives within the pattern of your certainties, I must come out, I must emerge" (*IM*, 580–81; emphasis in the original). The final result of the continuous pattern of trickery found in *Invisible*

43. Nichols, "Slave Narrators," 290, 292.

Man, then, is not so much an *actual* transcendence by the self of the pain experienced when tricked as it is a *sense* of transcendence, an understanding that "there *is* a death in the smell of spring and in the smell of thee as in the smell of me" (*IM*, 580; italics in the original). The Invisible Man's "underground existence," his sense of being as the picaro, Brer Bear, or Brer Rabbit therefore acts as the manifestation of a simultaneously simple and enormously complex pattern: the ever-frustrating and -satisfying mediation of the intricacies of social discourse, social action, and social politics. The narrator offers us a final symbol of these intricacies, these eternal contradictions, near the close of the novel with two telling phrases—a warning and a teasing query: "But don't let me trick you. . . . Who knows but that, on the lower frequencies, I speak for you?" (*IM*, 580, 581).

The sort of artistry displayed by Ellison in *Invisible Man* had an incalculable effect upon African American literature and culture. As the first black novel given international acclaim as more than "Negro literature" (though it has never escaped this label), *Invisible Man* had the impact of turning modern black experiences and perceptions into material both critics and reading public found eminently fascinating and astute. More important, *Invisible Man* proved that black folklore and its concomitant ironies and satirical commentaries could and should form the bases for black arts. In this sense, the novel represented a radical step forward for black literature, despite the criticism laid upon it by leftist and Black Arts critics in the 1960s that it was too conservative or failed to advocate a specific course of action for African Americans. The first criticism might be somewhat tenable in the sense that satire tends to call for more "rational" or acceptable modes of being (especially those followed in the past and laid aside in the present), but *Invisible Man* does not call unequivocally for a return to the past. Rather, it points out that no single interpretation of black history or identity will suffice to describe black experience. T. V. Reed correctly posits that "Ellison as storyteller is in a double bind; . . . like Trueblood he risks all manner of (white) misreadings, all manner of minstrel interpretations. In constantly working on the edge of stereotype in his satiric characterizations, . . . in trying to use laughter to shatter the minstrel mask from within, he is in danger instead of confirming that mask," which he does ironically, as if to say that the stereotypes of African Americans only make sense to the reader who is as naive as the Invisible Man was early in his quest. Thus, Reed notes,

Invisible Man has been attacked on a number of occasions by left-wing critics who find it insufficiently "committed" or "political" in its treatment of black life in America. Some of these attacks have been reductive and self-justifying, others have been serious and thoughtful. Most have tended to extrapolate from Ellison's own allegedly aestheticist or formalist statements about his book or from his often seemingly moderate political statements to find grounds for attacking his novel.[44]

As with the Invisible Man himself, interpretation of Ellison and his text is often based more on what the reader of the man and his work would like to see. What that reader might see is a text that seems somehow less than serious, unmindful of the purposes of its satiric humor and alleged stereotyping.

This tension between the representation of stereotypes and the need for new images of and critical discourse about African Americans ran beneath much of black culture and literature in the 1940s and 1950s. At the dawn of the Civil Rights era, when anger over the continued denial of African Americans' rights flourished with the simultaneous occurrence of new atrocities against and new social and economic advances for them, debates around the same issues highlighted in *Invisible Man* continued. In the next chapter, I shall discuss the revival of the spirit of Jesse B. Semple undertaken by African American satirists in the 1960s, who channeled his iconoclasm to face familiar adversaries: black nationalism's latest embodiments and the Black Power and Black Arts and Aesthetic movements.

44. Thomas Vernon Reed, *Fifteen Jugglers, Five Believers: Literary Politics and the Poetics of American Social Movements,* 58, 78.

CHAPTER 4

※

"Nation Enough"

Black Politics in the 1960s and the Advent of the Multicultural Iconoclast

Nevertheless and basically, this is a Black comedy. I mean a Black black comedy. Dig it. And I meant to do myself some signifying. I meant to let it all hang out.

—John Oliver Killens, *The Cotillion, or One Good Bull Is Half the Herd*

America in the 1960s became a land of gut-wrenching political turmoil on many different fronts. Between the election—and assassination—of President John F. Kennedy, the beginning of the American phase of the Vietnam War (with the concomitant antiwar movement), the rise of a new brand of feminist political activism, and the Civil Rights movement, America's mainstream had more radical social change than it could comprehend. We now rightly consider the Civil Rights movement in particular as both leader and emblem of the nation's changes; it forced America to confront its appalling oppression and brutal failure to live up to the democratic ideals Ellison privileges in *Invisible Man*. Equally important, the Civil Rights movement ushered in a period of national awareness and appreciation of African American politics and culture unparalleled since the Harlem Renaissance. As seen in the previous chapter's discussion of Langston Hughes's Jesse B. Semple stories, the Civil Rights movement's grandest victories and most troubling defeats dominated much of the American discourse on race. In the forefront of the public's consciousness were the rhetoric, actions, and posturing of black and white integrationists, Black Nationalists and separatists, white segregationists and racists, white liberals, and many other groups that had a stake in the elimination or preservation of America's racial caste system. Considering "the centrality of race in shaping American politics and culture," as elucidated by Michael Omi and Howard Winant, the debate encompassed most communities, ideologies, and organizations in the American political spectrum.[1]

Nowhere did this debate rage more hotly than within African American communities and organizations, where the residents and members were forced to redefine the parameters of political strategy when faced with the possibility that national de jure segregation might actually be eliminated through the efforts of the mainstream Civil Rights movement and, to a lesser degree, legislation and other actions stemming from the Johnson administration's public sympathy toward the social plight of black Americans. Perhaps inevitably, the outcome of the debate would be a set of revised approaches to interpreting African American culture and art. And just as inevitably, several African American satirists would chafe against the boundaries set by these new approaches, demanding greater diversity. In the process, they would echo the concerns, complaints, and styles of their predecessors of a prior generation.

It should hardly be surprising, then, that the terms of the intraracial debate over "racial" and cultural identity, the course of black political organizing and action, and the individuals or organizations that made up the diverse positions within the debate itself bore remarkable likenesses to those of the 1920s and 1930s. At the simplest level, the debate raged between those who believed in racial integration as the most effective means of obtaining social justice and civil rights and those who advocated racial separatism or Black Nationalism as the primary means of reaching complete social, political, and economic freedom. As in any serious debate, of course, numerous individuals and groups supported positions that fell between these poles, sometimes combining their rhetoric and ideologies. Despite the basic goal of complete freedom the integrationist and nationalist camps shared, some of the most vitriolic exchanges of the time occurred between extremists in the two groups. Significantly, the type of support given

1. Michael Omi and Howard Winant, *Racial Transformation in the United States: From the 1960s to the 1980s*, 6.

to particular positions could also be mapped out along regional and class lines. Black Nationalism's strongest support, for example, generally came from the northern, urban segment of black communities, whereas integration received some of its strongest support from, and appealed most often to, the disenfranchised southern African American, though many working- and poverty-class blacks also lent their political support to integration. The class factor substantially heightened existing conflicts between the two poles, however, as lower-class blacks began to view the middle class as that portion of the community that sought to escape its less fortunate brethren, whether for moral or social reasons, while the middle class viewed the lower classes as the people who could potentially disrupt or destroy efforts to appeal to the government and the rest of society to implement and enforce civil rights laws and integrative policies, due to their alleged inability or unwillingness to assimilate. This conflict was not contained within the black community; most of the discussion and arguing occurred in public, via debates between integrationists such as Dr. Martin Luther King, Jr., and Ralph Abernathy and such nationalists as Malcolm X, Elijah Muhammad, and later, Stokely Carmichael. Underlying the debate was the popular understanding of black identity; that is, how would black people identify themselves from that moment? What would be the (dis)advantages of a particular sort of identification? If black people perceived themselves as part of a group that should remain aloof from the rest of society to form cohesive bonds among its members, how would that affect their social and economic position? If, conversely, black people attempted to integrate with and possibly assimilate into mainstream American society, would that result in the advancement or destruction of black communities?

To the participants in these debates, these questions were not simply matters of rhetorical or ideological posturing; the answers to them were inextricably linked to the well-being of most African Americans. To that extent, they were debated at all levels of black society in the 1960s. In the writings and work of black artists in particular, though, the debate centered on questions of images, social value, and aesthetics; more specifically, they were "about the business of destroying those images and myths that have crippled degraded black people, and the institution of new images and myths that will liberate them."[2]

2. Hoyt W. Fuller, "The New Black Literature: Protest or Affirmation," 346.

The premise behind this particular belief and practice was that white Americans' traditional considerations of the cultural value of black people were poisonous if black people themselves ingested such ideas or tried to practice them. The notion that black culture and aesthetics (when their existence was even recognized by critics) was forever inferior to or dependent upon European-derived aesthetics would inevitably lead to practices that would cause black people to detest, perhaps even destroy, themselves. According to critics like Addison Gayle, Maulana Ron Karenga, Amiri Baraka (formerly LeRoi Jones), and Larry Neal, the responsibility of the black artist was to use the word, to use language as a tool invested with the power to transform ideas generated by black people into action, especially revolutionary action. Karenga argues in his 1968 essay "Black Art: Mute Matter Given Force and Function" that it "becomes very important . . . that art plays the role it should play in Black survival and not bog itself down in the meaningless madness of the Western world wasted. In order to avoid this madness, black artists and those who wish to be artists must accept that what is needed is an aesthetic" that would allow for a more balanced assessment of the validity and beauty of black art. Furthermore, "art must expose the enemy, praise the people and support the revolution"; it should be "collective," with the individualism of the artist being a commodity that is "nonexistent" something that African Americans "cannot afford" given the necessity of "committing . . . to revolution and change" on a mass level.[3] Or, put in Amiri Baraka's terms, the "Black Artist's role in America is to aid in the destruction of America as he knows it" and pursue a "correct" realism that would show America as it is and then guide the reader to the means of destroying it.[4]

This ideal of using literature to help change social and political conditions and to bring about a revolution in thought and action and effectively powered the Black Arts movement of the 1960s, one of the most significant literary movements in African American history. This was not the first such movement toward an aesthetic for African Americans, of course; as I discussed in chapter 2, one focus of the

3. Maulana Ron Karenga, "Black Art: Mute Matter Given Force and Function," 477–78, 479–90.
4. Imamu Amiri Baraka, "State/meant," in *The LeRoi Jones/Amiri Baraka Reader*, ed. William J. Harris, 169–70.

Harlem Renaissance was the debate over the direction and content of African American art. Reginald Martin suggests, in fact, that a movement toward a black aesthetic can be traced in a long historical arc from the nineteenth century. The first phase began in antebellum times with the 1829 publication of David Walker's *Appeal in Four Articles; Together with a Preamble, to the Coloured Citizens of the World, but in Particular and Very Expressly to Those of the United States of America* and ended with the 1881 publication of Frederick Douglass's *The Life and Times of Frederick Douglass.* The second phase began in 1895 with Booker T. Washington's speech at the Cotton States and International Exposition in Atlanta, and ended with the assassination of John F. Kennedy in 1963; the third phase began with Martin Luther King, Jr.'s "I Have a Dream" speech at the 1963 march on Washington and ended with Clarence Major's introduction to the 1969 collection *The New Black Poetry.* The fourth phase began in 1971 with the attention that black academics began giving to African American literature in a number of journal articles and anthologies and continued at least until 1988, the date of Martin's writing. Martin marks the arc of the search for a black aesthetic by publications, essays, and statements that defined different epochs.[5] While I would agree that it is possible to divide the arc of black literary thought and production loosely by epochal statements, I'd disagree that the third and fourth phases are so neatly demarcated, especially since many of the essays contained in the major collections Martin lists were published before 1971. Toni Morrison's debut novel, *The Bluest Eye,* which drew upon and made manifest some of the literary ideals of the 1960s, was also published in 1970. Needless to say, Martin's divisions do not include changes since 1988.[6]

Despite my misgivings, though, Martin's attempt to mark discernible boundaries for the changes in content and direction for African American literary criticism is well taken. It is more important that we be able to see the commonalities within the critical enterprise in the late 1960s and early 1970s, which had a substantial impact upon

5. Reginald Martin, *Ishmael Reed and the New Black Aesthetic Critics,* 21–22, 20, 22–24. Among these publications are Addison Gayle, *The Black Aesthetic,* Houston Baker, Jr., *Black Literature in America,* Amiri Baraka, *Raise, Race, Rays, Raze: Essays since 1965,* and Ishmael Reed, *19 Necromancers from Now.*
6. I discuss the publication of Trey Ellis's "Towards a New Black Aesthetic" and other changes in African American literature in chapter 5.

current trends. Two notes from Larry Neal's informative outline of the 1960s' Black Aesthetic provide a particularly illuminating view: "Word is perceived as energy or force"; "[m]ore concerned with the vibrations of the Word, than with the Word itself."[7] This new set of narratives is thus devoted to elevating the most valuable and cherished aspects of the African American and criticizing those who would stand in the way of black progress and empowerment. In essence, then, the advocates of the new Black Aesthetic perceived the black artist's role to be that of a direct advocate of the black masses and a staunch adversary to any agency that upheld oppressive stereotypes, whether that agency originated inside or outside black communities. Subsequently, black aestheticians found some of the more dangerous agents were white critics, even those who were somewhat sympathetic to black causes. This skepticism toward whites grew out of the tenets of various black nationalisms, such as this passage from Stokely Carmichael and Charles V. Hamilton's *Black Power*, wherein they quote Lewis Killian and Charles Griggs: "[M]ost white Americans, even those white leaders who attempt to communicate and cooperate with their Negro counterparts, do not see racial inequality in the same way that the Negro does. The white person, no matter how liberal he may be, exists in the cocoon of a white-dominated society." Carmichael and Hamilton use this quotation to conclude "that no matter how 'liberal' a white person might be, he cannot ultimately escape the overpowering influence—on himself and on black people—of his whiteness in a racist society."[8] Hoyt W. Fuller similarly takes white critics to task by arguing that

---

7. Larry Neal, "Some Reflections on the Black Aesthetic," 14–15. Neal describes his outline as "a rough overview of some categories and elements that constituted a 'Black Aesthetic' outlook," to be further elaborated in a later essay. The outline is apparently designed to provide a cursory history of the mythologies created by African diasporic peoples and those mythologies' cultural manifestations, both of which led to the Black Aesthetic. Some of the most famous African mythological figures, such as Legba, Urzulie, and shamans, find a place here alongside the cultural figures or phenomena inspiring the Black Aesthetic's ideology in a column on the left (entitled "History as Unitary Myth"), while the basic beliefs of the aesthetic itself lie in the right-hand column. This article, while somewhat fragmented, provides an excellent tacit summary of what primary cultural forces the Black Aesthetic was intended to embody and push forward to transform not only African American arts, but also African American communities in general.

8. Stokely Carmichael and Charles V. Hamilton, *Black Power: The Politics of Liberation in America*, 61.

"[c]entral to the problem of the irreconcilable conflict between the black writer and the white critic is the failure of recognition of a fundamental and obvious truth of American life—that the two races are residents of two separate and naturally antagonistic worlds."[9] He is essentially rephrasing a cornerstone of nationalist belief: all whites, even the most well-meaning ones, are irredeemably tainted by a racist culture, which places them in direct opposition to the wants and needs of black Americans, whether they are conscious of this opposition or not. In a hostile white's eyes, this taint will result in complete disregard for the value of black literature and culture. A more sympathetic white critic may find some value in black literature but may dismiss any literature that does not appeal to a "universal" aesthetic. The conclusion of the Black Aesthetic, therefore, is that only black artists are capable of creating and judging literature that represents black communities, a literature that would replace negative myths about African Americans with new narratives that extolled the virtues within the community that those outside the community had previously classified as vices. Simultaneously, a progressive black art would provide an internal apparatus for political and cultural critiques that served purposes not unlike that of African American satire itself. Reginald Martin highlights, in fact, the integral role that cathartic humor plays in all phases of the Black Aesthetic. "[E]ven in the midst of a serious text," Martin says, "a joke will be told or phrasing will be arranged in such a way that it attempts to evoke laughter from the audience" to relieve tension even as it provides an important critique.[10]

The move toward making a new aesthetic for African American literature in the 1960s proved, however, to be far more convoluted than the new narrators had hoped. These convolutions would eventually cause marked disagreements between thinkers and writers originally on the same ideological page. Though proponents of Black Nationalism and the Black Aesthetic rightly advocated a revaluation of African American literature and culture, their political rigidity potentially precluded dissent from the definitions of progressive black art outlined above. Specifically, Karenga's and Baraka's arguments for revolutionary and lucid writing, positive portrayal of African Americans,

9. Hoyt W. Fuller, "Introduction: Towards a Black Aesthetic," 7.
10. Martin, *New Black Aesthetic Critics*, 17.

and an accent on cultural and political collectivism within the black community were driven just as strongly by Marxist influences as they were by concerns for black progress. These unities could only be obtained by subsumption underneath an unequivocal aesthetic. Hoyt W. Fuller's qualifying statement that "the black writers themselves are well aware of the possibility that what they seek is, after all, beyond codifying" and acknowledgment that black writers "are fully aware of the dual nature of their heritage, and of the subtleties and complexities" while being "even more aware of the terrible reality of their outsideness, of their political and economic powerlessness, and of the desperate racial need for unity" does not fit the sort of dogmatic position Baraka and Karenga advocate. While Fuller agreed with their imperative need to establish some "unity" and "indoctrination of black art and culture," he also understood that some ambivalence in artists' thinking was unavoidable, but it should not be the *focus* of black art. The focus should be upon the form and goal of urban realism. But as Madhu Dubey points out, "Black Aesthetic critics, and especially those who wrote on the novel, regarded form as a transparent medium of ideological meaning." The critical problem was though selected 1960s black aestheticians were "[s]uccessfully challenging a formalist aesthetic at one level, by insisting that all art is ideological, Black Aesthetic theorists, by default, allowed the category of form to remain immune and peripheral to the field of ideological analysis."

Dubey provides a succinct interpretation and application of Bakhtin's "Discourse in the Novel" as an aid to reading the project of the Black Aesthetic as well as that of black women writers. In Dubey's argument, black aestheticians fell into the same trap as the white critics before them of dividing literature among a fallacious form/content split. The problem with the demand for a reflective/realistic aesthetic "is that an exclusive focus on themes helps to maintain the form/content split that usually justifies a nonideological analysis of literary texts," which was a major failing of white critics. Conversely, a bias toward the content side of this split prevents recognition of the diversity of social and political histories with which specific forms are invested. More accurately, "[i]n Bakhtin's terms, the novel, in its fictive construction of competing social and ideological discourses, forces the recognition that 'language is not a neutral medium that passes freely and easily into the private property of the speaker's intentions;

it is populated—overpopulated—with the intentions of others.' "[11] In other words, the realistic, reflective form of literature went relatively unquestioned, becoming an ideal model for all black art.

Where, then, in this breach between the new assessment of black literature and culture and the traditions assigned by white culture, including the form of satire, did black satirists in the 1960s find a place for themselves? A few, such as John Oliver Killens and William Melvin Kelley, would not have bucked the Black Aesthetic's tenets and, in Killens's case, actually preceded them, although some trepidations surfaced in their works. Others, most notably Ishmael Reed and Cecil Brown, agreed strongly with the basic premises of most black aestheticians, but after a point frequently defied their proscriptions, thus drawing heavy criticism of their novels and, at times, of themselves. Reginald Martin, in his volume on Ishmael Reed, illustrates precisely why Reed, for one, was a target of widespread censure by black aestheticians:

> Reed uses humour, especially satire . . . in dealing with subjects only entertained with seriousness before. Humour was an early insertion in the tenets of the original black aesthetic, but the tenor of the times in the 1960s, when the new black aesthetic was solidifying, demanded a direct confronting of social issues, and this was most often done in serious prose. For example, critics still have a difficult time handling Reed's *The Freelance Pallbearers* (1967), which was extreme satire containing negative black characterizations. Some critics have seen Reed's use of humour as a shirking of responsibility on his part; that is, he should be responsible (read serious) toward the serious problems which face black Americans.[12]

In the main, Reed agreed with the Black Aesthetic's goal of offering a richer portrayal of African Americans' complexities, free of demeaning stereotypes. Reed also posits a vision of history in his novels that places African and African American history and culture in the center rather than at the margins, where they had been cast by Western hierarchical thinking. Finally, Reed's novels demonstrate that art should be functional to the extent that it forces an alteration of the way the reader views and interprets history and culture; his goal is a multicultural history.

11. Fuller, "Towards a Black Aesthetic," 9; Madhu Dubey, *Black Women Novelists and the Nationalist Aesthetic*, 9, 10.

12. Martin, *New Black Aesthetic Critics*, 42.

Reed disagreed strongly, however, with Addison Gayle, who attacked the "imagists" and black "propagandists" whose "'artistic' offerings," "infantile rationalizations," and "inability to dedicate themselves to what is noble and beautiful in a race of people" were despicable. The imagists Gayle attacks include not only writers who eschew "racial" subjects in favor of so-called "universal" subjects—the elision of difference—but also those, like Reed, who are interested in the will to diversity and difference found within the Black Aesthetic but accept no "blueprints" for their art.[13] Ironically, however, the critical valuation of black satire and satirists as somehow "irresponsible" vis-à-vis black realities resides on rocky ground for several reasons: First, while satire's essence as a form of discourse devoted to the ridicule of certain norms in favor of other, more virtuous or sensible ones (for example, the norm of realist fiction being ridiculed in favor of the surreal) remains intact in black satire of the 1960s, this satire rarely, if ever, qualifies as a form that denies the realities with which African Americans are faced. Satire does not simply ridicule; the force of its ridicule depends upon its status as "a mode of aesthetic expression that relates to historical reality . . . and demands the pre-existence or creation of shared comprehension and evaluation between satirist and audience."[14] Satire, then, does not necessarily qualify as a denial of a perceived reality; its efficacy is intrinsically bound to historical events, figures, and circumstances. It may differ from realistic texts by choosing the fantastic over the naturalistic, as we shall see below, but it "always involves collusion between author and reader based on 'shared values, beliefs and expectations.'"[15] Instead of denying a particular reality, satire necessarily depends upon and attempts to alter it.

Second, black aestheticians, intent upon forming a *new* aesthetic for Black Arts, neglect or downplay the degree to which satiric irony and signifying has contributed to the artistic success of preceding authors, up to and including the creators of African and enslaved African folklore, as discussed in chapter 1. Karenga asserts, for example, that

13. Ibid., 30–31, 35.
14. M. D. Fletcher, *Contemporary Political Satire: Narrative Strategies in the Post-Modern Context*, ix.
15. Ibid. Fletcher quotes Richard Finhold, "Northup [sic] Frye's Theory of Countervailing Tendencies," *Genre* 13 (1980), 211.

"the blues are invalid; for they teach resignation, in a word acceptance of reality—and we have come to change reality," a reality that does not depend upon the past.[16] Such an argument ignores the agency of the blues as a renewable and renewed artistic form, one that has as much relevance to the present as the past through its frequent ironic indictment of the blues artist's circumstances. (Reed's *Mumbo Jumbo*, in fact, demonstrates the form's relevance.) This aversion to overt humor closely resembles that held by antiseparatist black leaders, such as W. E. B. Du Bois, who suggested that artists should "abandon the comic depiction of Negroes," since such a depiction supposedly perpetuated stereotypes about African Americans. This criticism, however, ignores many of the basic principles underlying humor in general and satire or irony in particular. Rather than being a passive means of critiquing social institutions, humor and satire issue

> most effectively from an *assumed* position of eminence and self-assurance based on some real or imagined trait such as physical prowess, social status or intellectual or moral superiority. Whether stoked by irreverence or self-righteousness . . . or nourished by worldliness or the underdog's eye for contradiction and pretension . . . humor reflects an aggressive thrust or ascendancy. It may assume the guise of modesty and self-effacement . . . but . . . it still extols and celebrates the perspicuity of that viewpoint. Perhaps most important, humor is seldom neutral; someone or something is nearly always the object of ridicule, the butt of the joke.[17]

Satire, then, has the marked potential to be more aggressive than straight polemics. Given the role irony played in winning rhetorical points in *The Black Aesthetic*'s essays, more overtly humorous or sardonic critiques of social problems should not pose a threat to the goals of the Black Aesthetic. Finally, if Fuller's concept of a black aesthetic was intended to obviate and supplant the white/Western bias in writing by and about African Americans' experiences, to be skeptical about the project of Reed or Brown might indicate a "Western cultural bias against allowing humor to represent serious and important cultural information."[18]

16. Karenga, "Black Art," 482.
17. Watkins, *Real Side*, 408–9. Emphasis in the original.
18. William G. Doty and William J. Hynes, "Historical Overview of Theoretical Issues: The Problem of the Trickster," 13.

Watkins's argument above, however, may lend some insight into the final reason for black aestheticians' rejection of most satire and satirists. Satire, indeed any form of humor, always has objects of ridicule. In the case of many *black* satirists, this object could easily include the black community itself, which directly contradicts the Black Arts movement's call for racial unity. The satirist's "eye for contradiction and pretension" does not limit itself to targets outside the satirist's group; intragroup satire, even that which may indict the satirist, is frequently well within the bounds of fair play. Thus negative black characters that reveal deep failings within African American society are anathema to a black aesthetic, but "the only truly negative black character to the aestheticians is the traitor to black causes; admittedly, causes whose validity is established by the aestheticians themselves."[19]

On the other hand, it would be inaccurate to place the Black Arts movement and black satire at opposing literary and ideological poles in the 1960s. Some black satirists worked primarily under the aegis of the Black Arts movement, albeit with a few significant reservations. John Oliver Killens's *The Cotillion,* for example, is based in the sort of thinking that Addison Gayle advocated later in *The Black Aesthetic.* Where satirists differed with the movement was in its frequently censorious edicts that had the potential to dictate which viewpoints would be published and advocated. Perhaps more important, the Black Arts movement and its aesthetic did not always allow for the type of critical ambiguity that was part of the foundation of African American literature. In seeking to engender unity, some satirists argued, this intolerance of ambiguity could serve to drive deeper divisions within African American literary arts. The major satirical works of William Melvin Kelley, Cecil Brown, John Oliver Killens, Hal Bennett, Charles S. Wright, and Ishmael Reed in the late 1960s and early 1970s thus critique the ideology of the Black Aesthetic— both directly and indirectly, in its interpretation of African American culture and its meanings, even as they provide their own perspectives on conflicts between the races.

Of the many ideas that gained popularity during the 1960s among African Americans, especially those within the Black Power and Black

19. Martin, *New Black Aesthetic Critics,* 60.

Arts movements, one of the most trenchant was a variation of the idea, supported by history, that America would be nothing, an obscure backwater nation, if it weren't for the enslaved Africans who made up a substantial portion of its labor force. This notion was made resolutely clear long before the 1960s, of course; Negro educator and politician Booker T. Washington's entire power base had been built upon exploiting this fact in the minds of southerners and northerners alike at the turn of the century, and the argument was made repeatedly during the Harlem Renaissance. As we saw in earlier chapters, George Schuyler's *Black No More* focused upon this fact with a bitterly satirical eye, as did Ralph Ellison's *Invisible Man* and "What America Would Be Like without Blacks." As the racial tensions engendered by the Civil Rights movement heightened, however, it became important to demonstrate that the sort of mutual cooperation called for in *Invisible Man* had to be reinforced in the public mind. At a time in which white Americans would have liked to be rid of the embarrassment that the Civil Rights and Black Power movements brought at the international level—to say nothing of the personal nuisance that continuous confrontations with one's own racism creates—authors such as playwright Douglas Turner Ward and novelist William Melvin Kelley revised the dystopic premise that Schuyler and Ellison wrote of through their most famous works. I wish to touch briefly upon Ward's 1966 play *Day of Absence*, one of the most powerful and hilarious one-act plays to emerge from the 1960s, to prepare the way for a discussion of the satiric works of Kelley, Reed, Brown, and Killens.[20] All of these authors either adhere to or counter the dystopic plot in their respective works as a means of exploring the shifting allegiances and cultural tensions of the 1960s and early 1970s.

Day of Absence's plot is fairly straightforward; the black citizens of an unnamed southern town disappear for one day, and the white townsfolk realize that their reliance upon this invisible labor force is so absolute as to drive them into decadence. A young married couple,

20. The other major African American satirical play to emerge from the 1960s would have to be Ossie Davis's *Purlie Victorious* (1961). In fact, Ward's play arguably borrows a significant portion of its material, including plot, location, and some characterizations, from Davis's precedent. We may also draw some parallels between *Purlie Victorious* and Bennett's *Lord of Dark Places*, discussed here, to the extent that both works use trickster figures to satirize the political and racial dynamics of the American South.

for instance, finds that in the absence of their black maid, they have no idea how to care for their child, cook, clean, or otherwise take care of their basic needs. The town's mayor finds himself embroiled in a political crisis as the townsfolk project their displaced racism onto his ineffective leadership, blaming him for the departure of "their darkies," nearly lynching him in the process. The mayor is eventually forced to grovel and plead for either the return of the town's erstwhile labor force, or its replacement, with the latter option mystically blocked as new laborers vanish upon hitting the city limits. At the play's conclusion, just after the situation has degenerated into utter pandemonium, the black townsfolk quietly return and resume their everyday schedules, with the secret knowledge of the effect they have had on the town intact.

In effect, Ward satirizes the types of political ploys that white politicians have traditionally used to keep African Americans in their place, literally. The mayor calls upon the state and federal governments to investigate the town's situation, not with a mind to create equality in the town, but merely to return the black denizens to the "rightful place." Members of the white clergy ("Rev. Pious"), white supremacist groups (mayoral candidate Mr. Clan), and ordinary citizens all place the blame for the black townsfolks' disappearance on every other source but their own negligence and racism, confusing the integrationist mission of the NAACP with the motives that drove the black population away. The absence of the town's black citizens actually operates in tandem with another, implicit "absence": a moral center within the American body politic. That is to say, while continually touting its sacred principle of self-reliance and independence, America has continuously relied and depended upon the people it has relegated to the bottom of the social heap, especially to define the contours and size of that social heap itself. Rather than recognizing that the social order needs to be drastically changed, the white townsfolk—and, by extension, the nation—eventually riot, destroying their own town because they refuse to recognize that the situation is entirely of their making.

Like *Day of Absence*, William Melvin Kelley's *A Different Drummer* (1962) probes the absence of a general American willingness to be self-conscious but opts for a more serious and provocative look at the complexity within Euro-American communities that allows for the existence of racism, rather than attributing it to mere idiocy as

Ward's play does. Kelley's renown as an author may be most easily attributed to *A Different Drummer* and another early novel, *dem* (1967). Each examines and satirizes white America's dependence upon both white supremacy and the continued presence and labor of African Americans, but *A Different Drummer* earned Kelley the Richard and Hinda Rosenthal Award of the National Institute of Arts and Letters in 1963 and paved the way for the more consistent satirical milieu of the later novel. The story is set in a mythical southern state *"bounded on the north by Tennessee; east by Alabama; south by the Gulf of Mexico; west by Mississippi,"* a state that is an amalgamation of the entire Deep South and its history.[21] The narrative revolves around the history of the protagonist, Tucker Caliban, a black sharecropper and descendant of an African chieftain. Caliban indirectly causes the migration of all African Americans from the state when he salts his fields, burns his farmhouses, and leaves the state. The departure of the state's black population leads to the inevitable confusion that follows when an essential labor force disappears. Confronted with its own oppressive practices, the state's whites are forced to consider what "whiteness" means in the absence of African Americans, not unlike the scenarios in *Day of Absence* and Schuyler's *Black No More*. As in those works, Kelley explodes the notion that American racial problems are natural consequences of inherent racial differences. He shows instead that "white" is a term that has meaning only to the extent that something "not-white" exists; the term is but one half of a binary construction that has no legitimate meaning on its own. As in *Black No More,* the novel's denouement occurs as a result of a lynching, done in this case to help the white townsfolk regain a sense of meaning to their lives after the people they used as eternal scapegoats have quit the dubious honor.

In the preface to his short story collection *Dancers on the Shore,* Kelley argues that as a writer he "should depict people, not symbols or ideas disguised as people," a notion that may cause "black literature [to stand] on its head; but it is by this measure that . . . *dem* is really raceless—beyond race."[22] The novel *dem* clearly rejects the sort of proscriptions set forth by the proponents of the Black Aesthetic. Kelley sublimates overt racial themes and references for a significant portion of the plot to focus on the lives of white primary

21. William Melvin Kelley, *A Different Drummer,* 3; italics in the original.
22. William Melvin Kelley, *Dancers on the Shore,* ix.

characters, especially the protagonist, Mitchell Pierce, an advertising executive and stereotype of the middle-class white American male, who is later exposed as the antithesis of this model via his marked racial chauvinism and inept acquiescence to American romanticism. An African American presence increases incrementally after the first of the novel's four books, becoming a crucial component of the novel in the last and longest book. The novel addresses the American obsession with miscegenation, especially through whites' eyes. For that purpose, most of the novel is told from Mitchell Pierce's view, via free, indirect discourse.

This is not to argue, however, that *dem* does not deal effectively with racial issues; on the contrary, concerns with race are integral to the novel's plot. *dem* places African Americans primarily in the background as foils used to reveal the complications and absurdities within white characters, not the converse; until the novel's fourth book, African Americans and their interactions with whites surface only once (though that event, told in the novel's short second book, contains several crucial plot details). This peculiar narrative position places *dem* in marked contrast with other black novels of the time. Aside from the fact that the protagonist is white, the text's critique of the white middle class is not expressed explicitly until its final pages. This is at least partially a reflection of Kelley's reluctance to utilize a single narrative form to "address himself to the Afro-American" and, simultaneously, his "dual commitment . . . to his craft and to black people."[23] It is Mitchell's unquestioning acceptance of the racial stereotypes held by the majority of the white middle class, combined with the sexual obsessions that blind him to his wife's desires, that leads us to declare him a dupe, buffoon, and quintessential cuckold. The satire aims to expose the degree to which bourgeois white America is so overconfident in its racial hegemony that it cannot comprehend that the subversive forms of that hegemony are always in motion.

The rhetorical force of Kelley's satire lies in the farcical pattern of Mitchell's misadventures. In each of the novel's episodes, Mitchell reveals that his obsession with keeping his purported masculinity and manhood intact must remain supreme. More specifically, his

23. Bell, *Afro-American Novel*, 296.

supremacy as a white *male* must remain beyond question. Mitchell's racial and sexual bigotries are too numerous to list in detail here, but they include a belief in the inferiority of Asians, which he learned in the military; an assumption that black people are thieves; necrophilia; an obsession with a soap opera actress, who happens to be "the daughter of a Jewish doctor," which "might explain why every so often she acted strangely"; profound fear and denial of miscegenation (*dem,* 10, 9, 39, 20–21, 43–72, 61, 75ff.).

When, therefore, Mitchell learns in the novel's last book that his wife, Tam, has given birth to fraternal twins, one of whom is phenotypically black, the narrative takes an increasingly comic turn. The doctor asks Mitchell how long he and his wife's "people" have been in the United States. When Mitchell tells the doctor that his family has been in the country for three centuries, while his wife is from Washington, D.C., the doctor concludes, erroneously, that Tam has black ancestors and therefore recessive genes:

> Mitchell did not at all understand the doctor, but something *terrible* was lurking in the air between them. He leaned forward into that terrible thing. "Is something . . . wrong . . . with one of the babies?"
>
> The doctor hesitated. "No . . . no . . . not the way I think you mean it. They're both . . . healthy. But one of them . . . its appearance . . . nothing is exactly wrong with it. In fact, if anything it's the *healthier* of the two. Tell me, Mr. Pierce, how much do you know about your wife's family?" (*dem,* 76–77; italics mine)

The doctor's reluctance to reveal that Mitchell's wife has given birth to a black child, a "terrible" thing, is a sign simultaneously of the unspeakability of miscegenation and the greatest fear of the racist: the possibility that a "foreign" element has somehow infected or tainted Mitchell's life and family history. The irony of the misunderstanding between Mitchell and the doctor is heightened by the ironies of Mitchell's other racialized memories running through the previous books in the text, including his memories of sex with Korean women while a soldier and his brief affair with a Jewish woman and, later, a black woman, all of which he accepts and even fetishizes with few reservations. The doctor's comment that the black baby is actually "the healthier of the two" veils Kelley's figuration of the irrational sickness that is white supremacy, a metaphor carried further in the nearly farcical fervor with which Mitchell rejects his child.

When Mitchell enters the nursery, then, and has a heated argument with a Cuban who has also had a son, accusing the man of trying to pass his "negrito" baby off as Mitchell's, this fever reaches an incredible pitch, with the Cuban calling Mitchell "crazy" and a nurse, ironically, commenting "[t]wo of them together and you have a riot," thereby playing to the stereotype of black violence and accusing Mitchell of "passing" for white (*dem*, 79–81). This particular insult is not lessened when the doctor reveals that the only way the child could not be Mitchell's is via superfecundation or, in the doctor's words, " 'your wife is an adulteress. . . . And, may I say, not a very lucky one' " (*dem*, 83).

Mitchell then embarks on a quest to find the father and make him take the child, for which he employs the services of his black maid's nephew, Carlyle, who leads Mitchell on a wild chase through Harlem and the Bronx, stopping at a house party where Mitchell is forced to "pass" as a very fair-skinned black man and endure the embarrassment and discomfort of being among the people he has most feared. Eventually, Carlyle leads Mitchell to a "Calvin" who knows "Cooley," the child's father. Mitchell pays Calvin a considerable amount of money to persuade Cooley to take the child, but Calvin eventually hands Mitchell a report that Cooley will not agree to Mitchell's terms because "he wasn't making it with your wife for no baby. . . . He saw her and wanted to find out how someone that messed up in the head would be in bed. It was so bad, so weak, he had to go back a couple times to make sure it was really bad as he thought it was the first time. . . . [Cooley's] got old scores to settle" (*dem*, 136–37). Those "old scores" are with the slave system and its amalgamation and subsequent splitting of black families that occurred regularly on slave plantations. According to Cooley, it is Mitchell's turn to experience the sort of destruction visited upon black families. When Mitchell asks " 'My turn? But why me?' " Calvin responds, " 'That's funny, because he said you'd ask that. And he told me that when you did, I was to ask you why his great-granddaddy?' " (*dem*, 137). Mitchell then pleads with Calvin to try again, placates him with more money, and, after Calvin has left, discovers that "Cooley" is, in fact, "Calvin," whom Mitchell did not recognize for the man he thought was the father's child. Mitchell has been the victim of an elaborate trick and has no means of redress; in fact, all of his neighbors are aware that Mitchell has been duped, and he must live with the shame that cuckoldom and being involved in miscegenation bring.

Kelley thus incorporates the tradition of black tricksterism into his text. Through his arrogance, his denial of the intelligence and worth of anyone besides himself and other whites, Mitchell falls prey not only to black tricksters, but to the irrationalities of white supremacy. The theme of *dem*, therefore, is not unlike that of Schuyler's *Black No More*, to the extent that the text's satire rests upon stale and staunchly held assumptions about constructed racial hierarchies. The difference, of course, is that Kelley uses the unusual device of sublimating his black characters' tricksterlike behavior to allow his portrayal of middle-class whites' assumptions about race to lead them into the trap of black trickery. The novel, therefore, posits Kelley's notion that if white America wishes to "help repair the damage done to the soul of the Negro in the past three centuries," it must demonstrate some consistency in its views of racial intermixing on at least the social and sexual levels.[24] Holding one group supreme for any reason can only lead to the same shock that Mitchell experiences out of a belief in a unidirectional racial purity; until the history of racial admixture, voluntary or forced, is openly acknowledged and confronted, white America shall continue to live a lie.

This same argument is used, for slightly different purposes, in Cecil Brown's *The Life and Loves of Mr. Jiveass Nigger*, though the narrative shifts back to a focus on black characters performing trickery on unsuspecting whites. Cecil Brown's most outrageous novel is a picaresque novel, a satirical bildungsroman that examines the exploits of George Washington, a young black man, as he fulfills and explodes the stereotype of the "black stud" or "bad nigger" who defies the accepted racial order despite the dangers of doing so. The title alone indicates the book's irreverence, even though this was not the only text from the late 1960s and early 1970s that used the term *nigger* in its title.[25] With its title and its exploration of the seamier side of African American life, the novel invokes the iconoclastic spirit of Harlem Renaissance authors Carl Van Vechten and Claude McKay, whose major novels (*Nigger Heaven* and *Home to Harlem*, respectively) outraged

24. Ibid.
25. Some notable examples include Dick Gregory's autobiographical *Nigger* and selected poems and songs by the Last Poets.

the black bourgeoisie. The novel's prologue writes Washington into the picaresque tradition; his distinguishing characteristics mark him as a true rogue. Interestingly, Washington receives a relatively sound education early in life: "Like all true students, George outgrew his teachers and became something his uncles never dreamed of: he became literate, which is to say, he became a voracious reader of any piece of printed matter he could lay hands on." Prior to and following Washington's self-education, though, he is surrounded, taught, and seduced by buffoons whose teachings eventually determine his worldview. During George's formative years, the uncles mentioned above "were very excellent models, indeed. Illiterate, generous, intuitive, simple, and hopelessly backwards, they were probably some of the finest men in the whole world. From them little Washington learned at an exceptionally early age how to swear, talk about women, talk *to* women . . . avoid unnecessary work, how to relax, how to tell when a white cracker is trying his best to get something for nothing (which is most of the time)." Not only is Washington "the cussinges' man ever born," full of lusts, obscenities, and lies, but his modus operandi is to be a "jiveass nigger," which means to honor superficially the authorities and social mores that guided the early part of his life while subtly subverting them through trickery and deceit. This behavior is an extension of Washington's singular personality; he possesses "the almost fanatical ability to remain *different* against all odds," to be able to walk in both high- and lowbrow worlds.[26]

In fact, this need to stand within both worlds extends itself beyond Washington. The novel's prologue itself is divided into two sections, the first written in a black vernacular, accusatory dialect ("There ain't a soul in this community he ain't cussed out, hardly a dog or cat either"), the second in a more formal, apologetic style ("Let us backtrack a moment. The most salient characteristic of George Washington's early childhood . . . was his *individuality*"). The novel, therefore, posits both itself and Washington as *double-voiced.*[27] In this sense, *Jiveass Nigger* and

26. Cecil Brown, *The Life and Loves of Mr. Jiveass Nigger,* 13, 12; italics in the original.
27. Brown, *Life and Loves,* 4, 12; italics in the original. The novel aspires, in the words of Henry Louis Gates, Jr., "to the status of oral narration" while directing "attention to the manner in which language is used," the possibility for black texts and characters to utilize two modes of discourse for the same purpose: triumph

George Washington exemplify common satirical modes of narration and satirical protagonists.

The body of the novel sustains the mode begun in the prologue by following Washington's sexual and other exploits as an American expatriate in Copenhagen. Washington's difference from previous protagonists in black novels, and thus the *novel's* difference from the naturalism of Wright's *Native Son* or Himes's *Lonely Crusade,* is established via a brief but devastating critique of the quintessential protest antihero, Bigger Thomas, who

> went through life living masochistic nightmares, who lived in fear of The Great White Man who in reality was a substitute for some psychic guilt . . . yes all those stupid ass Biggers who think violence is sex, who don't have enough cool to seduce a "white" woman but who end up *stealing* a kiss from "white" girl when he should have fucked her . . . so beautifully . . . that she would come away feeling he was a man, and not a nigger or an animal or an ex-gorilla or something. But no, Bigger's fear was so great that a mere kiss . . . has to be smothered in a fiery furnace. George Washington could not relate to demoralized Bigger (Nigger Chigger) Thomas. He could relate to . . . the nigger in Malcolm X, LeRoi Jones, James Baldwin, and Eldridge Cleaver. . . . to the Outcasts of Life and of Literature. . . . to the protagonists of *The Satyricon* and *The Golden Ass.* . . . He could not relate to stupidity, fear, and demoralization.[28]

The character of Bigger Thomas is not all that is satirized here; the passage also subverts the notion that mindless violence is necessarily part of the solution to black America's problems. It is rather the *cleverness,* the *cunning,* that may lie within African Americans, that should be promoted; the liberating role models should not be cultural icons who advocate random destruction but those who use their fullest faculties (especially their rhetorical skills, best exemplified in the black cultural figures Washington cites) to subvert racism's oppressions. Additionally, this passage problematizes the valorization of Bigger Thomas as an antihero to which numerous critics subscribed. Hoyt W. Fuller quotes Brown as saying that " 'White America branded [Richard] Wright the Official Negro Protester, the genuine article . . . to reject him was to reject official, genuine Negro protest, no matter

---

over a nonsensical world. Henry Louis Gates, Jr., *The Signifying Monkey: A Theory of African-American Literary Criticism,* xxvi–xxvii.

28. Brown, *Life and Loves,* 22–23.

what your own experience as a Negro might have been.'" Fuller goes on to say that "Brown is not opposed to protest, he is opposed to what he terms 'negative protest . . . which is . . . a raging, ferocious, uncool, demoralized black boy banging on the immaculate door of White Society, begging . . . so that in the final analysis, his destiny is at the mercy of the White Man.'" George Washington, then, is the negation of that negative protest; he embodies Brown's concept of a "destiny . . . not at the mercy of the white man" and lives "in a world with options."[29]

As one of the novel's most literate and intelligent characters, George Washington attempts to emulate these models and, as a result, fulfills the traditional roles of the picaro and the trickster, embracing signifying in the form of "shucking and jiving" practice. The novel switches between scenes from Washington's youth and events in Copenhagen, where he continually hustles money and women (frequently white) for his own benefit, to feed himself and fuel his own cynicism regarding absolute truths and stabilities. Each scene from Washington's youth in the early part of the novel further establishes his role as a trickster and picaresque figure. At one point, Washington tells his friend Reb, who is considerably less endowed in wit, that "everything is a lie. Life is a lie. But people don't know that, see. Only smart people like me know that. . . . I am jiving because jiving is the truth, and I'm the living truth." Appropriately, in the scene immediately following the compatriots' conversation, we see George lying his way through the consul at the U.S. embassy in Copenhagen to acquire funds to lengthen his stay in the city, where he spends most of his time carousing with friends in two local bars. These bars serve two significantly different sets of clientele. The Drop Inn "is the place you go to meet the 'intellectual' bloods" and is "close to being the Big House" while the Cassanova caters to American black servicemen, "has the smell of the slave quarters," and is considerably more rambunctious than its rival. The disparity between the classes exhibited by these two bars shows in George's choice of friends as well, who range from the intensely intellectual "Doc" to the coarse Jero.[30] Each of these characters and places reveals the conflicts within George Washington as he negotiates

29. Hoyt W. Fuller, "The New Black Literature: Protest or Affirmation," 367.
30. Brown, *Life and Loves*, 31, 19. Furthermore, in a thinly veiled reference to Shakespeare's *Hamlet*, the gaggle of friends counts a Falstaff among its number.

two different worlds, the high- and lowbrow. This negotiation is a common feature among trickster figures; Henry Louis Gates notes that in the case of the African trickster Esu, "his legs are of different lengths because he keeps one anchored in the realm of the gods while the other rests in this, our human world."[31] The tension within *Life and Loves* rests upon George Washington's determining which of his friends and which of his worlds is "human" and which is godly.

George's many liaisons with Copenhagen's white women—done to destroy white repression and its concomitant myths—find marked contrasts in his relationships with the few black women in Copenhagen, one of whom (Michele, who is *passing* for white) George actually attempts to befriend.[32] Numerous characters, including George himself, continually confront George's seeming obsession with white women and with destroying the myths that revolve around white women and black men, an obsession that could in turn destroy him. Though virtually all of George's most satisfying sexual encounters occur with white women, each of them eats away at his conscience, though he resists this deterioration by rationalizing his obession as a great conquest: "the black lover was a true warrior, a true soldier who is doomed, cursed, to fighting a perpetual battle with an elusive enemy, and with the foreknowledge that he can never be the victor, and fighting every day with this foreknowledge that he can never be the victor makes him victorious every moment of his life. His only security being in knowing that, as a black man, there is no security." This particular stance on his own degeneration, however, shifts as the novel progresses. Each encounter with white women (especially the American consul, Ruth Smith, a sign of the southern "Miss Ann" or slave mistress whom George *must* conquer) makes George feel more humiliated, until he finally concedes that the roles of the gigolo, the pimp, or the sexual trickster are ultimately fruitless. Only a full

---

This character indeed acts the buffoon and gets soundly humiliated for his sexual inadequacies by the other barflies later in the novel.

31. Gates, *Signifying*, 6.

32. In a fascinating reading of John Milton's *Comus*, George and Doc determine that the tale is actually about protecting white virginhood from black manhood and magic in the guise of Comus, "a witch doctor [who] changes his appearance and shit like this." The reading is concluded by a declaration that "ain't no power strong enough in the world to undo Black Magic," hence the impetus behind George's sexual conquests (Brown, *Life and Loves*, 55).

confrontation of racial issues can ever yield a sense of closure and satis-
faction to his existence; he must abandon his obsession with the "dirty
lives of white people" and focus instead on fighting "whiteness"
as a construction of power to which even he himself unconsciously
reacts. Washington is, therefore, shifting away from a celebration of
the sexual and social indeterminacy of the picaro/trickster toward
a more coherent (if highly problematic) perception of blackness. He
subsequently tells Doc that

> "[i]t is a tragedy if a black man lets himself love something in white
> women, just as it is if a man lets himself be fucked by another man, and
> it is not beautiful because it is based on a weak will. Somebody must
> have a strong enough will to set standards, to set up a guideline, or
> we won't be able to tell who's black and who's white, or who's man
> and who's woman. . . . I'm black and a man and that's my identity. If
> somebody comes up to me and tells me I'm white and a woman . . . then
> I lose my identity, my existence, my meaning, and my life becomes petty,
> meaningless, immoral and useless, I die. And I don't want to die, I want
> to live."[33]

If George's and the novel's inclusion of a heterosexist viewpoint to
confirm his move from weakness is somewhat appalling, it is consistent with a concatenating arc common in satire. Guillermo Hernández
observes that satirical works frequently move resolutely toward one
side of the hegemonic spectrum, most often toward the side that both
brings a palatable degree of cohesion to the personal psyche and helps
make sense of the individual's place in society. Such moves, however,
"are intelligible only within particular cultural contexts, since their
significance is evident only in relation to the specific conventions of
a group."[34] In George's case, resolving the problems facing African

33. Brown, *Life and Loves*, 110, 204, 205.
34. Hernández, *Chicano Satire*, 4. His hegemonic spectrum organizes the values
that determine the quality of "human existence" in a table consisting of contrast-
ing sets of positive and negative values and the characters who normally represent
them in literature. Each set of values lies on either side of the "historical axis,"
which societies cross over as they experience shifts in the values deemed integral
to continued prosperity. Thus, for example, the negative emotion of "fear" is
the property of the literary "coward"; he is contrasted with the "hero," whose
ideal emotion or characteristic is "courage." Most societies consider the former,
obviously, to be counterproductive, and the latter, a paragon of virtue. Over time,
however, the contrast between these two often becomes blurred in literature,

Americans, specifically African American males, must take precedence over the power that defiance of social, sexual, and racial norms provides.

If Brown, through Washington, elides the question of homophobia among African Americans—and he certainly does—I do not wish to endorse such a move or elide the issue. It is important to point out, however, that if homophobia in black communities is still a marked problem today, it had not reached the forefront of African American critical discourse in 1969, when upholding a construction of African American manhood was the crux of nationalistic visions of the salvation of African American communities. Resolution takes place by making a *physical* move toward a stable locus, "the dirt farm where [George] came from," where he will write "a book about the race problem with a dynamite stick concealed inside it. I mean a *real* stick of dynamite, so that when liberal ass crackers picked up the book . . . it'll go off and take [their] motherfucking head[s] with it. I won't mind writing a book, but I'd hate to be a black author in America. . . . All the publishers are interested in selling books and if you say something about sex and being a nigger then you got a bestseller." George's outrage is made ironic, of course, by the fact that it lies within a novel with precisely the subject matter he describes. He effectively signifies upon the reader, who has bought into the standards for black authorship even as George bought into particular racial standards.

George's farm thereby becomes the site from which he will be able to write novels that will figuratively explode in the faces of their readers, insofar as they will exploit their acceptance of racial and artistic standards that make sense only in the context of America. His plan is to use cynically American obsessions about race to the fullest: "Every liberal would go around reading the book and not understand . . . it, you know. So I'd be asked to go to universities and the Elks Clubs and ladies' teas to explain it. And I'll tell them the book is autobiographical, and that it reflects a black man's struggle to live in a white society." Finally, then, George has become a different type of picaro. Instead of exploiting reactionary social stereotypes about black men to make a subsistence living, George shall exploit the liberal end of the sociopolitical spectrum for enormous profit. It is not unlike the

---

especially as marginalized authors provide their own view of normal societal values (2, 3).

profit found at the end of Voltaire's *Candide;* in the end, it is better for George to "cultivate [his] garden" and rise transcendentally to a new level of tricksterism.[35]

Prima facie, *The Life and Loves of Mr. Jiveass Nigger* is at best an incomplete view of American race politics, since it is concentrated primarily in Copenhagen. This assumption proves to be false, however, since the novel's discourse never fully leaves American political shores. Perhaps it offers us a clearer view of America's racial dilemmas than most novels set in America and is no more isolated from the truths of the American scene than Wallace Thurman's *Infants of the Spring.* In fact, George's decision to write "a book about the race problem with a dynamite stick concealed inside it" is almost identical to Raymond Taylor's wish to "spend [his] life doing things just to make people angry" (*Infants,* 221) out of frustration with African American apathy and decadence.

Kelley's and Brown's notable concern with the miscegenated composition of "race" relations in America and abroad could easily leave the impression that the African American satirical novel in the 1960s and 1970s fit a general framework of obsessive phallocentrism and crude homophobia. Even a cursory look at any portion of Hal Bennett's contemporaneous oeuvre both confirms and troubles that impression considerably. If his novels are overtly phallocentric—each has at least one black character with a magical penis—it is not necessarily a call to his reader literally to worship the black male's sexuality. Instead, Bennett highlights the way that America is always already worshiping this icon through its own obsession with it. For Bennett, black males must be fully aware of their sexuality within the American milieu if they wish to be liberated.

Although Bennett's string of novels, published between 1966 and 1976, are written in the same picaresque mode and are as concerned with the black male's sexuality as are Kelley's and Brown's works, they also disregard the era's nationalistic image of manhood via characters that defy any easy sexual categorization. Bennett's obsessions are pointedly different; he regards America as the product of the incestuous confluence of humanity's streams, with the barriers between black/white, North/South, male/female, "queer"/"sissy"/"manly,"

35. Brown, *Life and Loves,* 205, 206; Jean-Marie Arouet de Voltaire, *Candide, or Optimism,* 77.

sacred/profane, formal/vernacular, and normal/taboo constantly in flux throughout the nation's history. While all of his novels explore this ambiguous terrain, it is his masterwork, *Lord of Dark Places* (1970), that is most successful in detailing what Bennett describes as "the black American's obsession with filth" that makes African Americans "feel unclean and impure and unworthy and inferior."[36]

Bennett's blunt assessment of African Americans' collective self-esteem, to say nothing of the sexually explicit content of all his novels, might help account for this remarkable work's being out of print from 1972 to 1997 and remaining, as of 2001, his only work in print under his own name.[37] In view of *Lord of Dark Places'* artistic accomplishments, any other reasons seem unfathomable. *Lord of Dark Places* essentially revises Ralph Ellison's *Invisible Man* without Ellison's continuous nods to modernism or the same degree of ambivalence regarding the promises of American democracy that ends Ellison's own master-work. Instead, Bennett offers a Christlike naïf and black Everyman in the form of Joe Market, whose worship of his own phallus coincides with American society's fanaticism regarding black sexuality. Joe, a "beautiful" manchild, is molested by his father, Titus, not without some cooperation on Joe's part. He subsequently works as a prostitute, engaging in sexual relations with men and women alike without considering himself "queer," in his own words. His complex sexual history is but part of extensive picaresque misadventures that effectively turn all of the myths America held about itself in the 1960s on their heads.

Joe's life begins as the sexual and religious icon in "The Church of the Naked Child Titus Market founded as an alternative to American Christianity, whose main error is that its primary icon is normally depicted as a white man whom African Americans must worship" (*LDP*, 15). In a wicked parody of Christian ritualistic practices, Titus and the teenaged Joe travel across America attempting to convert African Americans to this new religion, in which converts purportedly worship Joe's naked body. Titus funds the sojourn with proceeds gained by literally prostituting Joe's penis, which Joe later gives the

---

36. Katherine Newman, "An Evening with Hal Bennett: An Interview," 358–59.

37. Newman, "Evening," 378. Bennett has also published novels under the pseudonyms Harriet Janeway and John D. Revere.

symbolic name *Christ*opher as a sign of its power. After Titus is raped and murdered by police persecuting him for his religion, the novel fuses the picaresque narrative with the bildungsroman as Joe wanders physically and psychologically, witnessing or participating in events ranging from the epic Civil Rights movement to the cataclysmic Vietnam War and the urban violence that hit hundreds of cities throughout the 1960s. His final assessment of these events illustrates the novel's central premise: American violence and racial tension ultimately undermine any interpretation of national history that glosses racial oppression in favor of pretense. "What gets me," Market says in one of the novel's key moments, "is *the pretense of virtue*. . . . [T]he white man's hypocrisy makes him *pretend not to hate*. . . . The white man's pretense is designed to make him feel better than the colored man. Superior. On the other hand, a Negro pretends in order to keep from being destroyed. It's as simple as that" (*LDP*, 209; emphasis in the original). Market's basis for this argument is well founded. In an early scene that is a but thinly veiled reference to the opening pages of *Invisible Man*, Joe Market's grandfather, Roosevelt, who "had achieved something of the status of a wise man by telling white people what a dumb, low-down, no-good nigger he was," is lynched after a white woman interprets his nervous tic as him winking at her. Being lynched is something that Roosevelt "certainly would have preferred they do, if he had only known why they were lynching him in the first place." When Roosevelt asks one of the white lynchers if he was "a good nigger," his killer affirms the title while "touching him on his shoulder with a kind of awkward affection" (*LDP*, 2–3). Unlike the Invisible Man's deceptively meek grandfather, though, Roosevelt actually believes in his own inferiority and dies an ignominious death that concludes with his castration. The price of his hypocrisy was not survival, but death, which raises questions about the efficacy of playing a trickster role. While the Invisible Man's grandfather was clearly acting as a trickster and fully intended for his progeny to improve upon his plan, Roosevelt's death resulted, first, from the absence of any plan for triumphing over oppression and, second, from his failure to realize that the oppressor's law necessarily fills the vacuum left by the absence of real power. In the end, his lynchers defined his death, using their own affection to salve their consciences.

Yet the incongruity between a savage ritual and personal affection Joe Market speaks of, represented in this scene, is commonplace within the novel, lending it a surreal and therefore comically unrealistic atmosphere. Although Joe Market is himself a victim of incest and child molestation, he is also a participant. At one point he wishes his father would perform fellatio on him to salve his tortured soul after he was raped by an openly racist white woman, whom he alternately loved and hated for her actions (*LDP*, 42–47). This latter scene is itself another reference to Ellison's *Invisible Man*, specifically Ellison's erotic description of the blonde stripper with an American flag tattooed above her vagina, whom the Invisible Man wishes he could both love and murder (*IM*, 19). In the context of the novel, the scene symbolizes the Invisible Man's ambivalence regarding America's seductive promises of democracy and crushing reality of discrimination. Joe Market's ambivalence, though, is significantly murkier than Ellison's. Whereas *Invisible Man* places sexual tensions between African Americans and whites in but a few select scenes, *Lord of Dark Places* continuously posits milieux in which the lines between accepted sexual norms—consenting heterosexual acts between adults—and their opposing sexualities are blurred. The Invisible Man agonizes over the way America confuses the "class struggle with the ass struggle"; it is so obsessed with black sexuality and fears of miscegenation that it ultimately halts any social progress that could lead to interracial sexual encounters, despite the fact that African Americans are "*part of*" white America even as they are "apart from" it (*IM*, 418, 575; italics in the original).

Bennett's approach to the mixing of blacks in white America takes a markedly different turn. In Bennett's conception, social progress, national politics, religion, and sexuality are inextricably intertwined to the point that they are virtually indistinguishable. Bennett's text consequently equalizes each of these categories. In one crucial scene, Joe and his white friend Tony Brenzo wrestle and fight in a homoerotic battle that begins "in hatred" but "had terminated on the edge of sex," indicating that they, like black and white men in general, fight "to keep from making love" (*LDP*, 212). Racial tensions may thus be relegated to a manifestation of erotic tension not only between black men and white women, but also between black and white men who cannot acknowledge the same possibility of male-male love that could be found in Joe's relationship with his father. The pretense "not to hate" that Joe despises is therefore given another nuance. America's racial dilemma is attributable not so much to the notion that whites pretend not to hate but to the idea that whites have lost the ability to tell the difference between the emotions of love and hate as they have built a nation grounded in an oppressive social structure. Unresolved erotic tensions between and among the genders therefore confuse the body politic.

Consequently these tensions and confusions extend equally to African American communities, allowing for corruption within the fundamental institutions of black society. When Titus Market places Joe's sexuality at the center of the Church of the Naked Child, for example, he simply makes explicit the eroticism within the black church. In one central passage, Bennett lampoons the African American clergy as libertines with a "mandate" to pursue "fried chicken, free pussy and chocolate cake, in that order of edibility," making the black preacher "especially fortunate, since devoted sisters of the church have long ago convinced themselves that to fuck their preacher is one and the same with fucking their God, which they consider the insanest and sweetest kind of love" (*LDP*, 177). Even in the sacred institution of the church, sexuality reigns, allowing the worst sorts of crimes and mass hoodwinking to continue. "Black preachers," the narrator notes, "are forever doing wrong, and are forever being pardoned by their people" because of their special mandate for licentious sexual activity (*LDP*, 177). Justice and fairness are again sacrificed to unresolved sexual tensions.

The propensity for sexuality to conquer justice eventually leads to Joe Market's execution by the state after he kills Mary, a lustful, elderly woman, with his penis. Joe considers this killing a form of salvation; he was "saving" the woman from the trap of her own lusts and her bigotry. The scene parodies and reverses key moments in the life of Christ, especially the Virgin Birth and the Passion; whereas the Virgin Mary gave birth to Christ, Joe kills a corrupt Mary in a sexual act that is both brutal and loving. As refrains from New Testament passages declaring Christ's position as the savior "who taketh away the sins of the world" ring in Joe's head, he makes love to Mary until she dies in his arms (*LDP*, 283). When he is executed, he symbolically owes his death—or sacrifice, given his past and present status as an icon—to a nation that cannot handle his message of salvation through fully acknowledged sexuality. Mary wanted to be free of the "tragedy of men and women trying to love one another" but failing because of greed engendered by racial inequality (*LDP*, 282). With his last words, Joe bitterly points out that "the very fact of being human panics us into the most grotesque play-acting imaginable; and we deal in absurdities to keep life from being a total waste, like one constant jacking-off party.

Now please suck my dick. All you slimy motherfuckers, black and white alike" (*LDP*, 284). The text's concluding irony is found within Joe's last thought, a parody of Christ's final cry of the Passion: "*Father forgive them, they know exactly what they're doing*" (*LDP*, 285). Bennett satirizes a divided nation *willing* to play the pretentious roles that lead to death and destruction.

The theme of racial, sexual, and political pretense wove itself deeply into Black Aesthetic–era satires. It can be found in Charles S. Wright's surreal *The Wig: A Mirror Image* (1966), which satirizes African American obsession with white-defined beauty standards. The novel posits an occasionally satiric allegory through racially ambiguous everyman Lester Jefferson, who believes his own salvation lies in "conking" (chemically straightening) his hair into a shiny "wig." Through his picaresque misadventures in African American, white, and Latino communities, Jefferson reveals the degree to which attaining power in America's racial climate depends upon the individual's desire to sacrifice racial or ethnic identity and assimilate white standards. His "wig" becomes the central focus for every person he encounters, as each tries to force him into easily identifiable racial categories. As Joe Market discovered in *Lord of Dark Places*, Jefferson realizes that Americans find it impossible to function without rigidly divided hierarchies and categories. Inevitably, the desire for a strict social order extends to African American communities. For this reason, John Oliver Killens's *The Cotillion, or One Good Bull Is Half the Herd* locates itself well in the thick of post–civil rights African America's intraracial conflicts to concentrate primarily on the black community's own class divisions, which threaten to destroy it.

The Cotillion represents the convergence of numerous literary and ideological aesthetics and conventions. Bernard W. Bell classifies the novel as part of Killens's attempt to " 'change the world, to capture reality, to melt it down and forge it into something entirely different,' " an ambition manifested via "critical realism." Critical realism, in its simplest terms, is "a negative attitude toward capitalism and a readiness to respect the perspective of socialism and not condemn it out of hand."[38] In the context of Killens's novel, this concept is translated as

---

38. Bell, *Afro-American Novel*, 248, 247. Bell quotes Killens's "The Black Writer Vis-à-Vis His Country," from his collection *Black Man's Burden* (New York: Trident, 1965), 34.

a skeptical, satirical eye turned on the divisiveness of the class system within the African American community, specifically the yawning divide between, on one side, a petit bourgeois black middle class that identifies and strives for assimilation with the white middle class and, on the other, unpretentious, working-class blacks. The theme of class division and exploitation is not unprecedented in satire's history.[39] Killens's explicit project of trying to find a common ground upon which the different *intraracial* classes can meet is remarkably rare, if not unique.

The Cotillion's events are seen through the cynical eyes of Ben Ali Lumumba, a principal character, whose narrative voice continuously switches between straight, conventional narrative and African American "street" argot, as well as from first to second or third person. This constant code switching marks Lumumba the *narrator* as a trickster; it is his means of creating an inclusive text, one appealing to all types and classes of African Americans. In fact, in the novel's foreword, he boasts openly of his training and fluidity in both types of discourse and their value in creating his narrative form:

> I used to write my novels as I lived them from Rio all the way to Zanzibar. In the oral tradition of my African ancestors. . . . with my blood and sweat and years of wondering as I wandered (thanks to Langston) carousing, reading, brawling, learning, looking, drinking, fornicating . . . with all races and religions. . . . I should state, categorically, I have a tendency to boast and brag, or, in other words, exaggerate, and sometimes I'm a liar, like most men who have been to sea. I was a seaman, see?
>
> Yeah, and like I can lie with the best of them. Which ought to put me in good stead as a writer, right? Once has to lie sometimes to get closer to the truth. (*Cotillion,* 1)

This instance of apodixis evokes the long-standing irony of the literary enterprise: using fictions and figurations to describe reality. It also posits Lumumba as something of a propagandist using argumentum ad populum—rhetoric appealing to the crowd—with the crowd being an ostensibly African American audience, to draw in the reader. Simultaneously, he calls upon the tradition of earlier crucial literary movements and texts within African American literature, specifically

---

39. Pope's *The Rape of the Lock,* the first two books of Swift's *Gulliver's Travels,* and Schuyler's *Black No More* being but a few notable examples.

the autobiography and such *lanx satura* (medleys) as W. E. B. Du Bois's *The Souls of Black Folk* (1903):[40]

> This book is kind of halfly autobiographical and halfly fiction, all based on facts as I have gathered them. I got my log together, baby, from the natural source, the horse's mouth and his hinder parts. . . . Dig it, and like I went to one of them downtown white workshops for a couple of months and got all screwed up with angles of narration, points of view, objectivity, universality, composition, author-intrusion, sentence structure, syntax, first person, second person. I got so screwed up I couldn't unwind myself, for days. I said, to hell with all that! I'm the first, second and third person my own damn self. And I will intrude, protrude, obtrude or exclude my point of view any time it suits my disposition. . . . I know all about the dialectical approach, character development, cause-and-effect and orchestration, the obligatory scene, crisis, climax, denouement, and resolution. I was uptight with the craft shit. Can you dig it?
>
> I decided to write my book in Afro-Americanese. . . . And I [mean] to do myself some signifying. (*Cotillion*, 1–3)

This integral passage marks the novel's strategic boundaries, informing us that Lumumba/Killens will be embarking on a narrative that will not be bound by mainstream expectations of a coherent narrative. Rather, the novel demands and utilizes an influx of black language, inasmuch as its primary concern is satirizing specifically *intra*racial class tensions, tensions that should be familiar to those readers who have witnessed the absurdities of class conflict.

In fact, Lumumba/Killens's use of such cultural markers as "signifying," "lying," and reference to Langston Hughes as "fornicating" with all sorts of people link the text inexorably to the black folk and literary traditions. The sort of "lying" and "exaggerating" spoken of here barely reside in their conventional senses; they are used here to describe the process of African American storytelling, which is used for expressly didactic purposes.

In this case, Lumumba directs his vernacular didacticism toward highlighting and subsequently satirizing the class differences within the African American community. His critique is born out of a view of the black bourgeoisie not unlike that of E. Franklin Frazier's *Black Bourgeoisie*, which argues that

40. Clark, *Modern Satiric Grotesque*, 51.

[t]he emphasis upon "social" life or "society" is one of the main props of the world of make-believe into which the black bourgeoisie has sought an escape from its inferiority and frustrations in American society. . . . [Thus] middle-class Negroes have rejected both identification with the Negro and his traditional culture. Through delusions of wealth and power they have sought identification with the white America which continues to reject them. . . . The black bourgeoisie suffers from "nothingness" because when Negroes attain middle-class status, their lives generally lose both content and significance. Thus in its pursuit of conformity to American middle class values, the growing black middle class simultaneously creates a dangerously unnecessary wedge within the African American community and follows an ultimately nihilistic and destructively materialistic path.[41]

The Cotillion's primary symbol of black middle-class aspirations is Daphne Lovejoy, mother of Yoruba Lovejoy. Lumumba's romantic interest, Yoruba is forced to participate in the "Cotillion," a black middle-class debutante ball. Daphne's continuous chastisement of her husband, Matthew, is informed by several dynamics: Daphne's mixed heritage as a "black Scotchm[a]n," fathered by a well-to-do white Barbadian plantation owner and in possession of light skin, gives her an exaggerated sense of her own beauty and importance, so much so that "[w]hen she reached New York, she walked the streets for a couple of weeks, and found that one could indeed pick up money out there on the turf, if one gave of one's self, generously, in return. But she loved herself too much for that kind of arrangement. So she got a job as a chambermaid in a downtown hotel in Manhattan" (*Cotillion*, 45). This particular understatement about Daphne's introduction to New York's corruptions highlights the irony of the "lady's" marriage to Matthew Lovejoy, who is, significantly, neither light-skinned nor of a bourgeois background. These conditions make their marriage increasingly ironic, inasmuch as she continuously counts him as one of her many "crosses" [to bear]; his purported coarseness is nearly unbearable for her. The fact that Matthew cannot and will not appreciate the most minor actions of whites horrifies Daphne. Matthew and Yoruba provide Daphne with two more crosses when they refuse

41. E. Franklin Frazier, *Black Bourgeoisie*, 237–38. The controversial *Black Bourgeoisie* expounds upon many of the notions about the middle class that Frazier posited in his voluminous *The Negro in the United States*, which is an excellent socioeconomic history of black Americans comparable to Harold Cruse's *The Crisis of the Negro Intellectual* in both scope and depth.

to fall at the feet of Father Mayfair, who "came all the way from Alabama," thereby, according to Daphne, "giving up his entire career as a white man, just to give us an integrated experience. He's the only white person left in the entire congregation. You should get down on your Black knees and thank God for progressive men like Father Mayfair" (*Cotillion*, 42–43). Matthew openly rejects the Father, and Yoruba refuses to join the choir. Thus anything that privileges Daphne's white heritage is invaluable to her, while black people and culture, despite her love for Matthew, are anathema.

This particular irony is further reified in view of Yoruba's phenotype; the "pure, beautiful, untampered-by-the-white-man Yoruba, Black and princessly Yoruba, as if she'd just got off the boat from . . . Nigeria" hardly fits into her mother's perception of the black intraracial color caste system. Yoruba's enrollment in the cotillion ultimately proves to be a bourgeois farce and the scene in which Killens indulges his propensity for the comic and the carnivalesque.

Most of the text's satire derives from the tensions between Daphne's aspirations to bourgeois life, Lumumba's nationalism, and Yoruba's independence from each of these positions. Thus the tension lies squarely within the realm of social class conflict, since Lumumba and Matthew represent the crux of African American culture, while Daphne functions as its negation. Killens continually foregrounds Daphne's inability to immerse herself in the culture in which most of her activities lie. When faced with a particularly humorous situation, "Lady Daphne," "lacking a sense of humor, which should have been her heritage as a colored woman . . . took the whole thing at face value, and she fainted standing up, notwithstanding she fainted with enormous dignity. Can you dig it?" (*Cotillion*, 126). The satire often effectively demonstrates the possibilities of desire within class conflict, giving way to the romances between Lumumba and Yoruba and, later, the resuscitated and revised link between Daphne and Matthew.

Killens's satirizing of black society is the novel's central impetus, and his use of black vernacular discourse acts as the satiric linchpin: "Can you dig it?" is common, as are references to such contemporary and past political figures as Malcolm X, Martin Luther King, Jr., Marcus Garvey, Elijah Muhammad and the Nation of Islam, and W. E. B. Du Bois, among many others. These figures and swatches of their rhetoric are included in the text, via the arguments of various characters, along with Lumumba and Matthew, to create the milieu of critical realism, in which the nationalistic and occasionally socialistic politics of African Americans are aimed at pointing out problems with the writer's contemporary world.

Moreover, the centrality of nationalist politics in the text makes the central event, the cotillion, that much more farcical since it eschews progressive politics. In fact, the event is structured to resemble the life on an antebellum southern plantation, slaves and all. It is obviously retrogressive, despite the fact that its organizers, the "Femmes Fatales" (whom Lumumba calls, punningly, the "Femmes Fat Tails"), have all the white attendees play the parts of slaves and the blacks play the masters; it still reproduces the structure of slavery, romanticizing it underneath the guise of ironic reversal. As Matthew says during the event, "Like brother Malcolm said, these Negroes don't want no liberation. They tryna sneak back on the old plantation" (*Cotillion*, 245). As an object of satiric attack, the cotillion serves to prove Lumumba's (and the novel's) essential belief about both Daphne and the black bourgeoisie, as told to Yoruba:

> your mother is not the enemy. . . . If she is, then we are in a real big hurt. Cause your mother is where a whole heap of the Black and beautiful people of the Black Nation are at. . . . Miss Daphne is a caricature of her own dear bourgeois self . . . I mean, most of the time, she ain't to be believed, okay. But face it, she *is* Black, she *is* of the Nation whether she wants to be or not, she lives in the blackest of Black neighborhoods, she is working class to the core. She's just got her head all messed up with bourgeois aspirations. I mean, your mother is the Black masses that we're supposed to be fighting for. (*Cotillion,* 204; italics in the original)

Thus Lumumba and Yoruba launch a plot to undermine the cotillion entirely by encouraging three of the debutantes to appear, and appearing themselves, in the current (1970s) fashions, which means, simply, Afro haircuts and dashikis. Traditional debutante cotillions require extremely conservative dress codes, including hoop dresses and tuxedoes, that evoke the old, antebellum South. As cornerstones of one segment of the black bourgeoisie, these gatherings are almost identical to traditional white southern cotillions.[42] The Afros and

42. Lawrence Otis Graham, *Our Kind of People: Inside America's Black Upper Class*, 47–48.

dashikis represent dress standards that signify black radicalism to the reactionary Femmes Fatales and to many of the guests at the cotillion, especially the white ones, who wish to see the ball's reaffirmation of the slave/master dichotomy underscored by African Americans during a period of black cultural awakening.

An encounter between Lumumba and a white liberal racist engenders one of the novel's most carnivalesque scenes:

> Lumumba opened the toilet door, and there was this four-eyed rosy-cheeked dude who had been giving Yoruba and him such a bad time, seated on the toilet stool. Apparently he had forgotten his gender, and had sat down to make his water. In any event, he had somehow managed to get his cutest little fellow caught between the toilet seat and the commode. And there he sat in sweat and tears and excruciating pain. . . . "Help me! Help me! I ain't got nothing against you people! . . . I swear to Jesus I love niggers! I'm a member of the Urban League, the N-double-A-C-P, the CORE, Snickers, Panthers and all the rest of it. I'm a Black militant all the way. Please have mercy on me!"
>
> Lumumba pondered the question briefly, held with himself a quick debate, hesitated momentarily. Then he slowly raised his foot and brought it down on the seat with great vigor and enthusiasm. The poor rich white dude's rosy cheeks lost color as he fainted clean away. Shouting "Nigger! Nigger! Nigger!" Even after he lost consciousness, . . . he kept mumbling "Nigger! Nigger! . . . Nigger." (*Cotillion*, 218–19)

Here we have not only an example of grotesque, black humor at work, but also an effective demonstration of Lumumba's general disgust toward hypocritical liberals who claim to be supportive of African Americans while holding on to clearly racist beliefs. This scene thus hearkens to Thurman's *Infants of the Spring* and the character Sam, who reproduces racism while claiming a radical position.

The appearance of Lumumba, Yoruba, and the three debutantes, consequently, has the effect of starting a "race riot" (*Cotillion*, 247) in the minds of the Femmes Fatales, who have taken great pains to exclude anything or anyone remotely representing black pride.

All of these events effect the novel's most significant change in Daphne, who, upon witnessing the violently oppositional reaction of the Femmes Fatales toward Yoruba, rejects her bourgeois aspirations in favor of the reality Lumumba represents (*Cotillion*, 263). In fact, the novel ends with an ironic evocation of the "real." The answer to the nihilism of the black bourgeoisie is an adherence to black community in general, to the one community that is a larger home, a larger family.

After Lumumba and the Lovejoys have left the cotillion, Lumumba the narrator observes that

> the famous Femmes Fatales would never ever be the same. Which just goes to show you, you can take democracy and freedom and integration and due process and all them damn amendments too damn far. Particularly when it comes to colored people. Especially them that's truly Black. The kind that's always screaming about Black manhood and dignity, peace and power and liberation and Nationhood. The Black extremist demagogues who can't be bribed, and so you know they can't be trusted. That's the thing you got to watch. Understand? (*Cotillion*, 264)

This clearly ironic evaluation of black politics offers a choice to the reader similar to that given to Daphne: Who is more trustworthy, those black leaders who argue for the most radical, uncompromising position or those who espouse endless moderate politics? The impossibility of believing that black progress has gone too far demands that we read the passage ironically, just as we are to read the Femmes Fatales and the black bourgeois ironically. Implementation of their aspirations would require adherence to a fantasy world beyond the absurd, a world that would be culturally and politically anathemic to post–Civil Rights African America.

Killens's *The Cotillion* thus stands as one of the finest examples of the satire emanating from the brand of black nationalism born in the 1960s and explored in African America in the 1970s. In fact, the relative obscurity surrounding the novel is indeed mysterious, given the force of its satirical message. In the last twenty years the novel, largely ignored in critical discourse, has received only brief, pro forma mentions in surveys of African American novels. This obscurity, however, may be attributable to the novel's politics; though it speaks to a continuing problem within African America, it is immersed in a period in which Black Nationalism was a more palatable option for black progress. On the other hand, we may find a comparative timelessness in Ishmael Reed's most accomplished work, *Mumbo Jumbo*, which examines the obscure within African American history as a means to understanding the dilemmas of modern black political struggles.

Near the midpoint of *Mumbo Jumbo*, the "HooDoo" priest/detective PaPa LaBas discovers a publisher's rejection slip his friend Abdul Sufi Hamid received after trying to get "The Book of Thoth" published for mass consumption. The publisher says that "the market is overwrought with this kind of book. The 'Negro Awakening' fad seems to have reached its peak," and that a "Negro editor here said it lacked 'soul' and wasn't 'Nation' enough" (*MJ*, 98). These few lines represent many of *Mumbo Jumbo*'s thematics and problematics, inasmuch as they demonstrate the novel's continuous tension between the canon and those literary texts at the margins. Indeed, this tension runs throughout both Ishmael Reed's life and his oeuvre, as he has steadfastly refused to fit within prevalent notions of what an African American author should write about, both as a creative artist and a cultural critic. Reed has been especially staunch in this refusal when faced with criticism from the African American critical community, primarily because he considers the "average Afro-American" to be living "in an ideological cloud. What's happening in New York and New England is a power struggle . . . over [white] liberal patronage among Afro-American writers and intellectuals."[43] *Mumbo Jumbo* represents Reed's largely satirical interpretation of this power struggle as it manifested itself in both the 1960s and during the Harlem Renaissance, including the effects it has had on African American life, art, and culture. Reed sees a reproduction of the monocultural impulse ingrained in Western cultures in the Black Aesthetic's developments in the early 1970s that threatens to curb intellectual, cultural, and artistic freedom. Although Reed was, of course, an advocate of the new Black Aesthetic's more inclusive approach to African American art, his novel reveals the extent to which this approach was being stifled by ideological orthodoxy. To that extent, *Mumbo Jumbo* is Reed's revision of Schuyler's *Black No More*, which itself questioned the tendency of black intellectuals with wider exposure to become arrogant and reckless in their assertions. Like Schuyler—whom Reed and Steve Cannon interviewed for the collection *Shrovetide in Old New Orleans*—Reed points out that American racial categories become difficult to uphold, given that "the real so-called pure African disappeared very early in this country"; "most *people* are descended from Caucasians and Indians."[44] Black Nationalism therefore becomes a problematic position. In addition, considering that both authors focus on the ways in which the formerly oppressed eventually attempt to become the

43. Peter Nazareth, "An Interview with Ishmael Reed," 126.
44. Reed and Cannon, "George Schuyler, Writer," 198.

oppressors, Reed and Schuyler are points on a continuum across the lines of African American literary and cultural movements.

Moreover, Reed's novel is an extended illustration of the realization Amiri Baraka himself had years later of the ideological problems within the Black Arts movement. In his autobiography, Baraka recalls,

> I didn't quite understand the difference then between bourgeois nationalism that just wanted to get in on the exploitation and a revolutionary democratic view that wanted to destroy it, so-called revolutionary nationalism. I thought they were all the same. This is the reason so many of us slept on what it meant that Malcolm [X] and Elijah [Muhammad] had split. That split between the politics of an oppressed bourgeoisie and the politics of the exploited and oppressed revolutionary black masses.[45]

Baraka writes of a problematic, but common confusion within African American radical organizations (here, his Black Arts Repertory Theater in Harlem) between political ideologies. The source of this confusion, for both Baraka and Reed, is that African American radicals, like other revolutionaries before and since, are just as susceptible to the temptations of the society against which they struggle, primarily because they are still very much part of those societies. Complete separatism is virtually impossible, so long as the cultural and political ideologies of the oppressive society remain within the minds of the separatists.

Even if separatism is not a viable option, finding an aesthetic that allows for true artistic freedom is an excruciatingly slow and complex process. One ironic trope in *Mumbo Jumbo* concerns the practically inevitable ideological compromises that follow when African Americans in a new cultural phase try to find their place by seeking white patronage. This is a trope that touches many characters, scenes, and actions within the text. Through such characters as Abdul Sufi Hamid, Hinckle Von Vampton, Woodrow Wilson Jefferson, and PaPa LaBas, Reed satirizes such time-honored ideological constructs as Black Nationalism and Western dualism as the cultural bases for racism. *Mumbo Jumbo* succeeds partially because the satirical spirit is not without some ambivalence. Though Reed satirizes the above ideologies, he also lends each at least a small degree of veracity, if only to demonstrate

45. Imamu Amiri Baraka, *The Autobiography of LeRoi Jones*, 322.

the ambivalence found within any culture. His objection is to the idea that any single staid, immutable ideology is capable of resolving social problems; in fact, any such ideology is doomed to fail, since it does not allow for new input.

In the place of monoculturalism, Reed substitutes his "Neo-HooDoo aesthetic," modeled upon the syncretism of Vodun/Voodoo. "HooDoo" is one of the names for the religions practiced by people of the African diaspora; the practices are based upon West African religions, especially Yoruban forms. HooDoo combines the pantheons of gods and spirits—*loa*—of these religions with the basic structure of Roman Catholicism; it also incorporates the mysticism and magical rites of both religions. The Vodun/HooDoo pantheon is generally divided into two major categories: the *Rada* and *Petro loa*. The former are generally benevolent and warm; the latter are more mysterious but may be malevolent or benevolent. The Petro loa include a number of tricksters, most prominently Legba Attibon, sometimes called Papa Legba or Papa LaBas; all are translations of the Yoruban trickster god Esu-elegbara into the terms of African diasporic peoples. In Zora Neale Hurston's analysis of Haitian "VooDoo" mythology, Legba/LaBas is "the god of the gate" who holds "the way to all things . . . in his hands." "Every service to whatever loa for whatever purpose," therefore, "must be preceded by a service to Legba." PaPa LaBas serves a similar purpose in *Mumbo Jumbo* as its protagonist and practitioner of HooDoo. His goal in the novel is to help "Jes Grew" find its text.[46] Jes Grew is a new loa and pandemic disease that causes its carriers to begin dancing, singing, and generally appreciating black folk culture.

Jes Grew is also a metaphor for the non-Western cultures of the world, of which at least one—African American culture—gained prominence in the 1920s during the Harlem Renaissance through the blues and jazz. Jes Grew is seeking its "text" (*MJ*, 6), the completed "Book of Thoth," which was divided into fourteen pieces to prevent Jes Grew from having a focal point. Once Jes Grew finds its text,

---

46. Reed includes Hurston's *Voodoo Gods: An Inquiry into the Native Myths and Magic in Jamaica and Haiti* (London: Dent, 1939) in his bibliography for *Mumbo Jumbo*; Zora Neale Hurston, *Tell My Horse*, 128. Reed takes the name of "Jes Grew" from a name James Weldon Johnson assigned to the earliest ragtime songs in his preface to *The Book of American Negro Poetry* (1922) (Reed, *MJ*, 11).

the millennia-long domination of monotheism and its concomitant monoculturalism will end. Jes Grew and its text began as the embodiment of the dances of the ancient Egyptian god Osiris, whose art becomes a polyglot folk culture that threatens the megalomaniacal (and monolithic/monotheistic) ambitions of his evil brother Set (*MJ*, 162–63). Once Set finds a way to topple Osiris and his popularity, he introduces an oppressive monotheism into Egypt that extends to designating any and all folk culture or creative practices as useless. Set's edicts are thus synonymous with the judgment of African diasporic art and culture that have predominated since the development of "race" as a social construct. *Mumbo Jumbo* also employs and revises the technique Hurston utilized in *Moses, Man of the Mountain:* the (re)appropriation of biblical and other mythical figures to allegorize the struggle of people in the African diaspora. Specifically, Moses is written into the text in a role similar to the one he plays in Vodun as "the great father of magic in Africa and Asia."[47] Reed, however, alleges that Moses, who tried to learn the secrets of "The Book of Thoth," approached the project at the wrong time and in the service of a monotheistic religion, making him a charlatan and the ancestor to the forces of monoculturalism (*MJ*, 182–87).

True to his calling as a satirist, Reed aims his barbs at the sacred figures and ideas of Western cultures not merely for the sake of humorous, nihilistic destruction of each ideology, but instead to force the reader to question their hegemony. Reed satirizes Christianity, freemasonry, American Ivy League schools (the "Wallflower Order"), and Islam, showing how each is a form of, or allied with, monoculturalism and imperialism. In each case, these institutions and their *official* histories construct romantic narratives that elide any information that contradicts them in much the same way that Western societies have cast different peoples as the Others to be marginalized or destroyed for the sake of expediency and greed. They also are what contribute to an American misreading of its history that sycophantically reveres Europe as the locus of "civilization," despite that region's overwhelming debt to non-Western cultures. The result is an America that hardly resembles its official history, which places white European-Americans at the center. Reed highlights this monoculturalism by making it part

47. *ZNH*, 258.

of the text's iconography; the number "1" is substituted for the word *one* to show how an obsession with individual desires is the organizing principle of the West and of American society. *Mumbo Jumbo* calls for a continuous (re)definition of "American" culture; as we shall see, this (re)definition is often *multi*cultural.

One of *Mumbo Jumbo*'s primary satirical purposes is to demonstrate the ideological and practical fallacies of the traditions of Western thought and philosophy by attacking some of the claims of Western philosophers. The novel offers proof that most forms of Western thought, when they have not been derogatory toward the black diaspora, derived their frameworks from non-Western cultures, religions, and philosophies. In the United States, this means that most "mainstream" culture is actually a diluted form of Native American, African American, and other cultures. Jes Grew is the latest manifestation of African American culture that Hinckle Von Vampton and the Wallflower Order (the order's motto: "Lord, if I can't dance, no 1 will") (*MJ*, 63) wish to dilute by patronizing black arts, letters, and culture, just as Carl Van Vechten patronized the Harlem Renaissance.[48] The Wallflower Order commissions Von Vampton to "use something up-to-date to curb Jes Grew. To knock it dock it co-opt it swing it or bop it. If Jes Grew slips into the radiolas and Dictaphones all is lost" (*MJ*, 64). The Wallflower Order, then, "is looking for a way to borrow the 'jargon' of Jes Grew without being absorbed by it" or coming under the influence of the same force that is anathema to the "West," which would mean the destruction of its control over national definitions of culture.[49] The Wallflower Order symbolizes and embodies the pattern of patronage that, in Reed's view, may be traced throughout European contact with African, Asian, and other cultures; by choosing select "native" representatives for patronization (thereby co-opting and weakening them), the West has managed to quell movements that seek to question and end the supposed supremacy of this monoculture.

In numerous interviews, Reed has expressed his objection to such patronage, for not only has it quelled progressive political movements, it has also neutralized some of the best work in African American culture and literature. White patronage via Hinckle Von Vampton

48. Hinckle Von Vampton is a pun on Van Vechten's name as well.
49. Robert Elliot Fox, *Conscientious Sorcerers: The Black Postmodernist Fiction of LeRoi Jones/Amiri Baraka, Ishmael Reed, and Samuel R. Delany*, 57.

acts as a sign for a long-standing conspiracy against people of color disguised in (often false) benevolence. The Harlem Renaissance was one example; for Reed, the pattern seems to have repeated itself among those Black Aestheticians who attempted effectively to delimit the appropriate aesthetics and ideologies of black arts and letters. This movement had specific economic consequences for Reed and other writers, as he points out in this interview with Reginald Martin:

> [Martin]: You mention in your interview with *Conversations* that certain people were in the right place at the right time and/or they were also "chosen" in the 1960s. Whites said to these people, "Here, we don't understand this literature so you guys tell us how to understand it and you guys handle the boat as far as black literature is concerned—"
> [Reed]: I think there was a nonaggression pact signed between the traditional liberal critics and the black aesthetic critics. They were brought into the publishing companies about the same time that I was, about the same time that Doubleday— . . . didn't renew my contract and this was about a week after I had been nominated for two National Book Awards, and then later I learned how these black aesthetic people had gone on . . . and I wasn't the only victim.

Mumbo Jumbo represents the conflict between the "black aesthetic people"—representatives of one type of monocultural thinking—and other writers through a particular exchange between poet Major Young, Woodrow Wilson Jefferson, and his patron, Hinckle Von Vampton. Jefferson not only serves as Von Vampton's personal servant, but he is also the "Negro Viewpoint" for Von Vampton's paper, the "Benign Monster," a position which is designed to groom Jefferson for the role of the "Talking Android," one of the weapons against Jes Grew. When Jefferson misunderstands a bit of black vernacular, Von Vampton chides him, "Get with it, Jackson, maybe it will enliven your articles a bit. You still haven't made a transition from that Marxist rhetoric to the Jazz prose we want" (*MJ*, 100). In this particular chastisement, Reed offers a barely veiled attack on the ideology and rhetoric of some black aestheticians, specifically Amiri Baraka, whose work commonly followed the form of jazz, then began to follow "Marxist [/Maoist] blueprints."[50]

---

50. Martin, "Interview," 177. Robert Elliot Fox describes Jones/Baraka's jazz-inspired poetry as follows: "[I]t is not the movement of, for example, Jack Ker-

When Hinckle Von Vampton subsequently strikes up a conversation with Major Young, the text's irony turns toward two targets: biased comparisons of African American literature to Euro-American texts and the limitations Euro-American critics have historically put upon African American writers. In attempting to recruit Major Young to his cause, Von Vampton commits two major gaffes. He tells Young that the poet's work

> soars and it plumbs and it delights and saddens, it sounds like that great American poet Walt Whitman.
> Major Young looks at him suspiciously. Walt Whitman never wrote about Harlem.
> Well . . . let's just say it is polished as Whitman's attempts are.
> Polished? I don't understand. Is writing glassware?
> Insolent coon on my hands, Hinckle thinks. (*MJ*, 101; italics in the original)

This exchange is a partial critique of the lack of focus within the Harlem Renaissance that Wallace Thurman satirized in *Infants of the Spring* allegedly due to an excessive dependence upon "decadent" European models. Henry Louis Gates, Jr., notes that "[a]lthough the Harlem Renaissance did succeed in the creation of numerous texts of art and criticism, most critics agree that it failed to find its voice, which lay muffled beneath the dead weight of Romantic convention, which most black writers seemed not to question but to adopt eagerly" (*DLB*, 226). Reed carries this critique further when Von Vampton compares Young to another poet, Nathan Brown:

> He's so arid and stuffy with his material that Phi Beta Kappa key must have gone to his head. Does he know what those references mean? Or is that just half-digested knowledge. He seems to pretend a good deal.
> Nathan Brown happens to be a very accomplished poet and a friend of mine [Young says]. Is it necessary for us to write the same way? I am not Wallace Thurman, Thurman is not Fauset and Fauset is not Claude McKay, McKay isn't Horne. We all have our unique styles. (*MJ*, 102)

As Reed notes in his anthology *19 Necromancers from Now*, traditional criticism of African American literature has been most reductive and

---

ouac's 'bop prosody,' which is as breathless and unpunctuated as the road itself; rather, it is an urban prose of jerky rhythms, full of starts and stops. It emphasizes the phrase, staccato notes. . . . I would analogize . . . Jones's [typewriter] to Lester Young's saxophone" (*Conscientious*, 16).

exclusive when critics, black and white, assume that black authors can write only in certain genres. This, despite the fact that "the history of literature is replete with examples of writers not being what their writing represents them to be." As Bernard Bell points out, Reed himself has been "cast aside as 'pretentious,' for it is assumed that the native who goes the way of art is 'uppity.' "[51]

Reed counters this particular criticism most pointedly in his novel *Yellow Back Radio Broke-Down*, during an argument between the "neo-social realist" Bo Shmo and the protagonist, Loop Garoo:

> The trouble with you Loop is that you're too abstract. . . . Crazy dada nigger that's what you are. You are given to fantasy and are off in matters of detail. Far out esoteric bullshit is where you're at.
>
> What's your beef with me Bo Shmo, what if I write circuses? No one says a novel has to be one thing. It can be anything it wants to be, a vaudeville show, the six o'clock news, the mumblings of wild men saddled by demons.
>
> All art[, Shmo says] must be for the end of liberating the masses. A landscape is only good when it shows the oppressor hanging from a tree.[52]

Bo Shmo's comments in the above passage, then, articulate some of the frustrations expressed by many critics when they encounter *Mumbo Jumbo*. Its structure as a "composite narrative composed of subtexts, pretexts, posttexts, and narratives within narratives," as a supposedly indeterminate text, prompts such critics as Theodore O. Mason to comment that "Reed takes up more than he is able to handle and invites a degree of scrutiny that the novel simply cannot withstand.[53] It breaks apart under the vastness of its own intentions" (*CLC*, 310).

Mason dismisses *Mumbo Jumbo* on the grounds that its continuous referentiality obscures most of its ideological meaning; thus the details of Reed's cultural critique get lost in its crowded space. Mason loses sight of the fact that the novel's organization and content are not uncommon for satire. Robert Elliot Fox argues that "Terry Castle's discussion of "the carnivalization of eighteenth-century narrative is apropos for our examination of Reed, especially if one considers the

51. Ishmael Reed, "Introduction," xiii; Bell, *Afro-American Novel*, 330.
52. Reed, *Yellow Back Radio Broke-Down*, 35–36.
53. Gates, "Ishmael Reed," 223.

role of Carnival in black culture. Bakhtin's suggestion, which Castle refers to, that 'the carnivalized work . . . resists generic classification and instead combines . . . a multiplicity of literary modes in a single increasingly "promiscuous" form,' is certainly applicable to works like *Mumbo Jumbo*." Furthermore, Alvin P. Kernan's description of the "disorderly and crowded" scene of satire demands that we keep Reed's ambition within the context of his generic lineage.[54] If the crowded satiric scene, full of "detail," "esoteric bullshit," and "mumblings of wild men," does not somehow fit the criteria of a black aesthetic, whether that aesthetic be dictated by white or black critics, then Reed is more than happy to distance himself from that aesthetic and lambaste it for its limitations.

The conscription of African American artists into a "landscape" that must have "the oppressor hanging from a tree" represents a grave problem in *Mumbo Jumbo*. This compulsory service under the aegis of a specific artistic plan often translates devastatingly into economic terms; that is, artists like Reed can be excluded from the publishing world. The ideological implications of such limits, however, are no less pernicious. Not only do the confrontations between Bo Shmo and Loop Garoo, and between Hinckle Von Vampton and Major Young, recall "the ideological warfare between 'committed' and 'individualist' forces during the Black Arts movement," they also parallel the ideological conflict between Abdul Sufi Hamid and PaPa LaBas's followers in *Mumbo Jumbo*, in which Black Nationalism confronts a form of organic black culture, one that does not depend upon Western perceptions and constructions for its survival.[55]

As PaPa LaBas attempts to explain Jes Grew's search for its text to his friend Black Herman, Abdul Hamid interjects, "You both are filling people's heads with a lot of Bull. Do you think that Harlem will always be as it is now? . . . The People will have to shape up or they won't survive. Cut out this dancing and carrying on, fulfilling base carnal appetites. We need factories, schools, guns. We need dollars." PaPa LaBas then replies, "[Black people have] been dancing for 1000s of years, Abdul. . . . It's part of our heritage," while Black Herman asks, "Why would you want to prohibit something so deep in the race soul?" (*MJ*, 34). Implicit in this portion of the exchange is the

54. Fox, *Conscientious*, 49; Alvin P. Kernan, "A Theory of Satire," 253–54.
55. Fox, *Conscientious*, 48.

ever-resonant conflict over an essential meaning for "Blackness" or "negritude." Whereas one strand of the argument posits a Jungian "collective memory" and spirit that allow for the proliferation of Jes Grew (LaBas and Herman), the other argues that such notions of African American spirituality are retrograde and fixed within limiting frameworks so long as they do not engage in dialogue with other cultures.

Of course, as PaPa LaBas demonstrates, nationalist constructions of black spirituality are by definition in flux. If Abdul's form of Islam represents all twentieth-century black nationalist movements, including Marcus Garvey's Universal Negro Improvement Association, Noble Drew Ali's Moorish Temples, the modern Nation of Islam, and at least one segment of black aesthetic, then it/they are parodied as pieces of ideological artifice necessarily riddled with an all-too-tempting weakness: essentialism. This essentialism necessarily excludes and often alienates many factions within the African American community, many times those in possession of the capital to further nationalist programs. As LaBas chides Abdul,

> I guess your teachings haven't made you realize your bad manners. The people who support your magazine are no longer available since some of your vitriolic remarks about them, and now you have turned against us. A new phenomenon is occurring. The Black Liberal . . . your former victims who became fed up with it and have withdrawn funds for your support. You are no different from the Christians you imitate. Atonists, Christians and Muslims don't tolerate those who refuse to accept their modes. (MJ, 34–35)

But Abdul responds with an important counterargument, one that points out a few of the considerable limits of LaBas's organic "Neo-HooDooism" and the materialistic aspirations of the black bourgeoisie, the most alarming limits being each ideology's failure to thoroughly criticize and castigate both Euro-American and African American cultures. For Abdul (and other Black Nationalists, including Reed's adversaries), the salvation of African Americans rests on their ability to experience both a sense of loss and a desire for complete intellectual and economic independence. Thus Abdul asks, regarding LaBas's relationship to the masses of poor black people,

> Where are these people going to work and who is going to feed them? Are they going to eat incense, candles? Maybe what you say is true

about the nature of religions which occurred 1000s of years ago, but how are we going to survive if they have no discipline? . . . Some of these people with degrees . . . shouting that they are New Negroes are really serving the Man who awarded them their degrees. . . . This is the reason for Garvey's success with the people. O yes, he may look outlandish, loud to you, but the people respect him because they know that he is using his own head and is master of his own art. No, gentlemen, I don't think I would be so smug if I were you. (*MJ*, 37–39)

When Abdul leaves the room after making his argument, though, he undermines it by outlandishly and loudly denying he knows LaBas and Herman and stumbling over two party-goers. Herman points out that despite Abdul's call for discipline, he's "doing a lot of damage, building his structure on his feet," improvising a version of Islam that "resembles fascism" in its adherence to one ruling ideology. Reed envisions art and culture in America as increasingly "multicultural," without any sort of exclusionary aesthetics. Thus it is significant that Abdul, the nationalist, is eventually murdered by Safecracker Gould for his attempt to publish "The Book of Thoth." In the end, LaBas's HooDooism is ascendant, reifying Reed's valorization of the cultural practice as a viable aesthetic. As Reed explains to Martin, "I take [Neo-HooDooism] very seriously . . . I take from it what I can use. Thats the beauty of Neo-HooDooism: there are European influences in my work, as well as African, Native-American, Afro-American, and that's what Neo-HooDooism is all about."[56]

Jes Grew has begun to wane when LaBas receives a posthumous note from Abdul that explains Jes Grew's decline: Abdul has burned "The Book of Thoth" ostensibly to protect African Americans from the "lewd, nasty, decadent thing" that Jes Grew and dancing represent to him (*MJ*, 202). Abdul's goal is to "change these niggers" (*MJ*, 201) and prevent what he considers a cultural disaster; in its place, he will hock the box the book came in to build a mosque where only "clean and decent books shall be kept" (*MJ*, 202).[57] After digesting

56. Reed tells Reginald Martin that he "encourage[s] Afro-American critics to become multicultural critics because that's the wave of the future as more and more the country becomes multicultural and multinational. . . . [I]t's very rare for an American critic to be able to [shuttle between different ethnic and racial literary traditions], but more and more that's going to be called upon as you move toward the end of the century" (Martin, "Interview," 185, 186).

57. The rest of the paragraph from which this quotation is taken is as follows: "Change niggers! Niggers, change! Change! Change! Niggers! Make them

this note, PaPa LaBas sighs, "[C]ensorship until the very last. He took it upon himself to decide what writing should be viewed by Black people, the people he claimed he loved. I can't understand. Apparently after Abdul burned the Book, Jes Grew sensed the ashes of its writings, its litany and just withered up and died. Better luck next time" (*MJ*, 203). It is with this "next time" that the remainder of *Mumbo Jumbo* is concerned. Although the original text has been destroyed, "Jes Grew has no end and no beginning. . . . We will miss it for a while but it will come back, and when it returns we will see that it never left. You see, life will never end; there is really no end to life, if anything goes it will be death. Jes Grew is life" (*MJ*, 204). Jes Grew is the possibility of expression itself, something that cannot be confined to a single form, including a *written* "text." If Jes Grew were to die with the destruction of its text, it would not be truly multicultural, since other cultures rely upon orality, dancing, and other media for the preservation and revision of cultural expression. The "return" of Jes Grew will be any new artistic movement in which marginalized cultures find their expression.

In the text's epilogue, we witness PaPa LaBas in the midst of a lecture on the phenomenon of Jes Grew many years in the future (presumably in the late 1970s, given that PaPa LaBas is over one hundred years old at the time), during which he explains to the audience the "signs which determine our spiritual heritage," of which Jes Grew is but one (*MJ*, 212). Jes Grew, LaBas reveals, is not gone, but without its written text, it must survive in the bodies of its "Carriers," as opposed to the "imitators," who are relatives and/or descendants of the Atonists, who are constantly attempting to dilute Jes Grew (*MJ*, 213–16). This cultural prescription is notable inasmuch as it resembles one of the essentialist arguments of nationalism: only black people can interpret and accurately discuss black diasporic cultures, primarily because they originated these cultures. Or as Jerry Bryant argues, "Reed employs the same techniques he accuses the Western rationalists of using, guilt by association. Reed labels as fraud any attempt by the Western mind to

---

baaaaaaad Niggers!" Remarkably, these exclamations closely resemble the lyrics of the highly nationalistic African American poetry/music group, the Last Poets, whose work was popular in the late 1960s and early 1970s and is experiencing a resurgence of exposure through sampling in contemporary rap music.

uncover some of the forces he celebrates. Only the properly initiated are authentic."[58]

If we take to heart Bryant's argument that Reed is exclusionary due to his desire to have only the "properly initiated" privy to the richness of African American culture, then *Mumbo Jumbo* is just as reprehensible as the Black Nationalist texts it satirizes. Bryant's argument ignores, however, the crucial difference between the aesthetics of *Mumbo Jumbo* and the "phase" that is Western rationalism: the former, *as* a multicultural aesthetic, "can absorb," while the latter is "monotheistic and nonabsorptive."[59] In other words, the first accepts, while the second co-opts and dominates for the purpose of creating and maintaining supremacy. While this argument does seem to essentialize all "Western" discourse (all discourse derived from Europeans), we must remember that Reed's primary opposition is to Western *rationalism* and its cronies, including Black Nationalists who "propose the establishment of separate states and countries while at the same time accepting all of the benefits of this 1" (*MJ*, 35–36). In *Mumbo Jumbo*, such forces work in tandem to limit African American cultural and artistic discourse, insofar as they do not acknowledge the influences of multiple cultures on black culture and its arts. We may, therefore, find some of PaPa LaBas's final words (as he argues with a descendant of the Atonists) particularly poignant: "LaBas [the neo-Atonist asks], why do you mystify your past? These youngsters need something palpable. Not this bongo drumming called Jes Grew." LaBas responds, "Bongo drumming requires very intricate technique. A rhythmic vocabulary larger than French English or Spanish, the 1-time vernacular languages" (*MJ*, 217). This passage is but a subtle reminder of the dangers of separating any cultural practice from its complete history, as it recalls the histories of different communicative cultural practices. Our question, then, for continuously comprehending and evaluating Reed is whether he succeeds in drumming "intricate rhythms" as a writer without participating in the system he condemns.

As one of the most prolific novelists and essayists of the 1970s, Reed became a de facto leader of the Black Arts movement generation. Like that of his peers from the 1960s and 1970s, Reed's influence

58. Jerry H. Bryant, "Old Gods and New Demons: Ishmael Reed and His Fiction," 201.
59. Martin, "Interview," 184.

and artistic success cannot be measured merely in terms of years in print. While novels like *Mumbo Jumbo, Flight to Canada,* and *The Last Days of Louisiana Red* did not sell very well or remain in print for long, they had a significant impact upon at least some of the younger satirical novelists of the 1980s and 1990s, most notably in their irreverence toward constructions of history that consciously exclude for the sake of maintaining inequities, oppressive hierarchies, and false dichotomies. The stakes—equality in fact rather than in principle—have remained essentially the same; the difference, as the next chapter shall demonstrate, is that the discourses in which the satirical novelist's struggles are written have become more subtle and complex. In the post–Civil Rights era, the distance between the sacred and the profane seems to have closed, leaving the satirist with the immense task of determining whether the two were ever really separate at all.

⬦

CHAPTER 5

New Politics, New Voices

Black Satire in the Post–Civil Rights Era

It's been a lovely five hundred years, but it's time to go. We're abandoning this sinking ship America, lightening its load by tossing our histories overboard, jettisoning the present, and drydocking our future. Black America has relinquished its needs in a world where expectations are illusion, has refused to develop ideals and mores in a society that applies principles without principle.

—Paul Beatty, *The White Boy Shuffle*

THE CRISIS OF THE BLACK INTELLECTUAL REVISITED

In his seminal essay "The Satirist and Society," Robert C. Elliott writes that ancient satirists' verses were thought to be magical:

The ancient Arabic satirist, for example, was the seer, the oracle of his tribe. His enormous prestige derived from his role as magician, for his primary function was to compose magical satires, thought always to be fatal, against the tribal enemy. The Arabs thought of their satires concretely as weapons, and as the satirist led his people into battle—his hair anointed on one side only, his mantle hanging loose, shod with only one sandal—he would hurl his magical verses at the foe just as he would hurl a spear; and indeed the satires might be dodged, just as a spear could be dodged, by ducking and bobbing and skipping off.[1]

Elliott's account of the Arabian satirist bears a close relationship to Mel Watkins's example of West African griots, or storytellers, who are

1. Ronald Paulson, *Satire: Modern Essays in Criticism*, 207.

"most often feared by fellow tribesmen because of the great power they are thought to possess." According to Mylene Remy, " 'The truth is the griot's greatest treasure and weapon. . . . When he is properly paid, he remembers only the pleasant, but the edge of his tongue is always ready for those who earn his anger.' "[2] Both the griot and ancient satirist are appropriate metaphors for recently published African American satirists, although none of today's writers garner similar respect and fear. Instead, the metaphor speaks to the extent to which African and contemporary African American satirists represent the humorous and often most scathingly critical extensions of battles within contemporary cultural thought. Contemporary African American satire, whether written in novel form or as apologues with satirical elements, forms one of the first lines in an ongoing ideological battle; the combative role is one satirists have historically assumed in cultures. The difference is that these battles are part of a larger, quieter war being waged within both African American and American literature and culture to save the former from the infiltration of ideas harmful to free expression. This struggle continues alongside the struggle for complete freedom and equality for African Americans in the post–Civil Rights era.

This war began decades ago and is now well into a more complex period as economic and political conditions for African Americans and the rest of the country undergo startling transformations. Michael Omi and Howard Winant have outlined several models for contemporary reactions to these changes. "In the pre–World War II period," for example, "change in the racial order was epochal in scope, shaped by the conditions of 'war of maneuver' in which minorities had very little access to the political system, and understood in a context of assumed racial inequalities. . . . Today all of this has been swept away." In contrast, "[r]acial politics now take place under conditions of 'war of position,' in which minorities have achieved significant (though by no means equal) representation in which the *meaning* of racial equality can be debated, but the desirability of some form of equality is assumed." Omi and Winant use Antonio Gramsci's terms "war of maneuver" and "war of position" to help describe

---

2. Mel Watkins, *On the Real Side: Laughing, Lying and Signifying—the Underground Tradition of African-American Humor That Transformed American Culture, from Slavery to Richard Pryor*, 65.

the transformation of the status of African Americans within the American political landscape, a status that can no longer be viewed in the light of the pre–Civil Rights era. In Omi and Winant's summary of the terms, "war of position" is "predicated on political struggle—on the existence of diverse institutional and cultural terrains upon which oppositional political projects can be mounted, and upon which the racial state can be confronted." "War of maneuver," on the other hand, "describes a situation in which subordinate groups seek to preserve and extend a definite territory, to ward off violent assault, and to develop an internal society as an alternative to the repressive social system they confront." In other words, African Americans are in a state that forces them continually to negotiate and renegotiate their social and economic status. At those points when the forces against which African Americans have had to struggle, such as Jim Crow laws, are clearly defined, combatants undertake a war of position. When those forces and structures become more subtle and difficult to define, as has occurred in the post–Civil Rights era, the strategy of a war of maneuver is most commonly adopted as the best means to maintain a relative equilibrium.[3]

One result of the Civil Rights movement's aftermath, then, is that African Americans face the challenge of articulating a new meaning for the social category of "race" and using this definition to determine the consequences of this new perception of "race" and "racial" issues upon black political and economic life. In contemporary black politics, the choices African Americans must make to redefine "race" are virtually always between two or within one of these positions. It is an internal struggle, fanned in part by outside forces, that has taken the ongoing conflict between Black Nationalism and integration to another, more complicated plane. How, for instance, does one argue that African Americans are faced with challenges similar to those of the past when substantial gains in black political and economic power are obvious? Conversely, how does one adequately argue that black morality is the sole barrier to progress when examples of continuing racism from whites and other cultural groups abound? These questions and the divergent viewpoints they engender are far from being answered; neither is it possible to predict where the arc of black progress will end except in the most tentative terms.

3. Omi and Winant, *Racial Transformation*, 83, 74, 80–81; italics in the original.

If the Nationalist Black Arts movement and its concomitant Black Aesthetic, as defined by Addison Gayle and others, were "largely structured by semiotic strategies by which the signs of black life were reflected and refracted" and therefore "to be further transformed by the artist into myths through which the black masses were to be 'interpellated' and thereby moved to political consciousness," this particular purpose became more complicated in a black nation that has openly fractured into several states divided by class.[4] Free from a clearly definable and defined opposition, African American literature, like the people who produce and inspire it, has entered and mapped out new terrain, informed by previously denigrated considerations of the place of gender, sexuality, and class issues within black America. As Madhu Dubey argues, without the "sheer possibility of blackness" that came out of 1960s–1970s Black Nationalist thought, the focus of contemporary black authors on black community would be rendered moot.[5] Despite its frequent appeals to cultural essentialism, the Black Arts movement correctly identified, theorized, and channeled the sense of negritude that had flowered in African American communities in the 1960s. In effect, it argued that it was possible to transcend W. E. B. Du Bois's conception of double-consciousness; African Americans could indeed reconcile the dual identities of "African" and "American" by fully embracing the African, however complex and contingent that identity might be.

After the last two decades' "war of maneuver," however, this "possibility of blackness" does not possess quite the same cultural cachet it once did, although it is still a guiding force for many authors. The problem is, in fact, the disjunction between the essentialism found within some segments of the Black Arts/Black Aesthetic movements and the complexity of the "African" side of African American identity. Differences along class, gender, and sexual lines cannot be elided easily, if at all, nor can one set of experiences common to many African Americans be accurately attributed to all. That is, the experiences an urban milieu can produce, such as claustrophobia, interethnic/interracial tensions and despair, are not necessarily identical to those created by rural or suburban settings and vice versa, even if both sets of experiences are defined and instigated by racial oppression. By the same token, neither

4. Butler-Evans, *RGD*, 31.
5. Madhu Dubey, *Black Women Novelists and the Nationalist Aesthetic*, 29.

are black women's and men's experiences identical. Yet the Black Arts movement's theoreticians often sublimated such issues under a rubric of "blackness" meant to trump all others. At least one goal of contemporary literature produced by African American authors, then, is the interrogation of the categories existing below the rubric.

Given satire's tendency to look skeptically at all changes in a particular culture, it is not surprising that the diversity within black politics exposed during the contemporary "war of maneuver" has provided sufficient fodder for satire's own missives in the war. The satirist frequently thrives upon heteroglossia, polyphonic scenes, or apparent chaos. As a discursive descendant of the griot, the contemporary African American satirist in turn draws upon the inherent complexity of the voices that are part and parcel of black existence for material, reducing those voices to their most ludicrous level to confront them ironically. With the increasing open conflict between groups on the edges of African American cultures, these voices have grown even more strident and diversified, and thus more susceptible to satiric critique. This heightened polyphony obviates an inquiry into the *purpose* of black satire in the post–Civil Rights era. Is it to continue to target oppressive forces within and outside African American communities? Is it to call for a return to a less complicated past? Is it to argue for or against black cultural and political solidarity?

Some possible answers to these questions lie in the theories of postmodernism that scholars have used to describe the transformation of national consciousness and literature in recent decades. While no single definition of "postmodern" could ever suffice to describe these theories' relation to black literature, Linda Hutcheon's, outlined in chapter 1, is helpful, insofar as it argues that postmodernism is "a contradictory phenomenon, one that uses and abuses, installs and then subverts, the very concepts it challenges." Furthermore, its central concept, the one that ostensibly unifies the myriad definitions of the term is that of " 'the presence of the past' . . . Its aesthetic forms and its social formations are problematized by critical reflection. . . . Herein lies the governing role of *irony* in postmodernism."[6] Postmodernism, then, is a rubric in which the dominant myths of and about the past and history, in all their manifestations, are subjected to critical and often ironic scrutiny, questioned at their very bases.

6. Hutcheon, *Poetics of Postmodernism*, 3, 4.

Ishmael Reed has rejected labels of Western origin such as "post-modern," inasmuch as the sort of maneuvers postmodernism makes in revising and subverting systems is like the critical work that traditional African American folk figures have performed for centuries.[7] Similarly, neither does it differ significantly from what African American intellectuals have done by continually calling for American society to take a revised look at its myths and legends about its greatness that would include the viewpoints of peoples of color as subjects, rather than as objects of history. Theories of postmodernism, therefore, could be interpreted as restatements of ideas African Americans have already developed.

Despite Reed's objections to the label of being a "postmodern" writer, his novels in the 1970s provide excellent examples of both ironic revision and theories of postmodernism at work; they revise vast swathes of history using pastiche, parody, irony, and satire. Reed would rather be called a "Neo-HooDoo" artist; that is, an artist whose work syncretically draws upon the characters, cultures, and morals of the pantheons of African Diasporic religions, especially vodun, as well as, says Martin, European, African, Native-American, and Afro-American influences. Via these figures, Reed's early novels challenge us to look past Western epistemologies to perceive, appreciate, and adopt the social and ethical systems of the diaspora, thus allowing us glimpses into entirely new and richly referential views of history.

Reed's novels of the 1980s and 1990s, however, do not reach the heights of referential frenzy found in his earlier works, nor do they utilize the "Neo-HooDoo Aesthetic" as consistently as his earlier novels. This is not to imply that these novels are necessarily inferior, but Reed's strategy does seem to have changed as his attacks upon numerous enemies—real or imagined—have escalated. Steven Weisenburger suggests that Reed's work has grown less degenerative over time, with his earlier experimental models being replaced by an overt didacticism.[8] While he is still clearly concerned with the problem of Western ideas dominating American intellectual and

7. See Martin, "Interview." In this interview Reed argues that most of the labels American critics have used to describe African American literature have been inadequate; they often rely upon Western notions that do not allow for the type of inclusion that African religions and philosophies posit.
8. *Fables*, 27.

cultural discourse, Reed's most recent novels have concentrated on two general topics: first, the advent of neoconservatism in recent years and its effects on racial and cultural politics; second, the philosophical relativism that can result when the concept of multiculturalism is misapplied by inept academicians. These concerns are shared by contemporary African American satirists, albeit in altered forms. All the satirists, however, are concerned with the apparent field of black leadership, both political and intellectual, that remains open to the present.

In the remainder of this chapter, I shall examine the historical and radical revisionism of Ishmael Reed's novels in the 1980s and 1990s and Toni Morrison's *Jazz* as an allegorical troping of black life during the heyday of the Harlem Renaissance. I conclude the chapter, and *African American Satire*, with an analysis of the satirical and critical writings of Derrick Bell, Trey Ellis, Paul Beatty, and Darius James, authors who are currently drawing upon satire as a means of describing their particular places within African American history and their visions of its future.

Ishmael Reed in the 1980s and 1990s

Ishmael Reed's most recent concentration on the rise of neoconservatism in recent years forms the crux of *The Terrible Twos* (1982) and its sequel, *The Terrible Threes* (1989).[9] Set in the 1980s, the two novels make up an extended, elaborate vision of American political conservatism reductio ad absurdum. In the novels' contexts, the principles underlying American politics, most prominently capitalism and jingoism, are stripped of their coded manifestations and expressed through characters who cynically understand what the American mainstream really wants and are relatively successful at satisfying those demands. Put simply, the American people (and, by extension, their leaders) are the equivalent of two-year-olds (hence the title, *The Terrible Twos*):

He throws tantrums until he gets what he wants. You'd like to whack

---

9. Since *The Terrible Threes* is indeed a continuation of the events begun in *The Terrible Twos* and, as Jacob Epstein argues, is "almost impossible to understand without first having read *The Twos*, even though Reed provides a précis of the earlier book," I shall discuss the novels together here, distinguishing between them only in the citations except where absolutely necessary. Jacob Epstein, "The Devil Wears a Beeper," 311.

him good across the bottom but your wife is reading childrearing books which advise against this. They counsel patience.

As the child grows he tells you things. He tells you about nations and individuals. About how civilizations come into being. You're glad that two-year-olds don't have access to ICBMs the way the responsible leaders in your government do. . . . The terrible twos are twins to the terrible nos. . . . Human beings at two harbor cravings that have to be immediately quenched, demand things, and if another human being of their size and age enters the picture, there's war. (*Twos*, 23–24)

The metaphor of the two-year-old as representative of American political and social concerns continually resurfaces throughout the text, primarily through the presence of Dean Clift (a composite character whose name is taken from the 1950s matinee idols James Dean and Montgomery Clift, and who is based, in part, on Presidents Ronald Reagan and John F. Kennedy), a former actor elected to the vice presidency not for his political skills, which are nonexistent, but for his good looks. When his running mate, former general Walter Scott, dies in office, Clift succeeds to the presidency and subsequently finds himself acting as a figurehead for the reactionary politicians who bankrolled his election campaign.

The meaning Reed posits here is that the American people have continually chosen such leaders as Reagan or Kennedy for the most superficial reasons, so obsessed are they with maintaining an intricate architecture of illusion. The maintenance of this architecture is of such importance that a politician's platform will inevitably take second place to his or her carefully orchestrated image. It is the platform undergirding Clift's presidency that becomes the novel's central concern and the primary site for exploration of American racial politics. "Operation Two Birds" is a wildly elaborate conspiracy that would consolidate power for a small, fascist elite of white men by convincing the American public that the "surps," or surplus people (read: people of color) are destroying both the country and the world.[10] *The Terrible Twos* tracks the unraveling of this plot and the efforts of numerous characters to derail it; *The Terrible Threes* is the chronicle of the plotters' attempts to hide the plot from the public, to whom it is exposed at the end of the former novel.

Some critics found the novels' conspiratorial milieu, in which clandestine government officials and organizations wage secret war

---

10. Jay Boyer, *Ishmael Reed*, 36.

against people of color, paranoid, delusionary, and therefore unworthy of Reed's talent. Stanley Crouch, for instance, avers that " 'for all the literary appropriations in *The Terrible Twos*, it hasn't the level of invention that made his best work succeed . . . *The Terrible Twos*, unfortunately, is mostly a shadow of his former work, and a shadow that tells us little that we didn't already know.' "[11] Darryl Pinckney similarly argues, "Reed's campaign to mention everything that has gone wrong in America results in a narrative that is all over the place, as if he were trying to work in everything from crime against the environment to offenses against the homeless. Instead of suspense or satire one is confronted with an extended editorial rebuttal."[12]

While each of these criticisms has considerable merit, with Pinckney's being the most persuasive, neither accounts for the fact that however vitriolic and cynical Reed's critique of American politics in the 1980s may seem, most of his predictions of the path of political sentiment came true, if not always to the extent his novels foresaw. Furthermore, Pinckney errs in declaring the novels bereft of satire inasmuch as they resemble "an extended editorial rebuttal" that still manages to be "all over the place." The error here is in Pinckney's conflicting assessments. While the narrative in the two novels does touch upon a panoply of political and social issues, it does so to a lesser degree than Reed's previous novels. It would be more accurate, in view of Leon Guilhamet's categorization of satirical rhetoric, to say that Reed's satire moves toward a model that combines the judicial with the deliberative while retaining the use of folk elements as the text's countervailing forces.

Guilhamet describes deliberative satire as that which "look[s] to the future" insofar as it examines a problem and proposes a course of action. In other words, "[a]fter a central question is asked somewhere early in the [text], the remainder . . . is devoted to answering it. Examples are abundant."[13] The central question of *The Terrible Twos* and *The Terrible Threes*, apparently, is "What hope is left for the United States (and by extension the rest of the world) when immense greed coexists comfortably with abject poverty?" *The Terrible Twos*'s first chapter contrasts the wealthy who "will have any kind of Christmas

11. Ibid., 39.
12. *CLC*, 314.
13. Guilhamet, *Satire and Transformation*, 33–34.

they desire," with "gifts rang[ing] from $100 gold toothpicks to $30,000 Rolls Royces" to the "seven point eight million people [who] will be unemployed and will do without poinsettias tied with 1940 pink lace or chestnut soup. They will be unable to attend the ski lessons this year, but they will be fighting the snow, nevertheless. On Thanksgiving Day, five thousand people line up for turkey and blackeye peas in San Francisco. In D.C., four men freeze to death during inaugural week, one on the steps of a church. The church's door is locked" (*Twos*, 5).

If the essential dilemma implicit in the skiff of American wealth adrift in a sea of poverty provides the novels with their central question, their judicial element comes into play with the answer to that question, an answer that avers that a small cadre of rich, privileged men will eventually attempt to eliminate all but the rich and white from the face of the planet while the remainder of the populace is too self-absorbed to care. Guilhamet describes the judicial element of satire as an "apparent disbelief in justice in our world or the hereafter . . . [that] places a grave responsibility with the satirist who must discover a basis for satire and then, himself, become the chief dispenser of justice." The problem of this particular model, of course, is that the satirist's idea of justice can be especially bleak and harsh, which is "increasingly dependent on [the satirist's] personal wit. If the satirist is able to reconstruct an adequate sense of genre, his audience is unwilling or unable to do so."[14]

For the *Terribles*, though, the problem is not so much that Reed has instilled an inadequate sense of wit and satire, but that the satire is buried under a polyglot agenda, one that attacks buffoonery at every level of society (though concentrating on the nation's political and intellectual elite). To this extent, Reed is allied with the likes of Thomas Pynchon, whose most accomplished novels, especially *The Crying of Lot 49* and *Gravity's Rainbow*, posit a world in which vast conspiracies of the "Elect" or "They" intend to control or destroy the "Preterite" or "Us." While this form of paranoia is certainly present in Reed's novels and threatens to undermine their plausibility, the works do find a

14. Ibid., 65–66. The characteristic of an absence of justice in the hereafter, however, does not apply to *The Terrible Twos* or *The Terrible Threes*. In one pivotal scene that parodies Charles Dickens's *A Christmas Carol*, Dean Clift has a vision of the afterlife in which Harry S. Truman and Nelson Rockefeller are tormented for their acquiescence to brutality via their approval of the atomic bombings of World War II and the raid on Attica State Prison in 1970, respectively.

distinctive saving grace in the form of the folk element that Reed has utilized successfully in the past. In this case, the figure of St. Nicholas, long since evolved into Santa Claus in the American popular consciousness, is reunited with "his blackamoor partner," Black Peter. The picaresque team sets out to stop Operation Two Birds with magic derived from HooDoo and conjure. Yet this team is insufficient in the fight against an evil born of complacency in American society. As Jay Boyer asserts, "Reed seems unable artistically to envision a hero with suitable powers to fend off [Operation Two Birds]. It's as if Reed's faith in the magic he's embraced for so long has begun to diminish . . . as if the weight and momentum of the historical forces in these novels is of such dimension that Reed can't envision a magic great enough to stop them."[15] Indeed, the novels' satire derives its rhetorical force less from St. Nicholas and Black Peter's picaresque roles than it does from the juxtaposition of the caricatures of Operation Two Birds' conspirators upon the canvas of a world mad enough to allow their existence and considerable success in enacting oppressive policies.

This is a problem not unlike those posed in *Reckless Eyeballing*, which was published in the interim between Reed's *Terrible* books and the more recent *Japanese by Spring*. Both *Reckless* and *Japanese by Spring* are firmly in the tradition of satire and the satiric extensions of Reed's disquisitions of American politics practiced in his essays and articles. The former novel is closely tied to, and partially based upon, the essays Reed published in *Writin' Is Fightin'* and is, moreover, easily his most controversial novel. Reed's satirization of certain types of feminisms and feminists (including, in utterly thin disguise, Alice Walker) as cynical, manipulative women, as enthralled by misanthropy and racist images of black men as the men they critique are enthralled by misogyny, created an uproar and backlash against his work that, upon examination, is not entirely deserved. As Boyer observes,

> A closer look at [Reed's] female characters suggests that there isn't a feminist to be found in the lot. Reed's main [black] characters . . . want . . . to make it in a world dominated by whites, and they'll take any political stance and mouth any political rhetoric they think will speed up this process.
>
> Feminism happens to be in vogue when Reed's protagonist, Ian Ball, is trying to get his second play . . . produced; and to see that the play

15. Boyer, *Reed*, 38.

does make it to the stage, he discovers that he's willing to do almost anything. He's willing to let Becky French, a white lesbian producer, turn his black hero into a malicious villain. He's willing to cow-tow to Tremonisha Smarts, herself a black writer who'll do anything to stay in favor. He's willing to do anything that will make him marketable.[16]

Ian Ball and Tremonisha Smarts, then, find themselves playing roles that are unnatural to them to assimilate and achieve bourgeois status, two goals that are ultimately hollow insofar as they require a malevolent strain of trickster behavior that benefits only the individual. Ball and Smarts must subsume their own desires as African American artists for the sake of a party line that can only choke the vitality of their readings of black experience. Reed issued similar warnings previously in *Yellow Back Radio Broke-Down* and *Mumbo Jumbo,* but here the enemy is not Black Nationalism. Rather, it is the materialism of the black middle class in the post–Civil Rights era and the overwhelmingly materialistic 1980s that indirectly cause black art and culture to suffer. The result is a black double-consciousness so pronounced that it forces the black psyche to become virtually schizoid.

In the text's denouement, we discover that Ian Ball has been leading a double life as a vigilante who humiliates feminists, including Becky French, who disparage the image of black men. This double life is a simultaneous manifestation of the "two-headedness or two-facedness" of Ian's Caribbean heritage and his American upbringing and the source of the novel's final, greatest irony.[17] By virtue of birth, Ian contains within himself a trickster in the tradition of black Caribbean folk culture, which his mother tries to sublimate via assimilation into mainstream American society. It is precisely this assimilation, however, that causes Ian to manifest his trickster heritage; the more he is imbued with such a strong sense of American materialism, the more Ian struggles to achieve his material goals yet remain loyal to his race and gender, two goals that are virtually irreconcilable in the novel's milieu. His split identity becomes another sign of the importance of African Americans' (especially black men's) need to keep their culture intact at all costs; the alternative is to become truly "wrong-headed" and watch black culture be co-opted and therefore destroyed by mainstream America.

16. Ibid., 41.
17. Reed, *Reckless Eyeballing,* 147.

Tremonisha Smarts, on the other hand, functions as a paradigm for the integrity that black people, especially black artists, need to achieve. She reveals,

> I was writing about some brutal black guys who I knew in my life who beat women, abandoned their children, cynical, ignorant, and arrogant, you know these types, but my critics and the people who praised me took some of these characters and made them out to be *all* black men. That hurt me. The black ones who hated me and the white ones who loved me were both unfair to me. . . . I thought they were my fans, those feminists, but some of them would have drinks and ask me about the "raw sex" and how black men were, you know. Others used my black male characters as an excuse to hate all black men, especially some of these white women. Then they wouldn't feel so guilty for taking their jobs. (*Reckless*, 129–30)

After this revelation, Tremonisha decides she will leave the world of the intelligentsia and "just . . . get fat, have babies, and write write write," free of the ideological limitations that crop up among American intellectuals. The best artistic course for her and other black artists to take is to remain true to the concerns that reflect their experience, rather than engage in romanticism:

> Though the critics and the white feminists fell for it, I knew that those working class characters that I tried to write about and their proletariat voices I attempted to mime were phony. All of us who grew up in the middle class want to romanticize people who are worse off than we are. . . . It won't be long before some of these teenage mothers will begin writing about places like Bed-Stuy themselves, and then all of us debutantes will have to write about ourselves, will have to write about our backgrounds instead of playing tour guides to the exotics. (*Reckless*, 131)[18]

Thus Reed offers his prescription for the maintenance of black artistic integrity: attention to and writing about experiences relevant to one's self that reveal the richness of small, yet important niches of black ontology. This may allow for a wider representation of black

---

18. In addition to being a reference to the Trueblood episode of Ralph Ellison's *Invisible Man*, in which the Invisible Man takes a rich white philanthropist on a tour of the poor black section of a southern town, Tremonisha's notion of young, middle-class black artists writing about their own experiences has been taken to heart, especially in the novels of Trey Ellis discussed below.

experiences, thus discouraging critics from engaging in the callous delimitation of African Americans as a whole, no matter those critics' race or gender. It is worth noting, though, that Smarts's play *Wrong-Headed Man* closely resembles certain aspects of Alice Walker's novel *The Color Purple*, especially in its inclusion of oppressive black men. In *Wrong-Headed Man*, Reed greatly exaggerates the amount of domestic and sexual abuse Walker utilized in *The Color Purple* for his parodic purposes. We should, therefore, view his critique of Smarts/Walker with a skeptical eye; few African American women authors have ever written works as damning as Smarts's.

Through its updating of the problems of academic racism and intellectual co-optation for the 1990s, *Japanese by Spring* is largely a revision of *Reckless Eyeballing*. It makes Reed's ideology increasingly explicit via the introduction of Reed himself as an eponymous character, one who actively contributes invective material to the novel's plot and discursive strategies. Reed confronts the reader with the same type of hard historical evidence that buoys his previous novels, but without the subtler mediative function that his other characters have served. Moreover, the eponymic stratagem may be a sardonic attempt to make Reed's personal views entirely lucid to a critical audience that has frequently attacked his satire, especially his novel *Reckless Eyeballing*. Reed (the author) excoriates one of *Ms.* magazine's "black house feminists" for attacking Ishmael Reed (the character) as " 'the ringleader' of black men who were opposed to black women writing about black male misogyny" by pointing out that "[r]ingleader Ishmael Reed has never called anybody a traitor to anybody's race and not only hasn't opposed black women writing about black male misogyny but published some of it" (*JBS*, 24).

Most important, though, *Japanese by Spring* represents Ishmael Reed's concatenation of the intensely fierce debates over the meaning of multiculturalism in United States academia in the late 1980s and early 1990s. It offers in novel form Reed's vision of what a productive, transcendent multiculturalism *should* be, as opposed to what it has become in the face of American cynicism. Moreover, it offers Reed's satiric assessment of the most extreme poles in the debates and their inanities. Set at fictional Jack London College in Oakland, California, an institution remarkably similar to the University of California at Berkeley Reed knew as a member of the faculty in the 1990s, the novel utilizes pseudonymous characters and Reed's particular brand of reductio ad absurdum to represent the most visible scholars in the so-called "culture wars." The setting is ultimately a synecdochal representation of American academia in which Reed's characters are, in Charles Johnson's words, "cartoons, where the cartoon is seen as a caricature, a boiling down of a person to the essential elements . . . [they] are intended to be like voodoo dolls constructed on the basis of generic qualities, dominant impressions, a single feeling perhaps."[19] In *Japanese by Spring,* this aesthetic has the purpose and effect of satirizing the presence of established, nearly unquestioned racist beliefs, as well as a marked lack of moral courage and minimal intelligence in some of the multicultural debates' primary players. The solution to these debates is for the public at large to realize how mainstream American culture is always already multicultural. This realization may be what ultimately saves the United States from a race war, and is, to all appearances, possible only insofar as the public (including public intellectuals) is briefed on the *facts* surrounding events that clearly involve race.

Jack London College's central problem is the existence of a dangerous relativism surrounding issues of race, class, and gender among the campus's denizens, fostered primarily by incompetent administrators and neoconservative gadflies. The novel's central figure, Benjamin "Chappie" Puttbutt, a black English professor, mindlessly refuses to declare atrocious acts against black students the racist acts they are and horrifically becomes a ludicrous apologist for the white perpetrators in front of the press, primarily out of his own interest in safely obtaining tenure:

> The black students bring this on themselves. . . . With their separatism,
> their inability to fit in, their denial of mainstream values, they get
> the white students angry. The white students want them to join in, to
> participate in this generous pie called the United States of America.
> To end their disaffiliation from the common culture. Black students,
> and indeed black faculty, should stop their confrontational tactics.
> They should start to negotiate. They should stop worrying these poor
> whites with their excessive demands. The white students become
> upset with these demands. Affirmative Action. Quotas. . . . And so it's
> understandable that they go about assaulting the black students. The
> white students are merely giving vent to their rage. This is a healthy

19. Charles Johnson, *Being and Race: Black Writing since 1970,* 65.

exercise. It's perfectly understandable. After all, the whites are the real oppressed minority. I can't think of anybody who has as much difficulty on this campus as blondes. (*JBS*, 6–7)

Puttbutt's discourse does not merely demonstrate the intellectual contortions he must go through to become an apologist for racists. It also reveals him as a thinly veiled caricature of Shelby Steele, reductio ad absurdum, whose eloquent 1990 essay collection *The Content of Our Character* received lavish praise from numerous neoconservatives and many liberals for its tendency to place the responsibility for improving racial relations on the shoulders of African Americans. In addition, Steele's opposition to Affirmative Action and most forms of black cultural nationalism eventually earned him an appointment to the Hoover Institute, a conservative think tank at Stanford University.

Reed thus parodies and satirizes the wave of black neoconservatives that arose in the late 1970s and 1980s and their alleged modus operandi of crass careerism. It is, moreover, Reed's means to exemplify what Derrick Bell calls one of the "Rules of Racial Standing":

> *Few blacks avoid diminishment of racial standing, most of their statements about racial conditions being diluted and their recommendations of other blacks taken with a grain of salt. The usual exception to this rule is the black person who publicly disparages or criticizes other blacks who are speaking or acting in ways that upset whites. Instantly, such statements are granted "enhanced standing" even when the speaker has no special expertise or experience in the subject he or she is criticizing.*[20]

Bell's rule astutely assails the quality of intellectual discourse emerging from the sort of black and other neoconservatives parodied in *Japanese by Spring*, as far as Puttbutt/Steele is concerned. The novel levels numerous criticisms against neoconservatism, all based on a central premise: opposition to multiculturalism and ethnic studies is grounded in racist, victim-blaming (il)logic that seeks to perpetuate the exclusion of people of color from mainstream university curricula.

Further examples of neoconservatives attempting to delimit the breadth of discourse by and about people of color are scattered throughout the text. Reed's rhetoric rests comfortably on pseudonymity and reductio ad absurdum, as in the case of D'Gunga Dinza, a

---

20. *Faces*, 114; italics in the original.

caricature of Dinesh D'Souza, author of *Illiberal Education* and *The End of Racism*, two of the most controversial texts in the "culture wars" begun in the late 1980s over multiculturalism in American universities. Dinza's role as a "high-pitched and high-strung" advocate of "antidiversity on panels and talk shows" reifies a premise that has run throughout Reed's work: multiculturalism is an inherent component of the American cultural fabric and was so long before it acquired that particular name and the various connotations that accompany it today (*JBS*, 126–27). As evidence, Reed provides the following anecdote:

> Glossos United, an organization of artists, were using the term "multicultural" in the middle seventies, a few years before the right brought Dinza from India, and before its cooptation by the academic planting machine. Look at it this way, using the central antidiversity argument that freedom and democracy are Western inventions. Suppose that André Derain, Maurice de Vlaminck, Henre Matisse, Pablo Picasso, [et al.] denied themselves the opportunity to borrow from the art of Africa, because the countries which contributed the African sculpture which influenced their art had no history of democracy. Or suppose Bud Powell, considering a concert of Bach music, said, "I can't play this music because the Germans have had little experience with democracy." . . . If artists had paid attention to the central antidiversity argument, the tanka and the haiku would never have been introduced into American poetry. (*JBS*, 127)

Reed thus foregrounds several conspicuously troubling problematics of the "culture wars": First, most of the opponents of curricular and cultural diversity in the American university have extremely flimsy credentials vis-à-vis the artists (like Reed) who actually produce the texts so hotly contested. Second, the tradition of intellectuals and artists borrowing from other cultural paradigms to create their own may be found in all cultures and is particularly well established in Western arts and letters. Third, academicians have a long-standing habit of co-opting the terminology of different egalitarian ideologies, such as multiculturalism, without either attempting to understand the implications of that terminology or applying it properly to academia itself; they become merely fashionable bywords for career advancement or uncritically accepted shibboleths.

Each of these problematics continually weaves its way throughout *Japanese by Spring*, especially the latter problematic of intellectual co-optation, which in many ways contains the former two. Puttbutt eventually finds himself in power as the "special assistant to the acting president of Jack London College" (*JBS*, 94) via the graces of a Japanese firm that purchases a controlling interest in the institution, after suffering the humiliation of being denied tenure. Puttbutt proceeds with a thorough purging of the humanities departments' radicals and racists alike, since those groups are not, as it turns out, mutually exclusive. In each case, Puttbutt is motivated by personal revenge and a rediscovered sense of moral outrage. So long the player who refused to take the moral stance of defending other black people in his career, Puttbutt puts on a different face and adopts a second consciousness not unlike the one he possessed as a young nationalist. Subsequently, Puttbutt reorganizes the university into components that reflect each discipline's ideological pursuits, such as forcing women's studies to merge with the European studies department as an ironic "reward" of sorts for statements the department chair, Marsha Marx, had made on behalf of white supremacy for the sake of being co-opted by the academy.

The university's reorganization, however, eventually goes too far. The Japanese owners soon rename Jack London College after the infamous General Tojo and require the faculty to endure various humiliations that reinforce Japanese supremacy. These humiliations are, ironically, virtually identical to the sorts of humiliations that students and faculty of color endured when the university was funded and run by whites, and have the effect of showing the faculty the folly of their previous beliefs in white supremacy or other bigotries. Eventually the United States government ousts the Japanese administration, but not without a generous dose of gratuitous patriotism from the faculty and students; they have reentered the cycle of jingoism.

The satiric thrust here demonstrates that while the pursuit of middle-class material values by African Americans, who thereby bring dangerous relativistic and neoconservative philosophies to the university, is indeed perilous, it is not exclusive to that particular marginalized group. In other words, when an individual or group previously excluded from the social mainstream suddenly gains access to power, that power is often squandered on frivolous ideologies and materialism in lieu of enacting the social changes that engendered the original push for power. This tragicomic translation of Omi and Winant's revision of the "war of maneuver" casts all notions of "racial" or cultural Utopias in Orwellian dramas that instantly beget corruption.

Eventually, via his eponymous character, Reed posits a multiculturalism that is neither faddish nor materialistic, one that will help restore the integrity and strength of progressive racial and cultural politics. This brand of multiculturalism would mean that intellectuals would need to "stop moving in swanky company" and become "dogged populists" who "no longer would associate with cultural bigwigs in the establishment" (JBS, 191). They would instead become involved in folk rituals, such as the humble service Ishmael Reed attends at the text's end to celebrate the resurrection of Olódùmarè, "a god who lies dormant in the African American experience. A god with whom African Americans lost contact after the breakup of the Yoruba empire and the slave trade" (JBS, 217). These combined events represent Reed's view of the point from which any reconciliation of American cultures and the easing of racial tensions must begin: recovery of individual cultures and their subsequent exchange via social and educational institutions.

THE PROJECTION OF THE BEAST: SUBVERTING MYTHOLOGIES IN TONI MORRISON'S *JAZZ*

Similarly, Toni Morrison's novels, highly praised and rewarded for their lyricism, reify and "evoke [African American] folklore and [African American] mythology, as well as recodings of Black oral traditions" in order to preserve them.[21] Contemporaneously, Morrison's fiction is notable for its understated *subversion* of totalizing African American mythologies, especially those of African American communities from the urban North to the rural Midwest or South. It is this subversion, in fact, that qualifies Morrison as a subtle satirist interrogating our attempts at fixing subject positions and identities within African America. Rather than being a fixed ontology, identity in Morrison's novels is formed and revised by a nondeterministic process in which one cause does not necessarily lead to a specific effect. As Melvin Dixon summates the Morrison oeuvre, "her novels are *bildungsromans* of entire communities and racial idioms rather than the voice of a single individual" with a central protagonist developing only after interactions with larger communities.[22] Once those interactions have been completed, though, these texts defer the necessity

---

21. Butler-Evans, *RGD*, 59.
22. Melvin Dixon, *Ride Out the Wilderness: Geography and Identity in Afro-American Literature*, 164; italics in the original.

to declare one narrative voice authoritative. To do so would mean Morrison's African American characters reproducing the hegemonic power of racism rather than dispersing and defying it, an outcome that would lead to the destruction of both communities and individuals, engendering what Orlando Patterson has called "social death."[23]

I argue that Morrison's 1992 novel *Jazz*, which refigures life in black America before and during the Harlem Renaissance of the 1920s, is an ironic allegory whose significance extends beyond a single epoch, signifying upon some sixty years of (African) American history. As Morrison has stated, her works contain and describe a culture—black culture—that is "like a moveable feast—you could take it anywhere, and you [don't] have to identify geographically with anything because it [is] all there."[24] That is to say, Morrison's novels, including *Jazz*, draw upon Ralph Ellison's metaphor of the "boomeranging" of history to show how major upheavals in African American history and culture are repeated and echoed yet allow for unexpected additions to the history. Through this ironic revision, *Jazz* comments, sometimes satirically, upon the current state of African American politics, stripping them of their romantic veneer and exposing the conflicting cultural voices that (re)create them.

The novel begins by casting life in Harlem and, by extension, black America as dependent upon contingency and hidden histories. Rather than portray Harlem and its renaissance as romantic temporal and physical spaces, Morrison contrasts life in urban America with that in rural settings to show how the urban milieu simultaneously robs the soul of identity and purpose while allowing for new identities and goals. Harlem becomes a community writ small and with irony, with characters living lives not unlike those presented in Wallace Thurman's 1932 novel *Infants of the Spring*, one of the novels that stripped the Harlem Renaissance's cultural life of its veneer of bohemianism and romanticism. As I discussed in chapter 2, Thurman's novel depicts African American and white artists and cultural critics living lives of Wildean decadence that anticipates the onset of the quiet desperation that would be Harlem and African America's fate in the 1930s. The novel also questions whether African Americans can agree

23. See Orlando Patterson, *Slavery and Social Death*.
24. Carolyn Denard, "Blacks, Modernism, and the American South: An Interview with Toni Morrison," 5.

upon a single interpretation or understanding of black experiences, especially through art. Similarly, Morrison posits an ironic, unreliable narrator—or narrators—to comment upon the ambiguity of black identity. Through this narrator, however, the text also upsets the reader's expectations regarding the progression of two plots: the plot of the novel's protagonists, Joe and Violet Trace, and that of the narrators' and our expectations about the possibilities surrounding African Americans' political future.

In both plots, Morrison writes against the idea of African American identity and its characterization as sets of discrete, predictable ontological positions. The novel focuses upon Joe and Violet Trace's relationship, one troubled—but not destroyed—by the middle-aged Joe's affair with a young woman, Dorcas, whom he murders when he discovers her with a younger man. The narrative proper begins with an account of Violet's assault upon Dorcas's body at the funeral. While this particular plot, reduced to such essential levels, reads like simple melodrama, Morrison layers it with shifts and generic conventions that fall well outside those of melodrama, beginning with the characters. Joe Trace's actions, for example, are not meant to foster a synecdochal representation of the black male, nor is he meant to be such, at least not in popular conceptions of that subjectivity. As Morrison remarks in an interview with Cecil Brown, her critics "are often trying to force my black male characters into some kind of nuclear white family with the father, the mother and the children, something they don't even like." Morrison goes on to wonder why a single black male who commits violence is so frequently misread as all black men.[25] Implicit in Morrison's musings is an objection to the underlying inductive logic of stereotyping and discrimination themselves: the actions and experiences of the one are extrapolated to be emblematic of the many. *Who* commits this extrapolation, moreover, is as significant as the (il)logical leap itself, since it colors the interpretation of the original act. In a court of law and through legal discourse, Joe would almost certainly be branded a murderer. But as the narrator describes the event itself in detail, it looks less like an act of passion and more one of affection. Yet as Jan Furman argues, the reason for this description cannot be discerned until the narrator discovers and

25. Cecil Brown, "Interview with Toni Morrison," 472–73.

reveals more details of Joe's personal history.[26] The narrator and reader both discover shortly that Joe's act of violence is no more emblematic of his personality than his personality exemplifies the experiences of African American men in general.

Morrison's questioning of a widespread problem within critical judgments of her work is the same the text forces us to perform in considering each character, up to and including the narrator. As many critics have already noted, the narrator of *Jazz* remains nameless, genderless, and almost entirely enigmatic. One effect of this narrative choice is to deflect attention from Morrison as the voice of the omnipotent narrator. It opens up the space for polyglossia in the narration or, as Judylyn Ryan and Estella Májoza argue, dispersion of the narrative voice to match the dispersion of the characters from their places of origin and from their original desires.[27] It reproduces the route of the Middle Passage that brought Africans to the Americas, a journey that forced diverse peoples with many different languages, customs, and voices to find ways to tell their stories in a new language, new settings, and with new rules.

While the migration John and Violet make from their original Virginia cannot and does not approach the Middle Passage's horrors, the telling of it is meant to evoke the latter experience's elusive truth and the process of transformation it engendered. While most critics assume that the narrator is a single unidentifiable person, I argue instead that it is several distinct voices, some unknown, others the voices of characters speaking in free indirect discourse; all are in conversation. Each chapter in the novel and subsections of chapters are told by one of these narrators, with each narrator beginning and ending his or her portion with the appropriate transitions. Although all the narrators are conversant with each other, their accounts do not always agree; in fact, some narrators are presumptuous to the point of making startling interpretive errors. Jan Matus points out that the narrators are "intimate, personal, gossipy, and . . . concerned with [their] own musings . . . misreadings . . . and false predictions."[28] As Morrison indicated in another interview, she

26. Jan Furman, *Toni Morrison's Fiction*, 87–88.
27. Judylyn S. Ryan and Estella C. Májoza, "Jazz . . . on 'The Site of Memory,' " 131.
28. Jan Matus, *Toni Morrison*, 122.

"does not want her reader to 'get any comfort or safety in knowing the personality of the narrator or whether the narrator is indeed a man or a woman or black or white or is a person at all.' "[29] The only certainty the reader has regarding the narrator is that she/he/they doggedly elude delimited ontological and epistemological positions and are, therefore, uncertain of what they know. In Phillip Page's words, the narrator is both "knowledgeable *and* limited, reliable *and* unreliable," leaving a trace rather than an indelible impression upon the story.[30]

I focus on the elusive narrators' role to show how irony is an intrinsic part of the text, irony that reveals the allegorical qualities of Morrison's work. One piquant example would be the description of Harlem early in the text, a place existing "when all the wars are over and there will never be another one. At last, at last, everything's ahead. The smart ones say so and people listening to them and reading what they write down agree: Here comes the new. Look out. There goes the sad stuff. The bad stuff. The things-nobody-could-help stuff. The way everybody was then and there. Forget that. History is over, you all, and everything's ahead at last." The dramatic irony, of course, is that neither world conflict nor history is over, but the advent of the New Negro deceives the narrator and Harlem's denizens into thinking otherwise. It is a shunning of the process of memory that is essential in all of Morrison's work. This denial allows for a mystery—an *unnecessary* mystery—to develop regarding the origins of American and African American culture. As Charles Scruggs and Lee Vandemarr argue, *Jazz* is "a Gothic detective story" that reveals "the inescapable knowledge of corpses"—in this case, the slain Dorcas—and forces us "to uncover history as the progress of a crime, and in the process to discover a *new* history of the republic."[31]

This progress is perhaps best represented in the seven "changes" Joe Trace undergoes in his life, which spans Reconstruction to the Harlem Renaissance. Read allegorically, these changes encompass both this crucial, dangerous time in African American history and the breadth

29. Veronique Lesoinne, "Answer Jazz's Call: Experiencing Toni Morrison's *Jazz*," 164.
30. Phillip Page, "Traces of Derrida in Toni Morrison's *Jazz*," 61–2, 60.
31. Toni Morrison, *Jazz*, 7; Charles Scruggs and Lee Vandemarr, *Jean Toomer and the Terrors of American History*, 223; italics are mine.

and depth of African American history until the novel's publication. Joe's first change was the moment he named himself, after being born the bastard son of a mentally disturbed woman named "Wild"; the second occurred when he trained himself to be a man; the third, when his hometown, Vienna, Virginia, was "burned to the ground" in a so-called "race riot" and he met Violet; the fourth was when he and Violet migrated to New York City; the fifth, when he fought the "dickties" (middle-class, light-skinned African Americans) for the right to live "uptown" in Harlem; the sixth was the 1917 race riot in Harlem; and the seventh was when Joe marched with the 369th Regiment up Seventh Avenue when they returned from France. Each of these events resonates with different phases that pushed African American communities and individuals into modernity. The first is a representation of the long, arduous process African Americans underwent to name themselves after being stolen from Africa, a continent that was, ironically, defined as "wild" by the West, specifically those unwilling to acknowledge the continent's history. Joe must name himself—create an identity—and align himself with the idea of "manhood," which means being independent and free, the same freedom African slaves sought. The third and fourth changes encompass the upheavals of Reconstruction and this century's great migration, while the fifth resembles the continuous intraracial struggles along class lines. It is the process of breaking down the color and class lines, the realization that emerged before and during the Harlem Renaissance that most African Americans shared common causes and origins. To that extent, it also approximates the unifying factor of the modern Civil Rights movement. The sixth may best be understood as the violence that exploded in the 1960s as African Americans saw the promises of the Civil Rights movement being undermined and withered by governmental inaction, while the seventh—the number of completion—dovetails simultaneously with the militancy that marked both the Harlem Renaissance itself and African American cultural politics in the late 1960s and 1970s.

Again, I do not mean to suggest that Joe, in and of himself, stands for all African Americans. His changes, however, not only reveal the transitory and contingent nature of African American history and identity, but also point toward a critique of that history itself. The most accessible critique may be found in the text's indictment of romanticism, especially in the Harlem setting. The city seems to be a haven, yet the narrator also notices the incompleteness of this particular paradise:

> [W]hatever the problems of being winterbound in the City they put up with them because it is worth anything to be on Lenox Avenue safe from fays and the things they think up; where the sidewalks, snow-covered or not, are wider than the main roads of the towns where they were born and . . . everything you want is right where you are: the church, the store, the party, the women, the men, the postbox (*but no high schools*), the furniture store, street newspaper vendors, the bootleg houses (*but no banks*), the beauty parlors, the barbershops, the juke joints . . . and every club, organization, group, order, union, society, brotherhood, sisterhood or association imaginable. . . . It makes you wonderful just to see it. (*Jazz,* 10–11; italics mine)

This passage highlights both the excitement and the possibility within Harlem and marked *absences* within its milieu. Though Harlem offers all of the pleasures that migrants from the rural South might desire, it still lacks the signs of control over the cultural framework to be found within educational institutions—high schools—and economic independence via capital or property ownership—which banks represent. Morrison doubles the irony by implicitly interrogating the *current* status of cultural and economic controls within contemporary African American communities, where curriculum and capital are still limited and often controlled by forces outside those communities.

Harlem is thus the locus of opportunity for black success, but it is a fleeting success in the absence of the cornerstones of socioeconomic stability that are as sorely needed in the North as in the South. These cornerstones are analogous to the signs of social stability absent from the Traces' relationship; Joe and Violet wrestle with the difficulty of maintaining their desire for each other in the face of an urban environment that celebrates the sensual, as opposed to the rural South of their origin, which Violet perceives as an idealized site for the bond she and Joe enjoyed in the early part of their marriage. In comparing herself as a girl growing up in the South to Joe's mistress, Dorcas, Violet says, " 'I was a good girl her age. Never gave a speck of trouble. I did everything anybody told me to. Till I got here. City make you tighten up' " (*Jazz,* 81). It is in the city that encroachment upon another's territory, whether that territory be a different organization or group as mentioned above or a woman's spouse, is supposedly more tolerable.

Violet's perception, however, becomes problematic given the rural South's lack of simplicity. In the quixotic narrative of the mulatto Golden Gray, we witness a character who comically attempts to perpetuate southern myths of valor and white supremacy, despite his well-concealed biracial heritage. His narrative functions as a sign of a South that has always been the site of blurred boundaries, especially insofar as clandestine interracial mixing is concerned. Furthermore, when Violet reiterates to her friend Alice that " '[b]efore I came North I made sense and so did the world. We didn't have nothing but we didn't miss it,' " Alice counters, " 'Who ever heard of that? Living in the City was the best thing in the world. What can you do out in the country? When I visited Tuxedo, back when I was a child, even then I was bored. How many trees can you look at? . . . And for how long and so what?' " Alice further admonishes Violet by pointing out that Violet has succumbed to a fatalism born of an essentialist view of regional differences: " 'What's the world for if you can't make it up the way you want it?' " In other words, Violet has allowed herself to be delimited by the vagaries of city life, rather than obviating them. Ironically, this makes Violet not unlike Dorcas, who, according to Alice, "let herself die" by refusing medical aid when Joe shot her (*Jazz*, 207, 208, 209–10). Both have failed to write their own narratives.

Violet and Dorcas's inadvertent membership in a sisterhood of despair and victimhood is one that the text's narrator rejects, suggesting that the reader similarly distance her- or himself from it. At a crucial moment, Alice reflects,

> Every week since Dorcas' death, during the whole of January and February, a paper laid bare the bones of some broken woman. Man kills wife. Eight accused of rape dismissed. Woman and girl victims of. Woman commits suicide. White attackers indicted. Five women caught. Woman says man beat. In jealous rage man.
> Defenseless as ducks, she thought. Or were they? Read carefully the news accounts revealed that most of these women, subdued and broken, had not been defenseless. Or, like Dorcas, easy prey. All over the country, black women were armed. That, thought Alice, that, at least, they had learned. (*Jazz*, 74)

The text argues, then, that black women, in both their identities as women and as black people, have always held the means to stave off oppression, which is transcendence of narratives of victimhood and fatalism.

In positing Harlem as a site in need of economic renewal and Violet's and Dorcas's lives as potential sites for revision and rejuvenation, is Morrison therefore advocating Black Nationalist and feminist solutions to current or past problems within Harlem, African America, and black women's lives? To place such a label on *Jazz* would be to do a disservice to the text's structure, yet Morrison's depictions certainly suggest several long-standing criticisms of the Harlem Renaissance and African American intellectualism and (sexual) identity formation. That is, the "New Negro" renaissance possessed every cultural resource for pushing African Americans forward in American society except two: *new economic* ideas and *control* over the production, distribution, and interpretation of black life through literature. If the Harlem Renaissance's cultural and literary politics have come under fire for being controlled too closely by whites, then that same situation is reproduced here. On the other hand, George Hutchinson argues convincingly in *The Harlem Renaissance in Black and White* that rumors of African America's helplessness in the face of overbearing white patronage constitute an incomplete myth at best. To recover America's true history, Hutchinson writes, "requires a recognition of the national (and therefore hybrid) character of our racial identities as well as the racial character of our American identities, for the national subconscious affects our ideas of the American nation."[32]

Accordingly, some key passages in *Jazz* suggest that the reality of white/black interactions cannot be reduced to white hegemony and exploitation over people of African descent. Through Golden Gray, the young "mulatto" man produced by a liaison between a male slave and his young mistress—a liaison the mistress initiated—the text revives the investigation into the long history of voluntary sexual relations within the South, nodding to Jean Toomer's *Cane* in the process. Golden Gray embarks upon a farcical chivalric quest to find and kill his black father, ostensibly to obviate the presence of the African part of his heritage. As Golden's father, Henry Lestory, taunted him, his true purpose was to "see how black [Lestory] was," because Golden "thought [he] was white" and therefore was guaranteed white skin privilege (*Jazz*, 172). Lestory's name itself, and the versions thereof, parallel the falsehood written into Golden's whiteness. The first version of Lestory's name that Golden learns is "LesTroy," evoking a

32. *B&W*, 26.

Trojan horse within Golden's genealogy as well as the destruction—or "Lestruction"—of his mythical genealogy. The reality, of course, is that there is more to "race" than whites and blacks who are "black and nothing. Like Henry LesTroy . . . there was another kind—like himself" (*Jazz*, 149). As Morrison writes in *Playing in the Dark*, images of "impenetrable whiteness" such as the one Golden sustains in his self-image frequently appear "in conjunction with representations of black or Africanist people who are dead, impotent, or under complete control . . . [and] function as both antidote for and meditation on the shadow that is companion to this whiteness."[33] Golden is thus forced to contemplate the possibility that blackness is at the very core of his whiteness.

The anxiety Golden experiences in discovering his "mulatto" identity stems from his fear of losing the white skin privilege, on the one hand, and being denied the authentic Americanness in fact that he believes comes with African American identity, on the other. The narrator thus asks, "What was I thinking of? How could I have imagined him so poorly? Not noticed the hurt that was not linked to the color of his skin, or the blood that beat beneath it. But to some other thing that longed for authenticity, for a right to be in this place, effortlessly without needing to acquire a false face, a laughless grin, a talking posture. I have been careless and stupid and it infuriates me to discover (again) how unreliable I am" (*Jazz*, 160). In seeking Henry Lestory, Golden seeks an Other who both terrifies and fascinates him as the embodiment of "blackness," one construction of heroic masculine identity, and America itself, insofar as Lestory engendered a hybrid man and therefore a hybrid *culture*.[34] Golden wants all of these slippery identities, yet realizes that they cannot be reconciled in the face of a racist hierarchy. His ideal authenticity would mean being "black" without taking on the multiple identities that African Americans have had to obtain for survival. Consequently, Golden is attempting to prevent the fragmentation of the self and his identity. His search for the Other is a search for that stable identity.

Yet the narrator frames Golden's goal as one marked by "self-deception" inasmuch as he attempts to "shap[e] a story for himself"

33. Toni Morrison, *Playing in the Dark: Whiteness and the Literary Imagination*, 33.
34. Henry Lestory is popularly known as "Hunter's Hunter" in his community.

and thus rewrite the memory of his own narrative, a revision of America's history. Ironically, this act of revising history is repeated like a jazz theme throughout the text. The multiple narrators attempt to write the characters' history but find it impossible to predict or frame their behavior in any reliable terms. In the case of Joe and Violet Trace, their relationship transcends the melodramatic plot; they reconstruct their marriage despite Joe's affair with and murder of Dorcas, leading the narrator to an aporia, a recognition of the impossibility of narrating:

> I thought I knew them and wasn't worried that they didn't really know about me. Now it's clear why they contradicted me at every turn: they knew me all along. . . . They knew how little I could be counted on; how poorly, how shabbily my know-it-all self covered helplessness. That when I invented stories about them . . . I was completely in their hands, managed without mercy. . . . So I missed it altogether. I was sure one would kill the other. I waited for it so I could describe it. I was so sure it would happen. That the past was an abused record with no choice but to repeat itself at the crack and no power on earth could lift the arm that held the needle. . . . Busy, they were, busy being original, complicated, changeable—human, I guess you'd say, while I was the predictable one, confused in my solitude into arrogance, thinking my space, my view was the only one that was or that mattered. (*Jazz*, 220)

Another level of unreliability is added here to the narration. Whereas the narrator criticizes Golden Gray for his "self-deception," she/he/it/they become the object of their own critique for attempting to narrate human life, for assuming a deterministic and paternalistic naturalism.

Morrison thus precludes a totalizing reading of the novel as a form of urban realism; instead, she uses the polyglossia of the narrative voice to foreground the impossibility of creating a complete historical record of the subject. Although some of Morrison's views apparently align her with the ideologies of the Black Arts movement, they are not executed dogmatically in her novels. She focuses exclusively but not uncritically on African American communities. The community is both a site for solidarity and the production of a rich culture. By the same token, it is not a panacea; it can be stifling and autocratic over time, becoming a surrogate form of oppression. *Jazz* relies upon narrators and characters who are grotesque in their conception and used "as . . . instrument[s] of social satire."[35] The satire never stops with only one object, though; in Steven Weisenburger's terms, it degenerates to the point where the text itself is unable and afraid to tell its own story. Instead of positing these grotesque characters as objects to be condemned, the text shows how they are "readymade allies, both semantically and pragmatically, because only the grotesque can inscribe, in a mere figure, those disruptions of codified knowledge peculiar to [contemporary, postmodern] satire."[36] Like jazz itself, any attempt to place a defining label or a codified knowledge, whether according to generic, political, or theoretical lines, will fail as the form and content change. The responsibility then falls to the reader as the narrator tells us, mocks us, by declaring and requesting, "If I were able I'd say it. Say make me, remake me. *You* are free to do it and I am free to let you because look, look. Look where your hands are. Now" (*Jazz*, 229; emphasis mine). The text's final act of ironic reversal, then, is to recede from the possibility or responsibility that Ellison's anonymous Invisible Man posited: Instead of the text "speak[ing] for you," we speak for it, yet find ourselves faced with the possibility that we might not possess a stabilizing voice—and perhaps never will.

Jazz posits, therefore, an ideology and structure of irony that undermines one basis of popular conceptions of the Harlem Renaissance. Morrison, like Wallace Thurman and Ralph Ellison before her, satirizes the concept of African Americans, male and female, as inextricably written into an overdetermined narrative of victimhood. Rather, in *Jazz* she argues for African Americans' total, active participation in creating their own narrative, in understanding the breadth of possible experiences in the diverse milieux in which African Americans live.

POSTSCRIPT: WHO'S NEXT?: THE FUTURE OF BLACK SATIRE

The concerns Reed and Morrison posit regarding the function of the narrator of African American experiences have become more urgent as the gains of the Civil Rights movement have been slowly but inexorably eroded. A generation has passed since the movement's glory days; what are the status and fate of this generation, which has not gone through the same struggle and uncertainty that were

35. Dubey, *Black Women*, 35.
36. *Fables*, 24.

common before and during the movement? Who are their leaders—if any obvious leaders exist—and how do they compare to those of the past? Should they be compared to those of the past at all, given that the present generation is within a war of maneuver? Derrick Bell, Darius James, Trey Ellis, and Paul Beatty have recently emerged to answer these questions as four of the more intriguing satirical voices of this generation. Their focus is varied, with James taking a more surrealistic look at contemporary American race politics, but tends to center primarily upon the segments of African American communities that have grown up with considerable privilege and unprecedented access to supposedly "integrated" American institutions, especially the public educational system and white-collar employment, yet experience various forms of racism from an America that still operates within a system of de facto segregation.

I mention above that *Japanese by Spring* illustrates one of Derrick Bell's "Rules of Racial Standing." That rule, excerpted from Bell's *Faces at the Bottom of the Well*, utilizes the *deliberative* satirical form—which offers a vision of the future to criticize present problems—in apologues that debate different views of racial problems.[37] Bell, an accomplished civil rights lawyer, was the first black male tenured at Harvard's Law School before he was dismissed from his position as a result of his protest of the law school's refusal to hire a woman of color. Three of his most recent books, *And We Are Not Saved*, *Faces at the Bottom of the Well*, and *Gospel Choirs*, are collections of essays that, through deliberations over American legal history, are devoted to a central premise that, in Bell's words, "will be easier to reject than refute":

> *Black people will never gain full equality in this country. Even those herculean efforts we hail as successful will produce no more than temporary "peaks of progress," short-lived victories that slide into irrelevance as racial patterns adapt in ways that maintain white dominance. This is a hard-to-accept fact that all history verifies. We must acknowledge it, not as a sign of submission, but as an act of ultimate defiance.* (*Faces*, 12; italics in the original)

Upon this premise, Bell constructs numerous scenarios in which contemporary racial politics, including *intra*racial politics, are examined

37. See Leon Guilhamet's definition of deliberative satire in *Satire and Transformation*. In addition, Guilhamet defines and illustrates the *deliberative* and *judicial* modes of satire, which utilize a first-person narrative voice and courtroom settings, respectively.

and frequently satirized for their inability to bring any permanent closure to the dilemmas of African American existence.

One narrative predicts what would happen if African Americans were given the opportunity to retire to the panacea of a rediscovered Atlantis; another, asks us to consider what would occur if a race of space aliens were to offer to solve all of the United States' material problems if it turned over all of its African Americans to the aliens. In each case, the illusory hopes of African Americans are snatched away from them: Atlantis disappears back into the ocean, and America ultimately sells African Americans into apparent slavery.[38] Each of these narratives is intended to illuminate the impossibility and fatal dangers of black reliance upon the goodwill of a nation steeped in white supremacy.

Two of Bell's most openly satirical and provocative narratives, "The Racial Preference Licensing Act" and "The Freedom of Employment Act: Affirmative Reaction," published in the *Nation* in 1994 and revised for *Gospel Choirs*, use an interlocutor, Geneva Crenshaw, a fictional civil rights lawyer, and Jesse B. Semple, named after Langston Hughes's famous satirical character, to posit possible solutions to current race-based controversies. The former would allow racism to exist as a practice to be licensed, while the latter would eliminate Affirmative Action policies and force beneficiaries of those policies into compulsory, minimum-wage labor.

Each of these solutions are in the vein of Jonathan Swift's "A Modest Proposal" because they both engage in reductio ad absurdum to criticize contemporary racial tensions and are well-designed proposals that have already been implemented to some extent, most noticeably in the state of California.[39] Simultaneously, however, the arguments between Bell and Geneva over these proposals launch the

38. In *Gospel Choirs*, though, once the aliens have America's black population, they offer them the opportunity to live in equality on their world or return to America. The population chooses to return, because it is a land for which they have fought for so long.

39. On November 4, 1996, the voters of the State of California approved Proposition 209, the California Civil Rights Initiative, which effectively eliminated Affirmative Action programs in public employment, education, and contracting. The initiative was the brainchild of California academics Glynn Custred and Thomas E. Wood, who were opposed to multiculturalism and legal preferences. The cannily named initiative was later championed by University of California regent Ward Connerly, who continues to fight Affirmative Action programs as of

narratives into the satirical mode. When, for example, Geneva points out the folly of blacks' reliance on the activist model of the Civil Rights movement and the weakness of the legislation that resulted, Bell replies, "Most civil rights advocates . . . would, on hearing that argument, likely respond by linking arms and singing three choruses of 'We Shall Overcome' " (*Faces*, 60). This particular broadside attacks the traditional civil rights leadership and its apparent inability or refusal to consider anything but the methods and ideals established in the 1960s. "The question," Geneva argues, "is whether [civil rights] activity reflects and is intended to challenge the actual barriers we face rather than those that seem a threat to the integration ideology" (*Faces*, 61).

Bell's concern is that solutions to race-based crises among contemporary civil rights leaders lack imagination, at best, and are hopelessly outdated and ineffective, at worst. To invoke the "war of maneuver" metaphor again, Bell's solution to the problems engendered by these imaginary policies would be to surrender, after a fashion. In the case of "The Racial Preference Licensing Act," one clause of the act would set up an " 'equality fund' used to underwrite black businesses, to offer no-interest mortgage loans for black home buyers, and to provide scholarships for black students seeking college and vocational education." The counterstrategy for "The Freedom of Employment Act" would be to offer minimal legal resistance to the bill and trick the public into opposing it by not focusing on "its disadvantage to blacks, but on its burden to whites," as the act would guarantee employment for a substantial number of black people as whites lost their jobs with no recourse. The crux of each of these strategies is a dependence, not on American ideals and goodwill, but on the irrationality of American bigotries. Bell cites numerous historical precedents that demonstrate effectively that white America as a body has moved forward on racial issues not out of kindness, but out of self-interest.

The arguments Bell and Geneva posit are concerns that have become more urgent as the gains of the Civil Rights movement have been slowly but inexorably eroded. Darius James and Trey Ellis have recently emerged as two of the more interesting voices of the new

---

this writing. See Linda Chávez's *The Color Bind: California's Battle to End Affirmative Action.*

generation, particularly the segment that has grown up with considerable privilege and unprecedented access to mainstream American institutions, especially the educational system and white-collar employment, yet still experiences various forms of racism.

Darius James's satirical novel provides us with perhaps the most controversial and difficult illustrations of Mikhail Bakhtin's notions of the grotesque body and the carnival in contemporary literature. Written in the form of a screenplay, James's *Negrophobia* is one of the most consistently scatological novels to emerge from the American literary scene since William S. Burroughs's *Naked Lunch,* and easily the most continuously grotesque fictional work in African American literature; most of its scenes far exceed the infamous "Brigadier Pudding" episode of Thomas Pynchon's *Gravity's Rainbow* for scatological and sexual transgressions. Written in the form of a screenplay, *Negrophobia* is the narrative of Bubbles Brazil, a young white woman with an acute case of the condition, who, after casting a voodoo spell on herself, embarks on numerous hallucinogenic, picaresque adventures in New York City, where she confronts her fear of African Americans via every negative stereotype. In the course of these adventures, James manages to satirize, parody, lampoon, or otherwise offend and rhetorically decimate most of the major figures in African American history, art, literature, music, and politics within the past one hundred years and beyond. The novel seems to consciously take the dizzying historical referentiality of Ishmael Reed's novels, especially *Mumbo Jumbo* and *Flight to Canada,* to their most acidic extremes. Whereas Reed's novels seek to shed light on contemporary political and social events in American, especially African American politics, James's novel forces us to confront, digest—and that latter act is more difficult than it sounds—and perhaps inure ourselves against the most offensive racial/racist images and ideas extant today.

In his most recent book, *That's Blaxploitation! Roots of the Baadasssss 'Tude (Rated X by an All-Whyte Jury),* a history of Blaxploitation filmmaking, James writes, "Nowhere is it written [that] Black people cannot take back the images of racism and use them as a weapon against those who oppress them."[40] A reader who had not yet encountered *Negrophobia* would find this argument useful for limning the novel's

40. James, *That's Blaxploitation! Roots of the Baadasssss 'Tude (Rated X by an All-Whyte Jury),* 5.

basic premise; James focuses most of his text on utilizing and flouting stereotypical images of African Americans to keep his audience off balance. This process begins with a false advertisement preceding the title page that confronts us with a racist image and asks us to choose from a continuum of epistemological positions as we view it:

> the racial moderate or liberal who enjoys the occasional racist joke or image; the racially ingenuous, who find no problem with racist images; the veteran of the Civil Rights Movement grown more cynical over time; the overt and highly paranoid racist.

Belief in any one of these positions represents, in one way or another, not only the standard definition of "negrophobia," but also some degree of acquiescence to institutionalized racism. The third position, in particular, seems to be the one that James is directing at an African American audience, which is in danger of taking itself too seriously by growing too aggravated over negative images.

Incidentally, this subtle critique proved to be a self-fulfilling prophecy. When the cloth version of *Negrophobia* was published in 1992, its jacket, depicting a scantily clad white woman with a gigantic Sambo figure standing over her shoulder, was protested by the employees of the book's publisher, Citadel Press. James said, in response to the protest, "I understand that these images were once oppressive. But I think we are at the stage where we can look at these images and not feel threatened. . . . All kinds of black artists have started to take control of these images, whether they realize it or not. . . . You see these rap and hip-hop artists wearing tiny little braids just like those stereotypical pickaninny pictures. But it's a statement of power instead of self-loathing. It's taking back our own mythology. It is subverting the perversion."[41]

James's own subversions continue when he further jars us —while informing us of his project via his disclaimer, which reads, "*Negrophobia* is a work of fiction, a product of the author's imagination. Any resemblance to any person, living or dead, is purely coincidental. *Negrophobia* is a work of fiction. Every word is true. Fuck you. The Author" (*Negrophobia*, viii). The gloves are off; from this point, the

---

41. Esther B. Fein, "Book Cover Is Questioned. The Cover of Darius James' Novel, *Negrophobia*, Called Racist," B3.

novel delves into an irreverent *pastiche* of graphic sexual, racial, racist, scatological, and grotesque images designed to offend readers of all the positions named in the opening plate. The novel opens with a pseudocitation from a new book on "voodoo's" ability to adapt to new environments in the United States, including the resurrection of Malcolm X as a new *loa,* or spirit, and the incorporation of hip-hop into voodoo rituals. Thus James posits a notion similar to that which runs through Ishmael Reed's novels: African American cultural forms may be used to subvert and alter the ideologies of Western civilization. In addition, James is drawing upon a simultaneously Bakhtinian and postmodern aesthetic of the carnival that, as Steven Weisenburger summarizes, "fosters a heterogeneous flux of discourse types: . . . underworld slang, cant, professional jargon, popular slang, standardized English, obscenities [especially obscenities], versions of lyric, and ethnic expletives." These are all part of a "semiotic [process] . . . of dismantling and exposure of which satire is a part."[42]

Although it would be excrescent—in all senses of the word—to review too many examples of James's grotesque images, a few demand some attention. For example, when a "200-Pound Black Muslim" hawks bean pies by suggesting that it would be possible for consumers to "fart all four sides of Brutha Miles's *Bitches Brew* out dey butts" before he is torn apart by machine gun fire; Mickey Mouse and Walt Disney are superimposed over Nazi propaganda films; in an allusion to Ralph Ellison's *Invisible Man,* Bubbles sees a sign for the "BUSH MASTER PAINT FACTORY," scrawled in sperm; James includes several plates of caricatured stereotypes of African bushmen, of which one carries the caption "National Geographic Bush Babe of the Month"; a pamphlet warns against the problem of "exploding Negroes," the result of hundreds of years of continuous racial oppression; Bubbles encounters cesspools, numerous filthy restrooms, human genitals, winos, buffoons, "Sambos," remnants of the UNIA, the Civil Rights and Black Power movements, such as "H. Rap Remus"; and so on.

Ultimately, *Negrophobia*'s carnival of grotesqueries is supposed to *cure* the fear, inasmuch as it, like the civil rights strategies played to death, can only limit progress on racial issues. Similarly, Trey Ellis's

42. *Fables,* 25.

first two novels, *Platitudes* and *Home Repairs*, satirize the petty concerns of the new black bourgeoisie even as they celebrate the fact that this same bourgeoisie has attained a new size and affluence. It is Ellis's expression of his essay "The New Black Aesthetic" that while not intended to supplant the Black Aesthetic of the 1960s, argues that no racial label, whether it be foisted upon African Americans by whites or fellow African Americans, will suffice to describe the full spectrum of black culture.[43]

This philosophy is perhaps best expressed in Ellis's debut novel, *Platitudes*, a parody of conventions or clichés in recent African American literature. Ellis's narrative is a mock Künstlerroman in which a young black artist, Dewayne Wellington, struggles to tell the story of his social, racial, and artistic awakenings through the eyes of his postmodern subjectivity, even as another, female artist, Isshee Ayam, cajoles him to see himself as part of a traditional black community by writing his story in a rural context that focuses more on black women. This particular convention, of course, parodies the subject matter and settings through which Zora Neale Hurston, Alice Walker, and Toni Morrison achieved some of their greatest literary triumphs.[44]

The narrative's tension rests upon the male protagonist's desire to write his story free of the *platitudes* of contemporary fiction, a desire that is continually undermined as he finds himself using every available cliché, but only for the sake of creating a satiric pastiche commenting on the impossibility of originality when every previous literary movement has already preempted a new aesthetic. Thus, for example, the narrators continually call attention to the process and impetuses behind the narrative's formation, as when Dewayne writes one chapter about a scene in a movie theater in which signs on the movie screen reflect the interactions between the narrative's main characters. Isshee Ayam later commends Dewayne on his "semiotics movie."[45]

The text contains many other instances in which each character criticizes and parodies the other's chosen form and content for the narrative. Each instance further illustrates how different narrative forms

---

43. Trey Ellis, "The New Black Aesthetic."
44. Some of Ayam's titles: "*Chillun o' de Lawd, Hog Jowl Junction,* and *My Big Ol' Feets Gon' Stomp Dat Devil Down*" (Ellis, *Platitudes,* 110).
45. Ellis, *Platitudes,* 150, 151, 157.

can romanticize the socialization process of African Americans in the twentieth century, whether that socialization occurred at the height of southern sharecropping or in contemporary, post–Civil Rights black America. Ellis's text portrays the latter form of socialization as being closely linked both to the new black middle-class dynamic that has emerged in the last three decades and to the fixtures of mainstream popular and intellectual cultures. Ellis thus lampoons such icons as standardized tests, popular music, and contemporary literary theories and society's tendency to accept and follow them blindly without thought to their social relevance. Moreover, Ellis is fighting for the space to insert not only a new generation of writers, but also a new type of narrative into our literary tradition, one that goes beyond the ontology of the previous generation to highlight the everyday concerns of this one. One charge that has been frequently levied against the subject matter and narrative forms of Morrison, Hurston, Alice Walker, and Gloria Naylor, among others, is that they shift too much of their focus away from the extreme harshness of black life in the rural South during the first half of the twentieth century to romanticize the mystical and sexual relationships among African Americans in that context.

While this charge of romanticism is hardly fair or accurate—all of the aforementioned authors implicitly and explicitly condemn southern racism in their texts—it is the basis of Ellis's parody. Ellis's text insists that African American narratives with rural settings are frequently problematic because they sometimes posit the pastoral as the site of spiritual healing. This setting is thus less connected to contemporary African American life, which is now primarily urban and suburban. Yet this supposition ignores the allegorical content of most narratives of this nature in favor of satire. Are not Morrison's *Beloved* or Naylor's *Mama Day*, for instance, truly more concerned with intergenerational tensions and politics—Ellis's own concerns—than pastoral histories or presents? While Ellis is correct to question the ubiquity of rural settings for contemporary novels, his act of reductio ad absurdum denies these texts their true power.

Yet Ellis is hardly alone in his concern about the state of African American literature. As the past glories of black culture and political work continue to fade and/or fall into decay in the post–Civil Rights era, some African American authors have increasingly turned to satire to pursue seemingly contradictory goals: a call for a return to intellectual, social, and political strategies that succeeded for African

Americans in the past and a push for solutions that will jettison the baggage of those ideologies that have lost their efficacy or popular appeal.

In 1996, poet Paul Beatty published a highly—and deservedly—praised first novel that points in the direction African American satire is most likely to follow. *The White Boy Shuffle* revises and parodies the classic *Künstlerroman*, James Joyce's *A Portrait of the Artist as a Young Man*, for the African American author in the late 1990s. The breadth of Beatty's satire is vast, but rather than leading to ideological chaos, this strategy allows the author to lampoon appropriately an African American—and American—cultural scene whose complexities have become more apparent over the last two decades. Perhaps most important, Beatty manages to display a thorough knowledge of the history that has led to current crises without resigning himself to complete misanthropy.

The central artist of *The White Boy Shuffle* is young Gunnar Kaufman, a poet who, in the course of his hilariously chaotic life, has found himself filling the role of "Negro Demagogue," who, according to the faux advertisement on the opening page, "Must have ability to lead a divided, downtrodden, and alienated people to the Promised Land. Good communication skills required. Pay commensurate with ability. No experience necessary" (WBS, 1).[46] Beatty's cynical summation of Gunnar's destiny addresses questions that have haunted African American politics since the assassination of Martin Luther King, Jr., in 1968: Who, if anyone, is fit to be the next great "Negro leader"? Is it necessary for one such leader to exist in the first place, or is the idea of having to choose itself a disservice—and insult—to highly diverse African American communities? Over a generation earlier, Langston Hughes's Jesse B. Semple questioned the competence and sincerity of Negro leaders via Dr. Butts, a caricature of all accommodationist African American leaders. Beatty, in contrast, interrogates the rise and prominence of Black Nationalist leaders since the Black Power movement of the 1960s. More specifically, the advertisement refers to such controversial leaders as minister Louis Farrakhan of the Nation of Islam, who rose to his greatest prominence among the black working

---

46. An allusion to Gunnar Myrdal, author of *American Dilemma* (New York: Harper, 1944), one of the most important, if occasionally controversial, studies of race relations this century.

class in the late 1980s and 1990s as a voice representing those who had not been enfranchised by the Civil Rights movement.

The issue for Beatty is not so much the *existence* of such leaders as the lack of viable alternatives in a post–Civil Rights, postmodern landscape made up of enough economic chaos, rampant classism, and cultural confusion to make the most strident black nationalism not just highly acceptable, but fashionable, preferable, and inevitably hegemonic. As the new "Negro Demagogue," Gunnar has "the ear of the academics, the street denizens, and the political cabalists. Leader of the Black Community? There is no better job fit. . . . I spoon-feed them grueled futility, unveil the oblivion that is black America's existence and the hopelessness of the struggle. In return I receive fanatical avian obedience" (*WBS*, 1). Before Gunnar reaches this dubious high mark, he must overcome a family history of fawning Uncle Toms, including one ancestor who escaped *from* freedom into slavery! Such a heritage prevents Gunnar from fitting into the more fashionable modes of contemporary African American literature. Gunnar explains to us that "[u]nlike the typical bluesy earthy folksy denim-overalls noble-in-the-face-of-cracker-racism aw shucks Pulitzer-Prize-winning protagonist mojo magic black man, I am not the seventh son of a seventh son of a seventh son. I wish I were, but fate shorted me by six brothers and three uncles" (*WBS*, 5). Gunnar goes on to explain that he is, instead, bereft of any sort of supernatural powers, unless one counts his poetic imagination. By stripping Gunnar of the characteristics that are most closely associated with the novels of Gloria Naylor, Alice Walker, and Toni Morrison, Beatty is staking a claim to the same sort of independence Trey Ellis demands in *Platitudes* for the contemporary African American novelist. Combined with Gunnar's further description of his early childhood in predominantly white Santa Monica, California, this particular claim acts as a cry for an opening of African American literature so that magical realism and romanticism may be replaced by *urban* realism. That is to say, various types of cultural mysticism and legends need not be revised or reproduced in African American literature for it to be authentically African American.

The existence of this criticism in the work of two contemporary authors begs analysis. Are Beatty and Ellis rejecting magical realism and romanticism altogether? The answer would seem to be a resounding no. In *White Boy Shuffle*, after all, several characters' lives drift into the fantastic. The most obvious example is Gunnar's friend Nick Scoby, who has the uncanny talent of never missing a shot when playing basketball. Moreover, as in many satires, the action and characterizations remain wildly *un*realistic. Beatty is rejecting, though, works that rely upon the magic and legends to examine the problems of the present. Such texts reproduce the problem with traditional satire that, as Guillermo Hernández illustrates, requires a prelapsarian past filled with hegemonic moral systems in order for the satire to operate effectively.

The White Boy Shuffle, on the other hand, examines the current limits that define cultural authenticity and normativity that can be humiliating, perhaps even dangerous. Most of Gunnar's personal narrative describes his transformation from an alienated beach bum in Santa Monica to an alienated denizen of Hillside, the inner-city community full of "[h]ardrock niggers, Latinos and Asians," the kind of area pathologized relentlessly in the 1980s and 1990s. Gunnar initially measures authenticity by the extent to which he is addressed in black urban lingo. When fellow black youth Scoby calls Gunnar "nigger" for the first time, Gunnar says his "euphoria was as palpable as the loud clap of our hands colliding in my first soul shake. My transitional slide into step two was a little stiff, but I made up for it with a loud finger snap as our hands parted" (*WBS,* 67). As Gunnar immerses himself in life on the streets, eventually establishing himself as a street poet of sorts, he realizes that African American culture—or any "ethnic" culture, for that matter—carries its own immense cultural cachet that the cynical artist may use for immense profit, not unlike Max Disher in George Schuyler's *Black No More.* Among black intellectuals—one from a Boston-area university is likely a caricature of Harvard's Henry Louis Gates, Jr.—street gangs, liberal white schoolteachers—including one Ms. Cegeny obsessed with multiculturalism—and his own mail-order bride, Gunnar is ensconced in a world in which clever use of key catchphrases, attitudes, and slang carry more meaning than any sort of sustained, effective action to alleviate social problems.

The existence of this world, combined with Gunnar's poetic skills, eventually casts him in the role of a black leader drawing African Americans toward mass suicide. In his keynote speech at an anti-Apartheid rally on a university campus, Gunnar condemns 1990s–style American political activism as, ironically, the height of hypocrisy and concealed apathy, a far cry from the commitment of the 1960s. In describing the plaque on a memorial to Martin Luther King, Jr.,

Gunnar decries the "[m]iddle minorities caught between racial po-
larities" and "[c]aring, class-conscious progressive crackers" who are
truly "[s]elfish apathetic humans like everybody else."

> "It says, 'If a man hasn't discovered something he will die for, he isn't
> fit to live. Martin Luther King, Jr.' How many of you motherfuckers are
> ready to die for black rule in South Africa—and I mean black rule, not
> black superintendence?"
> Yells and whistles shot through the air.
> "You lying motherfuckers. I talked to Harriet Velakazi, the ANC
> lieutenant you heard speak earlier, and *she's* willing to die for South
> Africa.
> She don't give a fuck about King's sexist language, she ready to kill
> her daddy and if need be kill her mama for South Africa. Now don't get
> me wrong, I want them niggers to get theirs, but I am not willing to die
> for South Africa, and you ain't either."
> The audience hushed, their Good Samaritan opportunism
> checkmated. There was nothing they could say. "I'm willing to die
> for South Africa, where do I sign?" (*WBS*, 199–200)

This leads to the statement that raises Gunnar into the ranks of black
leadership, "Negro demagoguery," and black national suicide: "Matter of fact, I ain't ready to die for anything, so I guess I'm just not fit
to live. In other words, I'm just ready to die. I'm just ready to die"
(*WBS*, 200).

As African Americans all over the nation subsequently begin to kill
themselves (after sending their suicide poems to their new "hero"),
Gunnar cynically requests the United States government to obliterate
Hillside with nuclear weapons, thus bringing the text's irony full
circle. Ultimately, Beatty directs his satire toward a cultural scene that
has mistaken style for substance, that, in the words of philosopher
Cornel West, is enthralled with "nihilism." Beatty seems to be allied
with West, to the extent that West calls for African Americans to adopt
a "politics of conversion" in which people learn to "believe that there
is hope for the future and a meaning to struggle," that "shun[s] the
limelight—a limelight that solicits status seekers and ingratiates ego-
maniacs. Instead, it stays on the ground among the toiling everyday
people, ushering forth humble freedom fighters—both followers and
leaders—who have the audacity to take the nihilistic threat by the
neck and turn back its deadly assaults."[47]

47. Cornel West, *Race Matters*, 18, 20.

All the contemporary satirists, in their own way, call for this same politics of conversion and reject the notion that the future of black America is hopeless simply because all of the promises of both the Civil Rights movement and American democracy have not been fulfilled. The sort of projects these authors pursue via their satires and parodies, then, shall continue to find their voices, as they continue to offer hope to a generation that has become cynical almost to the point of complete despair.

The key question that African American authors, especially satirists, must ask is: What shall be the place of the current generation of African Americans in history? In fact, this question seems to be the underlying premise of Paul Beatty's most recent novel, *Tuff* (2000), in which Winston "Tuffy" Foshay, another young, urban African American male ensconced in the criminal justice system—the darling of the same sociological inquiries Ralph Ellison distrusted—attempts to make a place for himself in mainstream society by running for New York City Council. While Beatty's second novel is not as consistent in its blend of absurdity, pop culture referentiality, and reductio ad absurdum as *The White Boy Shuffle*, *Tuff* maintains the former novel's unrelenting cynicism toward current African American leadership. Foshay's picaresque exploits document the ease with which Americans tend to stigmatize neighborhoods made up primarily of African Americans and Latinos as crime dens. When Foshay delivers his climactic, damning stump speech against his middle-class opponent, Beatty reiterates *The White Boy Shuffle*'s essential argument, the same that concerned Jesse B. Semple over four decades ago: African American leadership has become alienated from its power base precisely because it has been most concerned with broad wars of maneuver rather than the present war of position.[48] The result is a cadre of leaders making generalizations about people who no longer fit into generalities, if they ever did.

How, then, shall African American satirists, whose genre virtually demands reliance upon some generalizations, help resolve this dilemma? The greatest possibilities are that African American satirists will continue to draw upon black vernacular discourse and cultural traditions, since they have served black literature so well and offer

48. Paul Beatty, *Tuff*, 236–37.

rich counterpoints to the vagaries of mainstream American culture by shedding new light on what satire means to African Americans. That meaning has numerous permutations, but the central stake is the continued *existence* of African Americans. When used for generative purposes, the African American satirical novel may help foster and perpetuate that existence. I would hope that it shall do so with the influx of new or younger talent that has appeared in the 1990s or perhaps with the return to print of some of the genre's strongest works from the 1960s and 1970s. It is not possible to predict when African American women satirists shall enter this overwhelmingly male-oriented area and reshape it, although I would like to. Yet the time is ripe and the talent is present; in addition to the authors I mentioned and studied in the previous chapters, essayists as diverse as Jill Nelson, Lisa Jones, and Joan Morgan have revealed a strong penchant for satire that has yet to be transferred into novelistic form. I suspect, however, that when the satirical novel asserts its place in twenty-first–century African American literary traditions, women will be at the forefront of the new movement. With luck, this will yield the benefit of forcing the old political directions of African American communities—and African American satire itself—to take fresh, new turns into more inclusive examinations of those same communities and their individual members.

BIBLIOGRAPHY

Abraham, Willie E. Introduction to *dem*, by William Melvin Kelley. New York: Collier, 1969.

Abrahams, Roger D., ed. *Afro-American Folktales: Stories from Black Traditions in the New World*. New York: Pantheon, 1985.

———. *Deep Down in the Jungle: Negro Narrative Folklore from the Streets of Philadelphia*. Chicago: Aldine, 1970.

Abrams, Meyer Howard. *A Glossary of Literary Terms*. 5th ed. New York: Holt, 1988.

Asante, Molefi Kete. *Afrocentricity*. 3d ed. Trenton, N.J.: Africa World Press, 1988.

Baker, Houston A., Jr. *Black Studies, Rap and the Academy*. Black Literature and Culture. Chicago: University of Chicago Press, 1993.

———. *Blues, Ideology and Afro-American Literature: A Vernacular Theory*. Chicago: University of Chicago Press, 1984.

———. *Long Black Song: Essays in Black American Literature and Culture*. Charlottesville: University Press of Virginia, 1972.

Bakhtin, Mikhail Mikhailovitch. *Rabelais and His World*, trans. Hélène Iswolsky. Bloomington: Indiana University Press, 1984.

———. "Discourse in the Novel." In *The Dialogic Imagination: Four Essays*, ed. Michael Holquist; trans. Caryl Emerson and Michael Holquist. Austin: University of Texas Press, 1981.

Baraka, Imamu Amiri. *The Autobiography of LeRoi Jones*. Chicago: Lawrence Hill, 1997.

———. "State/meant." 1966. Reprint. In *The LeRoi Jones/Amiri Baraka Reader*, ed. William J. Harris with the cooperation of Amiri Baraka, 169–70. New York: Thunder's Mouth, 1991.

Beatty, Paul. *Tuff*. New York: Knopf, 2000.

———. *The White Boy Shuffle*. 1996. New York: Houghton Mifflin, 1997.

Bell, Bernard W. *The Afro-American Novel and Its Tradition*. Amherst: University of Massachusetts Press, 1987.

Bell, Derrick. *And We Are Not Saved: The Elusive Quest for Racial Justice*. New York: Basic, 1987.

———. *Confronting Authority: Reflections of an Ardent Protester*. Boston: Beacon, 1994.

———. *Faces at the Bottom of the Well: The Permanence of Racism*. New York: Basic, 1992.

———. *Gospel Choirs: Psalms of Survival for an Alien Land Called Home*. New York: Basic, 1996.

Bennett, Hal. *Lord of Dark Places*. 1970. Chappaqua, N.Y.: Turtle Point, 1997.

Bergenholtz, Rita A. "Toni Morrison's *Sula:* A Satire on Binary Thinking." *African American Review* 30.1 (1996): 89–98.

Blake, Susan L. "Ritual and Rationalization: Black Folklore in the Works of Ralph Ellison." *Publications of the Modern Language Association* 94.2 (1979): 121–36.

Blakely, Allison. *Blacks in the Dutch World: The Evolution of Racial Imagery in a Modern Society*. Bloomington: Indiana University Press, 1993.

Booth, Wayne C. *The Rhetoric of Fiction*. 2d ed. Chicago: University of Chicago Press, 1983.

———. *A Rhetoric of Irony*. Chicago: University of Chicago Press, 1974.

Boyer, Jay. *Ishmael Reed*. Boise, Idaho: Boise State University Press, 1993.

Brown, Cecil. "Interview with Toni Morrison." *Massachusetts Review* 36 (1995): 455–73.

———. *The Life and Loves of Mr. Jiveass Nigger*. New York: Farrar, 1969.

Bryant, Jerry H. "Old Gods and New Demons: Ishmael Reed and His Fiction." *Review of Contemporary Fiction* 4.2 (1984): 195–202.

Bulmer, Martin. *The Chicago School of Sociology: Institutionalization, Diversity, and the Rise of Sociological Research*. Chicago: University of Chicago Press, 1984.

Butler-Evans, Elliott. *Race, Gender, and Desire: Narrative Strategies in the Fiction of Toni Cade Bambara, Toni Morrison, and Alice Walker*. Philadelphia: Temple University Press, 1989.

Carmichael, Stokely, and Charles V. Hamilton. *Black Power: The Politics of Liberation in America*. New York: Vintage, 1967.

Carroll, Rebecca. *Swing Low: Black Men Writing*. New York: Crown, 1995.

Chapman, Abraham, ed. *New Black Voices: An Anthology of Contemporary Afro-American Literature*. New York: Mentor, 1972.

Chávez, Linda. *The Color Bind: California's Battle to End Affirmative Action*. Berkeley: University of California Press, 1998.

Chesnutt, Charles W. *The Conjure Woman and Other Conjure Tales,* ed. Richard H. Brodhead. Durham, N.C.: Duke University Press, 1993.

Clark, John R. *The Modern Satiric Grotesque and Its Traditions.* Lexington: University Press of Kentucky, 1991.

Connery, Brian A., and Kirk Combe, eds. *Theorizing Satire: Essays in Literary Criticism.* New York: St. Martin's, 1995.

Cruse, Harold. *The Crisis of the Negro Intellectual.* 1967. New York: Quill, 1984.

Dance, Daryl C. *Shuckin' and Jivin': Folklore from Contemporary Black Americans.* Bloomington: Indiana University Press, 1978.

Davis, Charles T., and Henry Louis Gates, Jr. *The Slave's Narrative.* New York: Oxford University Press, 1985.

Davis, Ossie. *Purlie Victorious: A Comedy in Three Acts.* New York: Samuel French, 1961.

Davis, Thadious M., and Trudier Harris, eds. *Dictionary of Literary Biography.* 112 vols. Vol. 33: *Afro-American Fiction Writers after 1955.* Detroit: Gale Research, 1984.

Denard, Carolyn. "Blacks, Modernism, and the American South: An Interview with Toni Morrison." *Studies in the Literary Imagination* 31.2 (1998): 1–16.

De Jongh, James. *Vicious Modernism: Black Harlem and the Literary Imagination.* Cambridge: Cambridge University Press, 1990.

Dick, Bruce Allen, and Pavel Zemliansky. *The Critical Response to Ishmael Reed.* Critical Responses in Arts and Letters, 31. Ed. Cameron Northouse. Westport: Greenwood, 1999.

Dixon, Melvin. *Ride Out the Wilderness: Geography and Identity in Afro-American Literature.* Urbana: University of Illinois Press, 1987.

Doty, William G., and William J. Hynes. "Historical Overview of Theoretical Issues: The Problem of the Trickster." In *Mythical Trickster Figures: Contours, Contexts, and Criticisms,* ed. William J. Hynes and William G. Doty, 13–32. Tuscaloosa: University of Alabama Press, 1993.

Dubey, Madhu. *Black Women Novelists and the Nationalist Aesthetic.* Bloomington: Indiana University Press, 1994.

Du Bois, W. E. B. *The Souls of Black Folk.* 1903. New York: Everyman's Library, 1993.

Dundes, Alan, ed. *Mother Wit from the Laughing Barrel: Readings in the Interpretation of Afro-American Folklore.* Englewood Cliffs, N.J.: Prentice-Hall, 1973.

Ellis, Trey. *Platitudes.* New York: Vintage, 1988.

——. "The New Black Aesthetic." *Callaloo* 12.1 (winter 1989): 233–46.

Ellison, Ralph. *Going to the Territory.* New York: Random House, 1986.

——. *Invisible Man.* 1952. New York: Vintage, 1990.

——. " 'A Very Stern Discipline.' " In Ralph Ellison, *Going to the Territory,* 275–307. New York: Random House, 1986.

——. "The World and the Jug." In Ralph Ellison, *Shadow and Act,* 107–43. 1964. New York: Vintage, 1995.

Epstein, Jacob. "The Devil Wears a Beeper." *Los Angeles Times Book Review,* June 4, 1989: 2.

Fabre, Michael. "Postmodern Rhetoric in Ishmael Reed's *Yellow Back Radio Broke-Down.*" In *The Afro-American Novel since 1960,* ed. Peter Bruck and Wolfgang Karrer, 167–88. Amsterdam: B. R. Grüner, 1982.

Fein, Esther B. "Book Cover Is Questioned. The Cover of Darius James' Novel, *Negrophobia,* Called Racist." *New York Times* (June 17, 1992): B3.

Fisher, Rudolph. "The Caucasian Storms Harlem." In *Voices from the Harlem Renaissance,* ed. Nathan Irvin Huggins, 74–82. New York: Oxford University Press, 1976.

——. *The Walls of Jericho.* 1928. Ann Arbor: University of Michigan Press, 1994.

Fletcher, M. D. *Contemporary Political Satire: Narrative Strategies in the Post-Modern Context.* Lanham, Md.: University Press of America, 1987.

Fox, Robert Elliot. *Conscientious Sorcerers: The Black Postmodernist Fiction of LeRoi Jones/Amiri Baraka, Ishmael Reed, and Samuel R. Delany.* Contributions in Afro-American and African Studies, 106. Westport, Conn.: Greenwood, 1987.

Frazier, E. Franklin. *Black Bourgeoisie.* New York: Free Press, 1957.

Frye, Northrop. *Anatomy of Criticism: Four Essays.* Princeton: Princeton University Press, 1957.

Fuller, Hoyt W. "Introduction: Towards a Black Aesthetic." In *The Black Aesthetic,* ed. Addison Gayle, Jr., 3–12. Garden City, N.Y.: Doubleday, 1971.

——. "The New Black Literature: Protest or Affirmation." In *The Black Aesthetic,* ed. Addison Gayle, Jr., 346–69. Garden City, N.Y.: Doubleday, 1971.

Furman, Jan. *Toni Morrison's Fiction.* Understanding Contemporary

American Literature. Ed. Matthew J. Bruccoli. Columbia: University of South Carolina Press, 1996.

Gaines, Kevin K. *Uplifting the Race: Black Leadership, Politics, and Culture in the Twentieth Century.* Chapel Hill: University of North Carolina Press, 1996.

Gates, Henry Louis, Jr. *Figures in Black: Words, Signs, and the "Racial" Self.* Oxford: Oxford University Press, 1989.

——. "Ishmael Reed." In *Dictionary of Literary Biography,* ed. Thadious M. Davis and Trudier Harris. 112 vols. Vol. 33: *Afro-American Fiction Writers after 1955,* 219–32. Detroit: Gale Research, 1984.

Gates, Henry Louis, Jr., ed. *"Race," Writing and Difference.* Chicago: University of Chicago Press, 1986.

——. *The Signifying Monkey: A Theory of African-American Literary Criticism.* Oxford: Oxford University Press, 1988.

Gayle, Addison, Jr., ed. *The Black Aesthetic.* Garden City, N.Y.: Doubleday, 1971.

——. "Cultural Strangulation: Black Literature and the White Aesthetic." In *The Black Aesthetic,* ed. Addison Gayle, Jr., 39–46. Garden City, N.Y.: Doubleday, 1971.

Goldberg, Whoopi. *Book.* New York: R. Weisbach, 1997.

Graham, Lawrence Otis. *Our Kind of People: Inside America's Black Upper Class.* New York: Harper Collins, 1999.

Griffin, Dustin. *Satire: A Critical Reintroduction.* Lexington: University Press of Kentucky, 1994.

Gruesser, John C. Rev. of *Black Empire,* by George S. Schuyler. Ed. Robert A. Hill and R. Kent Rasmussen. *African American Review* 27.4 (1993): 679–86.

Guilhamet, Leon. *Satire and the Transformation of Genre.* Philadelphia: University of Pennsylvania Press, 1987.

Hall, Ernest Jackson. *The Satirical Element in the American Novel.* New York: Haskell House, 1966.

Harper, Donna Akiba Sullivan. *Not So Simple: The "Simple" Stories by Langston Hughes.* Columbia: University of Missouri Press, 1995.

Harris, Norman. "The Black University in Contemporary Afro-American Fiction." *CLA Journal* 30 (1986): 1–13.

Harris, Trudier, and Thadious M. Davis, eds. *Dictionary of Literary Biography.* 112 vols. Vol. 51: *Afro-American Writers from the Harlem Renaissance to 1940.* Detroit: Gale Research, 1987.

Hemenway, Robert E. *Zora Neale Hurston: A Literary Biography*. Urbana: University of Illinois Press, 1977.

Hernández, Guillermo. *Chicano Satire: A Study in Literary Culture*. Austin: University of Texas Press, 1991.

Highet, Gilbert. *The Anatomy of Satire*. Princeton: Princeton University Press, 1962.

Himes, Chester. *If He Hollers Let Him Go*. 1945. New York: Thunder's Mouth, 1990.

——. *Lonely Crusade*. 1947. New York: Thunder's Mouth, 1992.

Huggins, Nathan Irvin, ed. *Voices from the Harlem Renaissance*. New York: Oxford University Press, 1976.

Hughes, Langston. *The Big Sea: An Autobiography*. 1940. New York: Thunder's Mouth, 1986.

——. "Conversation at Midnight." *Chicago Defender* 40.44 (February 17, 1945): 10.

——, ed. *The Langston Hughes Reader*. New York: George Braziller, 1958.

——. "The Negro Artist and the Racial Mountain." *Nation* 122.3181 (June 23, 1926): 692–94.

——. "Simple Pins on Medals." *Chicago Defender* 38.43 (February 13, 1943): 15.

——. *The Ways of White Folks*. 1934. New York: Vintage, 1990.

Hurston, Zora Neale. *Moses, Man of the Mountain*. 1939. New York: Harper Perennial, 1992.

——. *Tell My Horse: Voodoo and Life in Haiti and Jamaica*. 1938. New York: Harper Collins, 1990.

Hutcheon, Linda. *Irony's Edge: The Theory and Politics of Irony*. New York: Routledge, 1995.

——. *A Poetics of Postmodernism: History, Theory, Fiction*. New York: Routledge, 1988.

——. *A Theory of Parody: The Teachings of Twentieth-Century Art Forms*. New York: Methuen, 1985.

Hutchinson, George. *The Harlem Renaissance in Black and White*. Cambridge: Belknap Press of Harvard University Press, 1995.

Hynes, William J., and William G. Doty, eds. *Mythical Trickster Figures: Contours, Contexts, and Criticisms*. Tuscaloosa: University of Alabama Press, 1993.

James, Darius. *Negrophobia: An Urban Parable*. New York: St. Martin's, 1992.

——. *That's Blaxploitation! Roots of the Baadasssss 'Tude (Rated X by an All-Whyte Jury)*. New York: St. Martin's, 1995.

Johnson, Charles. *Being and Race: Black Writing since 1970*. Bloomington: Indiana University Press, 1988.

Johnson, Charles S. "The New Frontage on American Life." In *The New Negro*, ed. Alain Locke, 278–98. 1925. New York: Atheneum, 1992.

Johnson, James Weldon. *Along This Way: The Autobiography of James Weldon Johnson*. New York: Viking Penguin, 1933.

——. *The Autobiography of an Ex-Coloured Man*. 1927. New York: Vintage, 1989.

Jones, Lisa. *Bulletproof Diva: Tales of Race, Sex, and Hair*. New York: Doubleday, 1994.

Jones, Norma R. "George Samuel Schuyler." In *Dictionary of Literary Biography*, ed. Trudier Harris and Thadious Davis. 112 vols. Vol. 51: *Afro-American Writers from the Harlem Renaissance to 1940*, 245–52. Detroit: Gale Research, 1987.

Karenga, Maulana Ron. "Black Art: Mute Matter Given Force and Function." In *New Black Voices: An Anthology of Contemporary Afro-American Literature*, ed. Abraham Chapman, 477–82. New York: Mentor, 1972.

Kelley, William Melvin. *dem*. New York: Collier, 1969.

——. *A Different Drummer*. 1962. New York: Anchor, 1989.

Kernan, Alvin P. "A Theory of Satire." In *Satire: Modern Essays in Criticism*, ed. Ronald Paulson, 249–77. Englewood Cliffs, N.J.: Prentice-Hall, 1971.

Kiley, Frederick, and J. M. Shuttleworth, eds. *Satire from Aesop to Buchwald*. New York: The Odyssey Press, 1971.

Killens, John Oliver. *The Cotillion, or One Good Bull Is Half the Herd*. 1971. New York: Ballantine, 1988.

Klotman, Phyllis R. "Wallace Henry Thurman." In *Dictionary of Literary Biography*, ed. Trudier Harris and Thadious Davis. 112 vols. Vol. 51: *Afro-American Writers from the Harlem Renaissance to 1940*, 260–73. Detroit: Gale Research, 1987.

Lemann, Nicholas. *The Promised Land: The Great Black Migration and How It Changed America*. New York: Vintage, 1991.

Lesoinne, Veronique. "Answer Jazz's Call: Experiencing Toni Morrison's *Jazz*." *MELUS* 22 (1997): 151–66.

Levine, Lawrence W. *Black Culture and Black Consciousness: Afro-Ameri-*

can Folk Thought from Slavery to Freedom. Oxford: Oxford University Press, 1977.

Locke, Alain, ed. *The New Negro.* 1925. New York: Atheneum, 1992.

Lundquist, Susan Evertsen. *The Trickster: A Transformation Archetype.* San Francisco: Mellen Research University Press, 1991.

Martin, Reginald. "An Interview with Ishmael Reed." *Review of Contemporary Fiction* 4.2 (1984): 176–87.

———. *Ishmael Reed and the New Black Aesthetic Critics.* London: Macmillan, 1988.

Mason, Elizabeth B., and Louis M. Starr, eds. *The Oral History Collection of Columbia University.* New York: Oral History Research Office, 1979.

Mason, Theodore O., Jr. "Performance, History, and Myth: The Problem of Ishmael Reed's *Mumbo Jumbo.*" *Modern Fiction Studies* 34:1 (1988): 97–109.

Matus, Jan. *Toni Morrison.* Contemporary World Writers. Ed. John Thieme. Manchester: Manchester University Press, 1998.

Matuz, Roger, et al., eds. *Contemporary Literary Criticism: Excerpts from Criticism of the Works of Today's Novelists, Poets, Playwrights, Short Story Writers and Other Creative Writers.* 70 vols. Vol. 60. Detroit: Gale Research, 1990.

Mayfield, Julian. "You Touch My Black Aesthetic and I'll Touch Yours." In *The Black Aesthetic,* ed. Addison Gayle, Jr., 24–31. Garden City, N.Y.: Doubleday, 1971.

McElvaine, Robert S. *The Great Depression: America, 1929–1941.* New York: Times Books, 1983.

McGee, Patrick. *Ishmael Reed and the Ends of Race.* New York: St. Martin's, 1997.

McKay, Claude. *Selected Poems.* New York: Bookman Associates, 1953.

Mitchell, Angelyn. " 'Sth, I Know That Woman': History, Gender, and the South in Toni Morrison's *Jazz.*" *Studies in the Literary Imagination* 31.2 (1998): 49–60.

Mitchell-Kernan, Claudia. "Language Behavior in a Black Urban Community." Ph.D. diss. University of California, Berkeley, 1971.

Morgan, Joan. *When Chickenheads Come Home to Roost: My Life as a Hip-Hop Feminist.* New York: Simon and Schuster, 1999.

Morrison, Toni. *Jazz.* New York: Knopf, 1992.

———. *Playing in the Dark: Whiteness and the Literary Imagination.* New York: Vintage, 1993.

Narrative of the Life of Frederick Douglass, An American Slave, Written by Himself. Boston: Anti-Slavery Office, 1845; reprint, New York: Signet, 1968.

Nazareth, Peter. "An Interview with Ishmael Reed." *Iowa Review* 13:2 (spring 1982): 117–30.

Neal, Larry. "Some Reflections on the Black Aesthetic." In *Black Aesthetic,* ed. Addison Gayle, Jr., 13–16. Garden City, N.Y.: Doubleday, 1971.

Nelson, Jill. *Volunteer Slavery: My Authentic Negro Experience.* Chicago: Noble Press, 1993.

Newman, Katharine. "An Evening with Hal Bennett: An Interview." *Black American Literature Forum* 21.4 (winter 1987): 357–78.

Nichols, Charles H. "Comic Modes in Black America (A Ramble through Afro-American Humor)." In *Comic Relief: Humor in Contemporary American Literature,* ed. Sarah Blacher Cohen, 105–26. Chicago: University of Illinois Press, 1978.

———. "The Slave Narrators and the Picaresque Mode: Archetypes for Modern Black Personae." In *The Slave's Narrative,* ed. Charles T. Davis and Henry Louis Gates, Jr., 283–97. New York: Oxford University Press, 1985.

Omi, Michael, and Howard Winant. *Racial Transformation in the United States: From the 1960s to the 1980s.* Ed. Michael W. Apple. Critical Social Thought. New York: Routledge, 1986.

Page, Phillip. "Traces of Derrida in Toni Morrison's *Jazz.*" *African American Review* 29.1 (spring 1995): 55–66.

Patterson, Orlando. *Slavery and Social Death: A Comparative Study.* Cambridge: Harvard University Press, 1982.

Paulson, Ronald. *The Fictions of Satire.* Baltimore: Johns Hopkins, 1967.

Peplow, Michael W. *George S. Schuyler.* Twayne's United States Authors 349. Boston: Twayne, 1980.

Pinckney, Darryl. "Trickster Tales." *New York Review of Books* 36:15 (1989): 20, 22–4. Rpt. in Matuz, 311–15.

Radcliffe-Brown, Alfred R. *Structure and Function in Primitive Society: Essays and Addresses.* Glencoe, Ill.: Free Press, 1952.

Rampersad, Arnold. *The Life of Langston Hughes.* Vol. 1, *1902–1941, I, Too, Sing America.* New York and Oxford: Oxford University Press, 1986.

———. *The Life of Langston Hughes.* Vol. 2, *1941–1967, I Dream a World.* New York: Oxford University Press, 1988.

Reed, Ishmael. *Japanese by Spring*. New York: Atheneum, 1993.

———. *Mumbo Jumbo*. 1972. New York: Atheneum, 1988.

———. *Reckless Eyeballing*. New York: St. Martin's, 1986.

———. *The Terrible Threes*. New York: Atheneum, 1989.

———. *The Terrible Twos*. 1982. New York: Atheneum, 1988.

———. *Yellow Back Radio Broke-Down*. 1969. New York: Atheneum, 1988.

Reed, Ishmael, ed. *19 Necromancers from Now*. Garden City, N.Y.: Doubleday, 1970.

———. *Shrovetide in Old New Orleans*. Garden City, N.Y.: Doubleday, 1978.

Reed, Ishmael, and Steve Cannon. "George S. Schuyler, Writer." In *Shrovetide in Old New Orleans*, ed. Ishmael Reed, 195–218. Garden City, N.Y.: Doubleday, 1978.

Reed, Thomas Vernon. *Fifteen Jugglers, Five Believers: Literary Politics and the Poetics of American Social Movements*. Berkeley: University of California Press, 1992.

Roberts, John W. *From Trickster to Badman: The Black Folk Hero in Slavery and Freedom*. Philadelphia: University of Pennsylvania Press, 1989.

Ryan, Judylyn S., and Estella C. Májoza. "Jazz . . . on 'The Site of Memory.'" *Studies in the Literary Imagination* 31.2 (1998): 125–52.

Schuyler, George S. *Black and Conservative: The Autobiography of George S. Schuyler*. New Rochelle, N.Y.: Arlington House, 1966.

———. *Black No More: Being an Account of the Strange and Wonderful Workings of Science in the Land of the Free, A.D. 1933–1940*. 1931. Ed. Richard Yarborough. The Northeastern Library of Black Literature. Boston: Northeastern University Press, 1989.

———. "The Negro-Art Hokum." *Nation* 122.3180 (June 16, 1926): 662–63.

———. "Our Greatest Gift to America." In *Ebony and Topaz: A Collectanea*, ed. Charles S. Johnson, 122–24. 1927. Freeport, N.Y.: Books for Libraries, 1971.

———. "The Reminiscences of George S. Schuyler." In *The Oral History Collection of Columbia University*, ed. Elizabeth B. Mason and Louis M. Starr. 1972. New York: Oral History Research Office, 1979.

Schuyler, George S., and Theophilus Lewis. "Shafts and Darts: A Page of Calumny and Satire." *Messenger* (April 1924): 108.

Scruggs, Charles, and Lee Vandemarr. *Jean Toomer and the Terrors of American History.* Philadelphia: University of Pennsylvania Press, 1998.

Singh, Amritjit. Foreword to *Infants of the Spring,* by Wallace Thurman. Boston: Northeastern University Press, 1992.

Smith, Valerie, Lea Baechler, and A. Walton Litz, eds. *African American Writers.* New York: Collier, 1993.

Steele, Shelby. *The Content of Our Character: A New Vision of Race in America.* New York: St. Martin's, 1990.

Stringfellow, Frank, Jr. *The Meaning of Irony: A Psychoanalytic Investigation.* Ed. Mihai I. Spariosu. Albany: State University of New York Press, 1994.

Sundquist, Eric J., ed. *Cultural Contexts for Ralph Ellison's* Invisible Man: *A Bedford Documentary Companion.* Boston: St. Martin's Press, 1995.

Swift, Jonathan. *The Writings of Jonathan Swift.* Ed. Robert A. Greenberg and William Bowman Piper. New York: Norton, 1973.

Talalay, Kathryn. *Composition in Black and White: The Life of Phillipa Schuyler.* New York: Oxford University Press, 1995.

Tate, Greg. *Flyboy in the Buttermilk: Essays on Contemporary America.* New York: Simon and Schuster, 1992.

Thurman, Wallace. *Infants of the Spring.* 1932. The Northeastern Library of Black Literature. Ed. Richard Yarborough. Boston: Northeastern University Press, 1992.

———. "Negro Artists and the Negro." *New Republic* vol. 52 (August 31, 1927): 37–39.

———. "Nephews of Uncle Remus." *Independent* 119.4034 (September 24, 1927): 296–98.

Thurman, Wallace, ed. *Fire!!: A Quarterly Devoted to Younger Negro Artists.* 1924. New York: Fire Press, 1995.

Tucker, Jeffrey. " 'Can Science Succeed Where the Civil War Failed?': George S. Schuyler and Race." In *Race Consciousness: African American Studies for the New Century,* ed. Judith Jackson Fossett and Jeffrey A. Tucker, 136–52. New York: New York University Press, 1997.

Van Notten, Eleonore. *Wallace Thurman's Harlem Renaissance.* Ed. C. C. Barfoot, Hans Bertens, Theo D'haen, and Erik Kooper. Amsterdam: Editions Rodopi B. V., 1994.

Voltaire, Jean-Marie Arouet de. *Candide, or Optimism.* Trans. and ed. Robert M. Adams. New York: Norton, 1966.

Walcott, Ronald. "The Novels of Hal Bennett, Part I." *Black World* 23.8 (June 1974), 36–48, 89–97.

———. "The Novels of Hal Bennett, Part II." *Black World* 23.9 (July 1974), 78–96.

Ward, Douglas Turner. *Day of Absence.* 1966. In *Contemporary Black Drama: From* A Raisin in the Sun *to* No Place to Be Somebody, ed. Clinton F. Oliver and Stephanie Sills, 340–64. New York: Scribner's, 1971.

Watkins, Mel. *On the Real Side: Laughing, Lying and Signifying—the Underground Tradition of African-American Humor That Transformed American Culture, from Slavery to Richard Pryor.* New York: Simon and Schuster, 1994.

Watson, Steven. *The Harlem Renaissance: Hub of African-American Culture, 1920–1930.* Circles of the Twentieth Century. New York: Pantheon, 1995.

Watt, Ian. *The Rise of the Novel.* Berkeley: University of California Press, 1957.

Weisenburger, Steven. *Fables of Subversion: Satire and the American Novel, 1930–1980.* Athens: University of Georgia Press, 1995.

West, Cornel. *Race Matters.* Boston: Beacon, 1993.

Wolfe, Goerge C. *The Colored Museum.* New York: Grove, 1985.

Worcester, David. *The Art of Satire.* New York: Russell, 1960.

Wright, Charles Stevenson. *The Wig, a Mirror Image.* New York: Farrar, Straus, and Giroux, 1966.

Wright, Richard. "Blueprint for Negro Writing." *New Challenge: A Literary Quarterly* 2.2 (1937), 53–65.

———. "Review of *Their Eyes Were Watching God.*" In *Zora Neale Hurston: Critical Perspectives Past and Present,* ed. Henry Louis Gates, Jr. and K. A. Appiah, 16–17. New York: Amistad, 1993.

Zumwalt, Rosemary Lévy. *American Folklore Scholarship: A Dialogue of Dissent.* Bloomington: Indiana University Press, 1988.

INDEX

Abrahams, Roger D., 28
American Mercury, 61
And We Are Not Saved, 194
*Autobiography of an Ex-Coloured
    Man, The:* influence on Harlem
    Renaissance, 40–41

Baker, Houston A., 102
Bakhtin, Mikhail Mikhailovitch: on
    the carnival in literature, 158, 199;
    definitions of novel form, 6, 119;
    "Discourse and the Novel," 119;
    and the grotesque, 96, 197
Baldwin, James, 86
Baraka, Amiri: on black art, 115, 118,
    119; on Black Arts movement, 151;
    satirized, 155
Beatty, Paul, 10, 16, 25, 30, 81, 164, 170,
    194, 202–6
Bell, Bernard, 7, 142, 157
Bell, Derrick, 10, 170, 179, 194–96;
    career of, 194
Bennett, Hal, 8, 10, 123, 137–42,
    138*n37*; pseudonyms of, 138*n37*;
    publication history of, 8, 138,
    138*n37*
Bergenholtz, Rita A., 16
Black Aesthetic, 1, 111, 114–23, 116*n6*,
    117*n7*, 126, 142, 150, 155, 158, 159.
    See also Fuller, Hoyt W.
Black and Conservative, 59
Black Empire, 61*n29*
Blacker the Berry . . . , The, 43
Black No More, 7, 8, 16, 31, 38, 41, 43,
    57–69, 82, 124, 126, 130, 143*n39*, 150,
    204; on American politics, 66–67;
    as basis for *Mumbo Jumbo,* 150; on
    black leadership, 64–66, 67, 69;
    critical neglect of 57; journalistic
    elements of, 8, 57, 59, 60, 61; as
    milestone, 57; on miscegenation, 7,

63, 130; parody in, 68; as picaresque
    narrative, 31, 63–64, 67, 204; on
    racial caste system, 7, 66; as science
    fiction, 57, 67; similarities to *Japanese
    by Spring,* 16. *See also Black and
    Conservative;* Du Bois, W. E. B.;
    Garvey, Marcus A.; *Messenger;*
    NAACP; Schuyler, George S.; UNIA
Blake, Susan L.: on flying metaphor in
    black folklore, 95
Bluest Eye, The, 116
Booth, Wayne C., 20–21, 24–25; on
    recognizing ironic statements, 20*n8*;
    on stable and unstable irony, 20, 21,
    24–25
Boyer, Jay, 174
Brooks, Gwendolyn, 6
Brown, Cecil, 10, 120, 123, 130–37, 184
Brown, Sterling, 82
Brown, William Wells, 38
Bryant, Jerry, 161, 162

Candide, 47–48, 137
Carmichael, Stokely, 114, 117
"Caucasian Storms Harlem, The"
    73–74
Chesnutt, Charles, 9, 38, 39
Civil rights, 65, 69, 70, 73, 85, 86, 194,
    195, 195*n39*
Civil Rights movement, 86, 89, 94,
    95*n29*, 98, 111, 112, 113, 114, 124,
    139, 142, 149; satire post–, 163, 164,
    165, 166, 168, 168, 175, 187, 193–94,
    196, 198, 199, 201, 203, 205
Color Purple, The. See Walker, Alice
Conjure-Man Dies, The, 70
Content of Our Character, The, 179
"Conversation at Midnight," 91
Cotillion, The, 7, 29, 70, 112, 143–49;
    critical neglect of, 149; as satire